THE NEXT
DIMENSION

THE NEXT
DIMENSION

TOM EMRICH

THE NEXT
DIMENSION

HOW TO USE
AUGMENTED REALITY
FOR BUSINESS GROWTH IN
THE ERA OF SPATIAL COMPUTING

WILEY

Published by John Wiley & Sons, Inc., Hoboken, New Jersey.
Published simultaneously in Canada.

For general information on our other products and services or for technical support, please
contact our Customer Care Department within the United States at (800) 762-2974, outside
the United States at (317) 572-3993 or fax (317) 572-4002.

Wiley also publishes its books in a variety of electronic formats. Some content that appears in
print may not be available in electronic formats. For more information about Wiley products,
visit our web site at www.wiley.com.

Library of Congress Cataloging-in-Publication Data is Available:

ISBN 9781394262564 (Cloth)
ISBN 9781394262571 (ePub)
ISBN 9781394262588 (ePDF)

Cover Design: Wiley
Cover Image: © Alexandr/Adobe Stock
Author Photo: © Kari Orvik

SKY10087161_101724

Dedicated to my dad, John Emrich,
who disassembled our childhood computer and,
in doing so, assembled my future in technology.
Your curiosity became my career.

Disclaimer

The information in this book is provided for general informational purposes only. While the author has made every effort to ensure the accuracy of the information contained herein, the publisher and author assume no responsibility for errors, omissions, or contrary interpretations of the subject matter. The reader should consult a professional before making any decisions based on the information in this book.

This book was written independently by the author and does not represent the opinions or positions of any organizations with which the author is currently or has been affiliated. The content in this book is based solely on publicly available information.

Contents

How to Use This Book

Congratulations! You are now the owner of an AR- and AI-enabled book! Follow the instructions below to use these two technologies to maximize your experience with this publication.

Bring the Cover to Life with AR

A book about augmented reality (AR) wouldn't be complete without using this technology to show it in action. The front cover of this book comes to life using web-based AR. EyeJack created the experience using Niantic's 8th Wall technology.

Follow these steps to activate the WebAR experience:

1. Grab your smartphone!
2. Scan the QR code on the back cover of this book with your smartphone camera or visit ar.thenextdimensionbook.com in your smartphone browser. Your phone must be connected to Wi-Fi or cellular data for the AR to function.
3. Tap on the "Start AR" button when the website loads.
4. Accept the permission prompts to give the web app access to your camera and motion and orientation sensors.
5. Tap the "Begin" button and point your smartphone camera at the front cover of this book.
6. Watch the book come to life with AR. Make sure your sound is on to experience the full effect.
7. You can record the experience and share the video with your friends and network using popular messaging and social media apps.

Talk to an AI About This Book

This book was used to fine-tune a GPT using ChatGPT so that you can talk with an AI chatbot about its content. You can use The Next

Dimension Book GPT to summarize chapters, find key points, or have a conversation about the book to deepen your understanding.

Follow these steps to chat with The Next Dimension Book GPT:

1. Visit ai.thenextdimensionbook.com in your browser on a smartphone, tablet, laptop, or computer. For the AI to function, your device must be connected to Wi-Fi or cellular data.

2. If you are using a smartphone, you can scan the QR codes found at the beginning of each chapter in the "Chapter Cheat Sheet Powered by AI" section to easily access this site.

3. Sign up or log in to ChatGPT to chat with this GPT.

4. Use the dialog box to message the GPT or choose from one of the suggested questions to get started.

5. Once you've talked to The Next Dimension Book GPT, it will automatically be added to your ChatGPT sidebar so that you can find and use it at any time.

Preface: The Man from the Future

I still remember the sound – the wrenching of bits and bytes tearing through a phone line that sounded as if it was being tortured to do something it wasn't meant to do. It was the sound of dial-up Internet – the sound of the future.

I was a young adult when I accessed my first online bulletin board with my dad in the basement office of our house in Kitchener-Waterloo, Canada. I still remember being amazed that my computer could now do something as powerful as connecting me with people worldwide. These early days of the Internet were interesting. It was fascinating that I could now go online to access the world's information, all while still expected to complete my university work using the traditional means of library books and microfiche. This feeling of living in the future while still footed in the present, where the new world and the old world intermix, would be a common occurrence in my life.

The next time I would find myself adopting new technology while the old working methods were still in play was around the emergence of the mobile Internet. I worked at a start-up in Toronto called m-Qube, an early innovator in delivering ads and content to mobile phones. There, I began to see firsthand the birth of the mobile web, the introduction of mobile media, and the new use of SMS and MMS, especially by advertisers. This was 2005, years before the iPhone, when feature phones and handheld devices from Blackberry showed us glimpses of the future of mobile computing. At that time, phones were mainly communication devices for many, but for me, it was clear that they were capable of so much more. Indeed, this became even clearer with the emergence of the smartphone.

Three years after the launch of the iPhone, the iPad was announced. Around that time, I was working in the publishing industry as a product manager. My mandate was to help the newspaper and magazine industry navigate the digital transformation mobile and tablets had ushered in as competition for printed products. I found myself again in familiar territory, where the old and new worlds meet. It was in this role that I was introduced to the power of augmented reality (AR), and I devised a strategy to leverage AR to build a bridge between the legacy world of print and the rapidly evolving mobile and tablet one. While the technology was there, the requirements for AR, often needing a computer webcam, downloaded software, and huge AR markers, made it extremely challenging to sell to brands. Regardless, I was convinced even then that AR would play a major role in blending the physical with the digital.

Not long after, I started a blog on Tumblr dedicated to exploring a world beyond the smartphone. I began the blog to channel my growing passion for wearable technology, including its use for AR and VR. It soon grew to nearly 100,000 followers before being acquired. Reaching this milestone inspired me to make the leap to become a writer full-time, and I wrote for various Canadian technology publications, including MobileSyrup and BetaKit, where I continued to focus on exploring the burgeoning world of wearable technology. It was the early days of wearables when crowdfunding enabled anyone to be a hardware manufacturer. The world of wearables at that time often felt weird and experimental, and too soon, it triggered that familiar feeling I had felt before of living in the future, and I knew that we were getting a glimpse into the next wave of computing.

I had promised myself at the mobile media start-up that if there were to be another wave of computing in my lifetime, I would spot it as early as possible and ride it toward opportunities. I had been early with mobile at m-Qube, but I was still green as a professional and had a lot to learn. This next time, I had hoped, would come when I was a little more seasoned and had even more to offer. It was clear to me that wearable computing was going to be that wave.

To find a way to be meaningful in this space, I started to host meetups. My first wearable technology meetup was in downtown Toronto in January of 2014. It was a seriously cold evening, and I showed up at the event space with pizza, beer, and a box of wearables that I had been collecting, including Google Glass. The plan was to have a few presentations and then mainly focus on demo time with the crowd, where they could go hands-on with devices, many for the first time. The event saw nearly two hundred people and convinced me to keep going. One meetup led to another, and I found myself building a community of over 120,000, hosting events around the US and Canada. My mission was to foster adoption and facilitate innovation in wearable tech by providing a platform for the entrepreneurs, start-ups, and organizations already making this happen and a place for those new to the space to be inspired to take action. In short, I wanted to bring people together to help accelerate the awareness and adoption of wearable tech.

My acquisition of Google Glass, one of a handful of Canadians who had one, was instrumental in my relationship with AR. I wore Glass for nearly one year, exploring ways to incorporate it into my daily life, witnessing the questions and concerns it raised while it was on, and giving hundreds of demos to anyone who asked. Because there were so few Canadian Google Glass users, my role shifted from writing about wearable technology to being written about. It was while wearing Google Glass at a Tim Horton's coffee shop in Toronto that a journalist gave me the moniker "Man from the Future." Wearing Google Glass that year was truly like living in the future, and it further cemented my belief that wearables and AR are the next wave of computing.

My passion for AR and wearables led me to Augmented World Expo (AWE), the world's largest spatial computing community, along with its founder, Ori Inbar. Like Google Glass, Inbar was pivotal in my journey with AR. A long-time believer in the power of AR to give us superpowers, Ori's long-standing passion and devotion to AR and the AR community are major contributors to its awareness and adoption. I had the opportunity to co-produce AWE and grow the community alongside him for nearly six years. It was there that I met fellow AR enthusiasts and true AR pioneers. During that time, I watched wearables and AR/VR go from parts on a table in the expo hall to complete solutions and next-generation products. When I left the team, I knew it was the right time to roll up my sleeves and get to work in this space.

When I left, I still had that familiar in-between feeling of the new world meeting the old, but AR and VR, in particular, no longer felt too early but rather ready for the masses. I was eager to find work that would allow me to go deep with the technology and deliver value in the market. I found this in 8th Wall, a web-based AR start-up in Palo Alto founded by Erik Murphy-Chutorian that had done the impossible and made the web a powerful place for AR. My time at 8th Wall felt like a full-circle moment from my product days in publishing. The 8th Wall platform was delivering on the promise of AR to brands I had envisioned nearly a decade earlier. WebAR was a game changer for marketers and brands, and according to the company, the platform has seen thousands of commercial launches for top brands across industry verticals since its launch. While at 8th Wall, and later Niantic (best known as the publisher of Pokémon GO), which acquired 8th Wall in 2022, I became intimate with how agencies and brands use AR to grow their business. This included witnessing how AR was delivering tangible results across the marketing funnel.

Marketers and advertisers have always been among the first to adopt new technologies. They play an instrumental role in introducing and acclimating the mainstream with new tech, and the insights from early campaigns shape the entire industry. I wrote this book to celebrate the early marketers, businesses, and brands who have innovated, iterated, and realized ROI using AR. My hope is that these examples will give you the confidence and inspiration to use AR in your own business plans.

With the emergence of mixed reality headsets, including the Meta Quest and Apple Vision Pro, I find myself again getting that familiar feeling that we are in the midst of a shift. The era of spatial computing is upon us, and it is the right time to harness the power of AR to futureproof and grow your business.

The future is now.

CHAPTER 1

Welcome to the Era of Spatial Computing

Once you learn to wear, you can learn anything. Right now, you're in a trap; it's like you're seeing the world through a little hole, just whatever your naked eye sees – and what you can get from that." She pointed at the magic foolscap that was tucked into his shirt pocket. "With some practice you should be able to see and hear as good as anyone.
— Rainbows End *by Vernor Vinge*[1]

Chapter Cheat Sheet Powered by AI

I asked an AI to read this chapter and create a cheat sheet. If you only have five minutes to spare, here are the three must-know insights to help you level up your spatial computing knowledge.

- **Presence and Perception:** As computing shifts from 2D to 3D, it gains the ability to perceive and interact with the world around it. This enables digital experiences to feel more natural and tangible, allowing us to be present in these virtual moments.
- **Spatial Awareness:** Devices with advanced sensors and AI enable them to perceive and navigate physical spaces, bridging the gap between the digital and the physical and making digital interactions more intuitive and natural.

◆ **Business Transformation:** This technological leap transforms digital experiences by making them more immersive and engaging, requiring businesses to invest in new skills and strategies to take advantage of this new dimension.

Want to talk to an AI about this book? Scan the QR code or visit ai.thenextdimension book.com in your browser to access The Next Dimension Book GPT.

Scan Me

We Are All Digital Flat Earthers

We are 3D beings living in a 3D world, yet almost half our waking lives are spent interacting with 2D screens.[2] We may be multidimensional, but our digital experience is flat. From computers and laptops to tablets and smartphones, our smart screens offer us access to an online cosmos that is now fundamental to our way of living. But while these devices have let us surf the information superhighway, we have never really been able to dive deep into its waters and are stuck skimming the surface. A single pane of glass keeps the digital universe always just out of reach, allowing us to engage with it using artificial interactions such as clicks, taps, and swipes. This separation between us and technology limits its potential impact on our lives, constrains its capabilities, and often conflicts with our ability to be present in the physical real world. When it comes to our digital experience, we are like Alice at the beginning of her story, observing a world of wonder beyond the looking glass but have yet to step through the glass to immerse ourselves completely.

But this is all changing, and it is happening now.

Enter the era of spatial computing, a new computing paradigm that is shifting technology into the next dimension. The time has arrived for our digital experience to move from 2D to 3D. Spatial computing blends the virtual world with the physical world by enabling computers to perceive, interact, and navigate three-dimensional space. In this next wave of computing, the barrier between the digital and the physical is removed, and we can engage with technology as a part of our world rather than something separate from it. Fueling the spatial computing revolution is the growing ubiquity of sensors, advancements in artificial intelligence (AI) and machine learning (ML), and the introduction of new devices, including augmented reality and virtual reality headsets, autonomous vehicles, and personal and enterprise robots.

Spatial computing will break our technology free from the pane of glass it has been behind for decades and allow it to exist among us. In some cases, computing will be able to enter our world, quite literally walking among us by using its newfound ability to independently sense and navigate. In others, we will be able to enter the digital world and interact with it in a very similar way to how we engage with the physical world around us. Both are made possible with technology now present with us in the same dimension. With less of a separation between the physical and digital worlds, technology can be much smarter, more contextual, and more intentional, resulting in immersive, personal, and meaningful digital applications.

Every wave of computing has proven to change the world as we know it. Spatial computing will be no different. It will introduce a new way of living, changing all aspects of the human experience, from leisure to work and everything in between. Now is the time to understand how to harness the power of spatial computing to enhance your life and supercharge your business.

I Sense, Therefore I Am

It all begins with awareness.

Today's computers provide us access to a wealth of information at our fingertips. But while they are great at storing and retrieving data, their ability to understand the world around them relies on us feeding them this information. Social media posts, vlogs and blogs, and Wikipedia pages are just a few of the explicit ways we have collectively empowered computers with knowledge we can access at any moment. Updating the collective digital mind is an active and ongoing process in the Information Age. This means that we spend a lot of our time generating this information, time that could be spent doing other things in the physical real world. It also means that computers may only have a partial understanding of our world as they are at the mercy of the quality and completeness of the information we provide. In turn, computing often lacks context, making applications less personal and meaningful.

Technology in the Age of Spatial Computing begins to wean itself off its dependence on us. Using sensors, it will gather information on its own, listening with microphones, seeing with cameras, and orienting itself with an array of sensors. This is an awakening for computing as it becomes aware of its surroundings, including the environment, objects, and people around it. This not only frees computing to learn beyond the silo of information it has access to today, but it also frees us from our active duty to build the collective digital mind. This changes our relationship with technology. Computers get to know us in a new, more intimate way, which enriches our digital interactions, making them more personal, meaningful, and valuable. And we no longer need to work so hard at providing technology with information about our world. This enables us to be more present with the happenings around us as we no longer need to stop and document them.

Spatial computing goes beyond just enabling awareness. Using AI and, in particular, ML, computers will be able to make sense of the large amounts of data they now possess. Interpreting and organizing this sensory information to produce a meaningful experience of the world will unlock the gift of perception. Computing will not just sense the world but make sense of it: images captured through cameras are recognized, and speech recorded using microphones is understood. This will enable us to do things such as talk to smarter virtual assistants embedded inside camera-equipped eyewear that lets them see what we see. Or ride in autonomous vehicles that can understand what is around them to safely drive us to a destination. And one day, it will also power robots that can navigate our space and interact with us as if they were humans.

Just as computing gains the ability to perceive the world around it, we will begin to use it to edit our own perception of the world. Wearable devices that merge our technology with our bodies will give computers access to our eyes, ears, and hands, influencing our senses. Robust sensors and advanced algorithms will lend our hands to the computer so that we can move digital objects in 3D space or allow computers to interface with our eyes and ears to edit what we see and hear. This will change our perception of reality by blending the digital world with the physical one. By harnessing technology that understands space, we will be able to transform our own experience of this world. This could be choosing to remove the physical real world completely to enter a simulation or experiencing both the virtual and the physical together in an augmented interaction.

Mind the Gap

By blending the physical with the virtual, spatial computing also promises to dramatically close the separation gap that exists between us and technology. This separation gap limits computing's capabilities and impact and often causes technology to distract and remove us from being fully present in physical, real-world moments.

Computing on flat screens keeps us separate from the digital world, making it intangible and requiring us to learn a new user experience language to interact with. With spatial computing, our technological experience breaks out from the screen into our physical space, which allows for complete immersion and more intuitive interactions.

Today's gap interferes with our ability to be intimate with technology and obstructs computing's capacity to truly understand us and the world around us. Both are due to computing not being present in our physical space. This results in applications with little context of the world's real-time happenings and a relatively cold computing experience based on taps of glass or mouse clicks. With spatial computing, this interference is diminished as computers join us in space where we can interact with the digital more tangibly, and computers can use their newfound senses to be more informed and deliver more personal and meaningful results.

Today, we cannot be present in a digital moment and a physical moment at the same time, which causes us to be constantly distracted as we try to multitask between the digital and the physical. Think about the simple task of taking a picture of your family at a theme park. Today, you need to remove yourself from enjoying the moment to document this and, in some cases, interrupt the moment completely to capture it. Or consider the times when you have engaged in text messaging or email or checked your social media feed quickly while at a dinner party. In all these instances, you chose to remove yourself from the present physical moment to engage quickly with the happenings in the digital world. The duality of our lives, one foot in the physical world with another in the digital, is a large reason why technology has a bad rap as being rude and antihuman. To be engaged with computing today, you can't be fully present in a physical real-world moment. With spatial computing, we will no longer have to choose between being present in a digital moment versus a physical moment. That is because the moment will be unified as a blended augmented moment. In this hybrid moment, where virtual and physical meet, we will be fully present with both virtual and physical interactions simultaneously.

Presence is a critical aspect of spatial computing. On the one hand, spatial computing enables us to feel physically present within a virtual environment or the digital elements realistically situated in our physical space. Feeling present makes the virtual experience feel more natural and intuitive and helps us react and interact just like we do in the real world. On the other hand, spatial computing enables computers to have a presence in our physical world. This includes embodied technology in robots, autonomous vehicles, or disembodied virtual assistants whispering in our ears through wearable technology. In both cases, presence is made possible because of computing's newfound ability to perceive, interact, and navigate 3D space.

Presence and perception are intricately linked in spatial computing. This synergy is an essential quality that allows it to blur the lines between the digital and physical worlds. Sharing space with technology in such an integrated manner opens new possibilities for businesses across industries. Harnessing these unique qualities of spatial computing as part of your digital strategy will be key to success.

A Leap in Dimension

A critical component of spatial computing is the shift from 2D to 3D.

Until now, our computing has been flat, using only the x and y axes, allowing content to exist in horizontal and vertical dimensions. Spatial computing introduces a third dimension, the z-axis, adding depth to our computing. This new dimension enables technologies such as robots that can walk, self-driving cars, and the creation of virtual worlds we can explore and interact with. 3D computing opens up new possibilities for applications focused on spatial understanding, intuitive and natural user interfaces (UIs), and enhanced realism and immersion. This will require a brand-new way of thinking about software design and development.

While this type of shift doesn't happen frequently, we have seen leaps like this before. In the 1980s, the personal computing era saw a transition from text-based interfaces to graphical user interfaces, also referred to as GUIs.[3] Made popular by Apple Macintosh and Microsoft Windows, the GUI revolutionized how users interacted with computers by introducing elements such as windows, icons, and buttons. Users could also see their actions on screen with pointing devices such as the mouse. Visual elements and common physical interactions came more naturally to users than text-based commands, making personal computing more accessible to more people, and were instrumental in the widespread adoption of the personal computer (PC).

Moving from command-line interfaces to a 2D graphical environment was a significant one, and it caused developers to rethink how to build software for users. The focus shifted from creating just functional software to emphasizing how user-friendly it can be. This led to the development of UI elements, such as drop-down menus, toolbars, and dialog boxes. These elements used visual cues and interactions that mimicked the physical world, such as dragging and dropping, to help users more intuitively engage with applications. At the same time, the way these elements looked – such as layout, color, and typography – also grew in importance to enhance usability and user engagement. This holistic approach to software design, which considers functionality and user experience, laid the groundwork for many of the design philosophies and best practices still prevalent today.

Like the introduction of the GUI, the move from 2D to 3D will trigger a new way of thinking about software development. Designers and developers will require a new approach to make use of spatial computing's environmental integration, spatial awareness, and a brand-new set of input methods. This will require a shift from designing flat planes to creating dynamic, immersive environments where users can interact with digital objects as if they were there. As software becomes more integrated with the user's physical space, developers must consider spatial logic, physics, and user movement and create interfaces that respond to hand movements, gestures, and gaze – which, in many ways, can be considered the new mouse. This spatial UI (SUI) will enhance user engagement by making digital interactions feel more instinctive, further blurring the lines between virtual and physical realities.

Developers and designers will need to familiarize themselves with 3D media and 3D software development. 3D models, textures, materials, shaders, particle systems, and animations are just some of the 3D asset essentials to 3D software development. Creating and integrating these assets requires a combination of artistic skills and technical knowledge, utilizing specialized software and tools. But luckily, not everyone will have to start from scratch. Many people working in 3D industries, such as gaming, will already be equipped with some of the fundamentals. In many ways, 3D games played on smartphones and game consoles can be seen as a precursor to spatial computing. We can look to 3D games to glean many of the same concepts that will be core to this next wave of computing, including the creation of 3D assets and environments. This expertise in 3D game development provides a robust foundation for the transition to spatial computing. Game developers have long tackled issues related to rendering complex environments, managing real-time interactions, and creating immersive experiences that react to a user's actions – skills directly transferable to spatial computing.

As we move into the era of spatial computing, specialized skills in 3D will grow in demand. Ramping up your teams with 3D talent will be a competitive advantage. There is also a major opportunity to contribute to creating a new set of design philosophies and best practices within spatial computing. Establishing these frameworks by innovating in this space early could be a competitive advantage for businesses, especially those in the creative field.

Our Post-Smartphone Future

In the personal computing era, the computer was the star of our digital lives. The PC began as an expensive, clunky device that was anchored to a desk in our house. In its early days, the PC was meant to boost professional productivity, extending work from the office to the home. As PCs became more affordable and more user-friendly with the introduction of the GUI, people quickly started to use them for education, gaming, and other use cases. The variety of uses grew exponentially as PCs became connected to the Internet, which gave rise to new applications, including new forms of communication and social interaction. Eventually, PCs began to leave the confines of the home in a more portable form factor, the laptop. The ability to carry this computing power outside the home made it possible to work from anywhere and paved the way for mobile computing.

In the mobile computing era, the smartphone is undeniably the new center of our digital lives. The smartphone goes beyond the laptop's portability, enabling us to use computing wherever we are, so much so that it feels like an extension of ourselves. But while we have been carrying around this supercomputer in our hands for over a decade now, it hasn't always been as powerful nor portable. Like the PC, the mobile device also had a journey in miniaturization, cost, and connectivity-driven use cases. Once carried in a suitcase or embedded in cars, mobile devices, like the PC, began to enter the mainstream as a work device. These devices were clunky, like the early days of PCs and laptops, and were also inaccessible to many people due to their high cost. Eventually, these devices became more powerful and smaller, moving from feature phones and PDAs (personal digital assistants) to the smartphone's modern form factor. Like the Internet in the PC era, connectivity was a major contributing factor to the widespread adoption of mobile devices. Cellular connectivity, beginning with 3G, expanded the use of mobile beyond communication and data management to eventually every facet of our modern-day lives.

So what will the new device be at the center of the spatial computing era? Wearable technology. While we may feel today that our smartphone is an extension of ourselves, wearables will truly deliver on this. Wearables will shift our computing experience from something we hold in our hands to something we wear on our bodies. We will likely have a myriad of wearables on our person that work in tandem with smart devices in our environments, creating a device constellation suited for 3D computing. This may include smartglasses, hearables, smart rings, brain-sensing smartwatches, and haptic vests. All these devices help to lend our body to computing, granting it access to better understand you and the environment around you to create more immersive and meaningful digital interactions. While we are early in our wearable journey, wrist-worn wearables such as the Apple Watch and Fitbit have already inched us toward this future. Millions of users now wear tech on their wrists, which senses their movement and biometrics and begins to merge their tech experience with their body.[4] This is the same with hearable devices, such as Apple AirPods, which put digital assistants and sensors for spatial audio in people's ears.

While a set of wearables will play a key role in spatial computing, the hero device in this computing era is expected to be head-worn wearables such as smartglasses and head-mounted displays (also referred to as HMDs or simply headsets). Like the mobile era, which saw car phones, feature phones, and PDAs before the convergence of the smartphone, we should expect to see a variety of different headworn wearables available for enterprises and consumers in the early days of this category. The device journey will follow similar patterns as the PC and mobile era in a stronger enterprise start before reaching widespread consumer use. Today's smartglasses and headsets are like the early days of PCs, clunky and expensive, and not expected to leave the office or home. These devices are also finding the most immediate value in professional use cases, including reimagining working from home with co-presence capabilities and an infinite canvas for applications for the ultimate multitasker as a monitor replacement. But it is only a matter of time until such devices become smaller and more powerful, making them more wearable and attractive to more consumers. And new use cases will be unlocked by advancements in connectivity, both cellular and Wi-Fi, making these devices more of a staple in our everyday lives and eventually replacing our smartphones.

We are still years away from fully realizing our post-smartphone future. In the meantime, we will see the role of the smartphone change as the adoption of wearable technology rises. Our smartphones will become computing hubs for wearables, allowing these devices to be smaller and more comfortable by offloading the computation to the phone. Early wearables will benefit from being tethered to the smartphone with the upside of making them more fashionable and comfortable to wear. This relationship will also extend smartphone applications and services to wearable devices, which will introduce a new opportunity for smartphone apps. This dependency on the mobile device will only strengthen the role the smartphone has in our lives. But it will begin to change our relationship with our phones, eventually seeing us leave them in our pockets as we interact with our wearable devices instead of tapping on the screen.

Smartphones will also act as companion devices to wearables such as headsets, extending its use. Here, smartphones will be used to bridge the indoors with the outdoors, giving headset-applications value outside or on the go, significantly increasing the time spent by a user. They will also be used to connect headset users and mobile users, whether they are in the same room or in different places, dramatically increasing the number of people that can engage with the app.

Understanding where we are in our wearable adoption cycle and the new role the smartphone will play through this journey will be essential to any successful spatial computing strategy.

The Age of Experience

Computers that are present and able to perceive the world are arriving just in time to bolster the Experience Age (also known as the Post-Information Age) that has already begun.

In the Information Age (also known as the Digital Age or Computer Age), technology is used for knowledge transfer at scale. Computers act as vast repositories, collecting, storing, and managing the world's information, which we then have access to at our fingertips using the Internet. The focus in the Information Age was on data. In the early days, few users contributed to the creation of this information; most only accessed and consumed it. With the emergence of social media, this balance changed as more consumers became creators, documenting and sharing the happenings of our world in real-time.

The Information Age has significantly reshaped our society in several profound ways. Access to information has changed education and self-improvement. Online resources, digital libraries, and e-learning platforms have made it possible for anyone with Internet access to educate themselves, learn new skills, and even earn degrees remotely. Text messaging, email, and video calling have transformed the way that we communicate with one another. These tools have made it possible to maintain personal and professional relationships across long distances, fostering a more connected global community and changing how we do business. Economically, the Information Age has emphasized data as a crucial asset, catalyzing the rise of the digital economy. This shift has led to the proliferation of e-commerce, digital marketing, and brand-new business models, including freemium, subscription, and on-demand services.

As information becomes a commodity, the value shifts from the data itself to how it is presented and consumed. The focus moves from managing and sharing data to using data to create more immersive and personalized experiences for users. In this way, The Information Age may have been about establishing the Internet on which we could "surf," and the Experience Age is all about getting off that board and diving deeper into its waters. The goal is to transform content into more human-centric experiences and engage us visually and emotionally. Content is valued beyond its function, assessed on its quality of engagement and the emotional connection it can create, aiming to make technology useful and enjoyable.

The Information Age may have emphasized access and utilization of data, but in the Experience Age, it is all about engagement and interaction. We have already begun this change in our modern-day use of social media. Here, we play two main roles: that of the creator and that of the consumer. As creators, we continuously feed the digital ecosystem with new content, including text, images, and videos. As consumers, we engage with a constant stream of digital content by searching, viewing, watching, and reacting to content through likes, comments, and shares. The latter creates a dynamic feedback loop where creators adjust their content based on the engagement they receive, driving a more interactive and responsive information environment. A shift to engagement and interaction is even more evident in popular gaming worlds such as Fortnite and Roblox, which are emerging as the new social media for younger generations. These platforms are realizing this by prioritizing in-world play and world-building over the photo and video feeds that define traditional social media. Similarly, virtual reality destinations such as RecRoom, VRChat, and Horizon Worlds are gaining adoption as new places to connect and play.

This new age reflects changes in consumer expectations, where people increasingly seek products and services that offer compelling experiences over materialism and utility. According to a study from Experian, "63% of Gen Z and 59% of millennials would rather spend money on 'life experiences' like travel and concerts now rather than save up for retirement."[5] Immersive technologies that transform content into experiences, such as augmented reality (AR) and virtual reality (VR), are maturing at just the right time when consumers are looking to connect through things to do rather than things they view and read. AR and VR are the new media for the Experience Age and will deliver on the growing consumer demand for more human-centric, visual, and emotionally connected digital content.

Just as new business opportunities were cultivated in the Information Age, so too are the prospects in the Experience Age. Understanding the changes in consumer expectations and how new immersive technologies can be used to harness these possibilities will position your business to not just benefit but lead from the front.

Sparking Spatial Strategies

Strike up strategic dialogue about AR's role in your business with these essential conversation starters:

- ◆ **In the boardroom:** What strategic investments in spatial computing should we prioritize to ensure we remain competitive and innovative in this evolving technological landscape?
- ◆ **For your team meeting:** How should we be thinking of spatial computing to engage our customers and achieve our goals as we construct our roadmaps?
- ◆ **Around the water cooler:** Have you seen any of the new 3D technologies in action yet? Do you think it'll make a big difference in our daily work?

Share this on your socials: Step beyond the screen with spatial computing! As we move from 2D to 3D, technology becomes an integrated part of our physical world, allowing for more natural and immersive interactions. Get ready for the next wave of digital evolution! #thenextdimensionbook

CHAPTER 2

Spatial Computing 101

Like any place in Reality, the Street is subject to development. Developers can build their own small streets feeding off of the main one. They can build buildings, parks, signs, as well as things that do not exist in Reality, such as vast hovering overhead light shows, special neighborhoods where the rules of three-dimension spacetime are ignored.

– Snow Crash by Neal Stephenson[1]

Chapter Cheat Sheet Powered by AI

I asked an AI to create a cheat sheet for this chapter. If you only have five minutes to spare, here are the three must-know insights to help you level up your spatial computing knowledge.

- **Spatial Computing History:** Spatial computing has evolved significantly since its inception in the 1980s, initially centered on geospatial information within the Geographic Information System (GIS) community and later expanded to include interactive 3D environments in the 1990s through innovations in virtual reality.

- **Integration of Multiple Technologies:** Modern spatial computing encompasses a broad range of technologies, including augmented reality (AR), virtual reality (VR), and mixed reality

(MR), which collectively enable computers to perceive, interact with, and navigate three-dimensional spaces. This integration is enhancing applications in numerous industries, such as
automotive, health care, and entertainment.

◆ **Evolution of User Interaction:** Spatial computing is shifting
how users interact with digital information, moving from
traditional flat screens to immersive three-dimensional interactions. This is facilitated by sophisticated sensor technologies
and artificial intelligence, which together enable more natural
and intuitive user experiences.

Want to talk to an AI about this book? Scan the QR code
or visit ai.thenextdimension book.com in your browser
to access The Next Dimension Book GPT.

Scan Me

40 Years in the Making

To many, "spatial computing" is a new term recently made popular
by Apple as part of its launch of the Apple Vision Pro in June of 2023
as its "one more thing." "Introducing the era of spatial computing"
was a campaign tagline for Apple's first MR headset, which it refers
to as a "spatial computer."[2] But while the 2020s will be looked back
at as a major milestone for spatial computing and certainly a major
leap forward toward its mainstream impact, this wave of computing
goes as far back as the 1980s.

According to Wikipedia, the GIS community first used the term
"spatial computing" in the mid-1980s to describe computing large-
scale geospatial information.[3] Geospatial roots make sense for spatial
computing, seeing that mapping the world around us is fundamental
to this next wave of computing. At that time, the GIS community
was focused on mapping much larger areas versus the more human-
centric scale that spatial computing also encompasses today.

In the early 1990s, when VR made its way out of academia and
the military into its first commercialization attempt for consumers, the
definition of spatial computing moved beyond its geographic use to
encompass machine-to-human interactions. A start-up from Seattle
named Worldesign used spatial computing to describe how people
interact with three-dimensional environments.[4] Specifically, Worldesign
used the term for its immersive CAVE-like space known as the Virtual

Environment Theater, which simulated a flight over the Giza Plateau in 3000 BCE. Robert Jacobson, who was the CEO of Worldesign, has said that this definition of spatial computing was largely influenced by the research conducted at the University of Washington's Human Interface Technology Lab, which was under the leadership of Thomas A. Furness III, who has been referred to as the grandfather of VR.[5]

But perhaps the most frequently cited definition of spatial computing in recent times is from the eponymous 2003 thesis by MIT researcher Simon Greenwold.

In his thesis, Greenwold states:

> *Spatial computing is human interaction with a machine in which the machine retains and manipulates referents to real objects and spaces. Ideally, these real objects and spaces have prior significance to the user. For instance, a system that allows a user to create virtual forms and install them into the actual space surrounding him is spatial computing. A system that allows a user to place objects from his environment into a machine for digitization is spatial computing. Spatial computing differs from related fields such as 3D modeling and digital design in that it requires the forms and spaces it deals with to pre-exist and have real-world valence. It is not enough that the screen be used to represent a virtual space – it must be meaningfully related to an actual place.[6]*

Greenwold's human-centric explanation still holds true decades later.

Spatial computing promises us a computing experience beyond the screen where our digital interactions take place in 3D space. The essence of spatial computing is to integrate digital information with our physical environment in a seamless and interactive manner. By blending the virtual world with the physical world, computing can then perceive, interact with, and navigate three-dimensional space. This greatly enhances applications in every industry by providing more intuitive, efficient, and immersive ways to interact with technology.

Today, spatial computing has become synonymous with augmented reality and virtual reality. While AR and VR are examples of spatial computing, it is more appropriate to think of spatial computing as an umbrella term for a broad range of technologies. These technologies all enable computers to be present in and perceive our physical real-world space. Spatial computing ushers in a brand-new wave of applications, including AR, VR, and MR (together often referred to as extended reality, or XR), as well as autonomous vehicles, virtual assistants, robotics, and the Internet of Things (IoT).

AR and VR devices represent the next phase of consumer hardware in the era of spatial computing, moving us beyond the smartphone. XR technologies benefit from all aspects of spatial computing, leveraging the computer's new sense of awareness to edit our perception of reality. This can be achieved by changing our experience of the physical world with the blending of digital content with the physical real-world experience, such as AR and MR or completely transporting us into a simulation that removes our physical world completely, as in VR.

Autonomous vehicles and robotics use technologies such as sensors, AI, and in particular, machine learning, to understand and navigate surroundings and perform complex tasks in the physical world. This includes manufacturing robots that can work alongside humans, drones for delivery and surveillance, robots used in surgery, machines that vacuum our houses, and, eventually, androids in our homes.

Virtual assistants and the Internet of Things are examples of technologies that benefit greatly from the context spatial computing brings. In smart homes, spatial computing can help devices understand the layout and context of their environment, improving how they automate tasks and respond to user needs. For virtual assistants, spatial computing enhances their ability to interact with users through more natural, context-aware responses.

While we are still in the early days of the spatial computing era, it is important to look back and understand that we have been on this journey for a while now. The innovations and advancements of the last few decades have made it possible for us to see the opportunity in this next wave of computing more clearly. Our job at hand is to continue this evolution by investing in technologies and applications that will allow spatial computing to deliver on its promise.

The Spatial Computing Tech Stack

To understand what opportunities there are for your business in spatial computing, it is important first to understand its technology stack. While there are various perspectives on the tech stack within the computer programming world, this approach is designed to provide you with what you need to understand from a practical business standpoint.

A technology stack is everything you need to build and run an app. It includes the physical computers or hardware where the app runs to the various software components that handle different tasks. The software stack has two main sides: the front end, often referred to as the client, is what you see and interact with on your device, and the back end, often referred to as the server, works behind the scenes to manage data and ensure everything runs smoothly. All parts of this stack are necessary to enable applications and use cases for your business.

HARDWARE AS THE FOUNDATION

If we consider the structure of a house as an analogy for the spatial computing tech stack, the hardware would be the foundation. The previous waves of computing introduced groundbreaking consumer devices such as the personal computer, laptop, feature phone, and, eventually, the smartphone. Each played a pivotal role in shaping user interactions and capabilities, paving the way for more sophisticated applications.

Similarly, this new computing wave is introducing categories of devices designed for everyday use. Like the wave before, we will see these hardware options evolve over time. Among these are MR headsets. These headworn wearables offer both AR and VR experiences, with AR made possible through the use of the headset's advanced color passthrough capability. Alongside this category are smartglasses, which range from AI-enabled camera glasses with virtual assistants that whisper in your ear to glasses that feature optical see-through displays that can overlay virtual objects onto the real world without obscuring vision.

Outside of the headworn wearable categories, spatial computing is giving rise to autonomous devices, including self-driving cars, which aim to revolutionize transportation; drones or unmanned aerial vehicles (UAVs), which offer everything from delivery services to aerial surveillance; and robots designed for both industrial automation and personal assistance.

CONNECTIVITY AS THE WIRING AND PLUMBING

If hardware is the foundation, then connectivity is the plumbing and electrical wiring of the stack. In the PC and mobile eras, we saw how essential networking and data communications were in enabling applications that helped these waves realize value. The Internet and cellular networks have powered use cases on computers and smartphones that have fundamentally transformed society.

The spatial computing era will also have its own connectivity requirements, which will be critical in helping this wave prove its value. The new hardware categories in this next dimension of computing will need more robust and sophisticated networking and data requirements to power immersive technologies and autonomous systems that will usher in our future. The high bandwidth and ultra-low latency of 5G networks provide the real-time, reliable data transfer necessary for AR and VR applications to deliver seamless and immersive experiences. On the horizon are 6G and Wi-Fi 7, which is anticipated to revolutionize connectivity further by enabling even faster speeds and lower latencies, facilitating more responsive and interactive AR and VR applications.

BACK-END TECHNOLOGIES AS THE SUPPORT BEAMS

Back-end technologies serve as the tech stack's support beams and structural framework and are essential to its workings. They handle the behind-the-scenes processing and data management tasks to run applications smoothly. This includes application programming interfaces (APIs) that let software programs communicate with one another.

For spatial computing applications, AI and, in particular, machine learning algorithms are necessary for computers to process and make sense of large volumes of data. These algorithms are fundamental for computers to perceive the world around them. The back end also supports 3D modeling and rendering tasks necessary to visualize virtual content in space. Advanced networking solutions such as cloud computing and edge computing server architecture will also be needed to ensure data integrity and fast, reliable communications of sensitive and sizable spatial data.

FRONT-END TECHNOLOGIES AS THE CURB APPEAL

Front-end technologies make the software usable. Using the same house analogy, front-end technologies are what people see, the tech stack's interior style and exterior curb appeal. They shape the user interface, which determines how people interact with machines.

Spatial computing is leading to a shift in how we interact with technology as it moves from flat screens to three-dimensional space. As computers become more perceptive, we no longer need to interact with them in the same way. This era of computing is introducing a user interface that's more intuitive and engaging, incorporating technologies such as gesture recognition, eye tracking, and voice control. Additionally, haptic feedback technologies are being developed to provide tactile responses that enhance the realism of experiences. These advancements aim to simulate real-world interactions when engaging with content.

The Eyes and Ears of Spatial Computing

Sensors are essential to spatial computing. Sensors are the "senses" of a machine, providing raw data about light, sound, motion, and more. Common sensors include cameras, microphones, accelerometers, gyroscopes, compasses, and GPS units. Each type of sensor feeds its data into the system where it is initially processed. In this way, sensors act as the eyes and ears of the system, gathering data about the user and the environment, which is then used to enable computers to perceive and interact with the real world. While there are many sensors at play in spatial computing, this era is truly the camera's time to shine. Cameras are powerful sensors that collect vital visual information. When combined with AI, this gives computers the sense of sight. This new capability equips computers with perception and presence, the major building blocks for spatial computing.

CAMERAS AND DEPTH SENSORS

The camera, of course, is not a new sensor. Our smartphone cameras have democratized photography and are now a very common part of our everyday lives, mainly to capture images and videos for social media. But these same cameras (also referred to as RGB cameras as these sensors capture light using an array of red, green, and blue photosensors) can also be used for object recognition, environment mapping, light estimation, face tracking, and more. All of these are essential for your smartphone to be a powerful AR machine. If you have ever used an AR face filter on a social media application with your smartphone, you have experienced this new use of the RGB camera.

Spatial computing also makes use of depth cameras to measure the distance between the camera and the objects in its field of view. If RGB cameras help computers see what we see, depth cameras give them superpowers to see the world in 3D. These cameras use technologies like time-of-flight (ToF), structured light, or stereo vision to capture in-depth information, which is crucial for understanding the geometry of the environment. Similarly, depth sensors such as light detection and ranging (LiDAR) use laser pulses to measure the distance to objects, essentially shooting laser beams out and measuring the time it takes for each beam to bounce back after hitting an object. Both measure distances and create three-dimensional representations of the environment, but LiDAR is typically more precise and capable of working over longer distances. Depth cameras and sensors are necessary to help autonomous cars navigate safely and accurately as they provide critical information about the distance and size of objects around them. They are also essential in AR and VR, mapping real spaces for AR to blend digital elements realistically and ensuring safe, immersive interaction in VR environments by tracking movements and surroundings.

MOTION SENSORS

Beyond cameras and depth sensors, spatial computing also makes use of motion sensors, which help computers know that they are moving, which way they are facing, and what's around them. Accelerometers act as tiny motion detectors inside devices, sensing whether and how fast they move in any direction by measuring changes in speed, which helps devices, such as smartphones or smartglasses, respond to your movements. Gyroscopes, internal spinning tops, track how something is turning or tilting, which is crucial for keeping your phone's screen oriented correctly or making VR feel real as you look around. Magnetometers, known colloquially as compasses, detect the Earth's magnetic field to determine direction, guiding you on map apps by showing which way you are facing. In AR and VR, these sensors are key to creating immersive experiences, tracking user movements and translating them into the virtual world for a realistic and engaging interaction.

If Computers Only Had a BrAIn

Sensors are only half of the equation when it comes to enabling computers with perception. While sensors give computers the ability to collect information about the world around them, it is the processing of this data using ML and, more generally, AI that transforms it into understanding, prediction, and decision-making. AI algorithms process and interpret the data gathered by sensors, turning these raw signals into actionable insights. This symbiosis unlocks the ability for systems to dynamically adapt and respond to their environment. For example, in an autonomous car, cameras act as the eyes, detecting obstacles, traffic signals, and road signs. GPS systems help the car understand its location on a map, and accelerometers measure acceleration (changes in speed or direction). But this is all just a collection of numbers and images until it is integrated and interpreted. AI uses this raw data to enable the vehicle to operate and drive.

The true power of AI systems lies in their ability to process and make sense of a large volume of data. These technologies help the system understand information and make decisions based on what it receives. The process starts with gathering and combining data from different sources, a step known as sensor fusion. This approach helps create a complete picture of the environment. From there, machine learning models take over to analyze this information further, allowing the system to respond intelligently to the world around it.

Large language models (LLMs) are advanced AI systems designed to understand, generate, and interact with human language in a way that mimics human-like comprehension and response. These models are trained on vast amounts of text data, enabling them to perform a wide range of language tasks such as translation, summarization, question answering, and creative writing.

Large vision models (LVMs) are a type of neural network designed to process visual data and play a significant role in spatial computing. These models can analyze extensive visual data from cameras to identify objects, classify them, and understand their spatial relations. When combined with LLMs, LVMs can use both text and visual information to build a semantic understanding. In AR applications, large vision models can sense and understand the objects, layout, and people in the environment.

AI systems can be single-modal or multi-modal, depending on their design and the tasks they are intended to perform. Multi-modal AI refers to the use of AI that can handle multiple types of data inputs (such as images, sound, and text) to make decisions. This is crucial in environments where different kinds of data must be analyzed simultaneously to understand the context fully. For example, multi-modal AI can enable you to ask your virtual assistant to use a wearable camera and tell you what it sees. This capability allows the virtual assistant to analyze the camera feed, understand what is being seen, and then describe or respond to the user based on this visual information.

Merging Our Body with Bytes

Embodying these algorithms and housing these sensors are new categories of hardware for spatial computing, including wearable technology. Wearables are a step change in personal computing, moving the computer from something we hold in our hand or place on a desk to something we wear on our body as a part of ourselves. Like the personal computer and the smartphone, wearable technology is set to transform how we live our lives in every aspect, from work to play.

The wearable technology category is quite diverse, with health and fitness trackers, smartwatches, wearable cameras, smart clothing, and headworn wearables such as head-mounted displays and smartglasses. While all play a role in the future of computing as a new device constellation for consumers, the hero device in this next wave of computing is headworn wearables. Headworn wearables, or wearable headsets, are connected devices that are meant to be worn on your head. These may be goggles you wear, which are fully functional computers or glasses that house sensors and a display but offload the computation to the smartphone in your pocket. With Meta, Apple, Microsoft, HTC and Bytedance all with devices in the headworn category, it's clear that the technology giants are convinced that the next big consumer device will be on your head. While we may eventually reach a point where we will swap our smartphone for a pair of spatial computing specs, in the meantime, we will see various eyewear become available, all aimed at different use cases, and expected to live alongside the devices currently in play.

Three major categories of headworn wearables are connected eyewear, smartglasses, and head-mounted displays.

CONNECTED EYEWEAR

Connected eyewear refers to any eyeglass-like device with connectivity features, such as Bluetooth or Wi-Fi, allowing it to communicate with other devices or the Internet. Connected eyewear can vary in functionality, ranging from playing audio or announcing simple notifications to more complex tasks such as navigation, translation, and fitness tracking. Connected eyewear is dependent on the smartphone, tethering to it for connectivity, app integration, device control, data and media streaming, and processing power. In this way, connected eyewear is not a stand-alone computer but acts as a smartphone accessory. The advantage of this dependency is a lightweight form factor that looks much more like the non-digital eyewear available today.

Ray-Ban Meta, a collaboration between tech gian Meta and eyewear leader EssilorLuxottica, are a great example of connected eyewear. The glasses feature audio and cameras, various custom frame and lens combinations, and enable livestreaming from the glasses to Facebook or Instagram. You can also use your voice to engage with Meta AI, an advanced conversational assistant. This includes asking Meta AI to "Look and tell me what you see" to use its multi-modal AI capability that uses the onboard camera identify what is front of the wearer.

Other devices in the connected eyewear space include Xreal Air and Rokid Max. These glasses prioritize audio-video use cases and feature OLED displays, allowing wearers to extend their smartphone screen to the binocular displays.

SMARTGLASSES

Smartglasses go beyond connected eyewear as a stand-alone computing solution. Most of these devices prioritize delivering AR content viewed through an advanced optical see-through display. These displays feature optics, such as waveguides or prisms, which allow wearers to see virtual content intermixed with the real world in much the same way we see the physical real world, making them more comfortable on the eyes. However, to make these systems, with a wide field of view and power and heat efficient while bright enough to see indoors and outdoors is a huge challenge.

Some smartglasses use these optical systems to project notifications and contextual information in front of the users. These are typically referred to as heads-up displays, or HUDs, and can either be monocular or binocular in nature. Google Glass is a great example of a monocular heads-up display. Others, such as the Microsoft HoloLens and Magic Leap, combine these optical systems with robust cameras and sensors, enabling the device to have spatial awareness to place virtual content in physical, real-world space. These devices are currently aimed at enterprise use, mainly because of their high price tag, clunky industrial design, and limitations in field-of-view, battery life, and energy efficiency. They are ready for work and are proving value in reducing errors and improving operational efficiency, but they are not ready for consumers. These devices have a way to go to become more fashionable, wearable candidates for everyday use.

HEAD-MOUNTED DISPLAYS

Head-mounted displays create immersive visual experiences using video displays – LCDs, OLEDs, and micro-OLEDs – which offer a wide field of view and high-resolution graphics. Most HMDs today offer 4K resolution displays, while higher-end devices, such as the Pimax Crystal and Varjo XR-4, boast 8K displays. For the most part, HMDs block out the physical real world and replace it with the digital environment, completely immersing the wearer in a virtual reality experience. It has become common for VR HMDs to offer color video passthrough (or color passthrough) as a feature that enables an AR experience, commonly referred to as mixed reality or MR when experienced this way on a headset. To achieve color passthrough, the device captures live video from the environment using cameras on the outside of the headset. This feature allows users to see their surroundings in color through the headset at the same time as virtual content, effectively blending real-world visuals with the virtual world.

While these displays offer a wide field of view and high resolution, the trade-off is in varifocal issues because these devices typically have a fixed focus, which can make it hard for your eyes to adjust naturally when looking at objects at different distances. This can cause visual discomfort and make the virtual experience feel less real. The introduction of eye-tracking systems that monitor the direction and focus of your eyes in real time could help introduce varifocal systems that tell the headset how to adjust its lenses or displays to match where your eyes are focusing, better mimicking natural eye behavior.

HMDs also track the user's head movements using inside-out tracking technology to provide a realistic interaction with digital content to further the sense of immersion. This system utilizes cameras or sensors mounted on the headset itself, allowing it to determine orientation and position without the need for external sensors. These same cameras are used for the device to sense the world around it, create guardian systems to keep users safe in VR and map out the environment for use in MR. Outside cameras can also be used to track hand movements, allowing wearers to interact with applications with their hands, while in-headset cameras are used for eye-tracking systems, which enable the use of your eyes as a precise input mechanism. Together, with hand tracking, you can use your eyes and hands to interact with applications without controllers.

HMDs can either be tethered to a computer or console, such as Sony's PlayStation VR or HTC Vive Pro, or stand-alone, such as the Meta Quest 3 and Apple Vision Pro, incorporating all necessary processing hardware within the headset itself. In some cases, such as the Apple Vision Pro, the device is untethered for computation but tethered to an external battery for power.

Software Development for AR/VR

The value of hardware is always proven by the software that runs on it. Developers play a critical role in creating applications that unlock use cases for AR/VR wearables that will resonate with people, causing them to not just buy the device but come back and use it time and time again. To do this, developers need to use platforms such as software development kits (SDKs), game engines, frameworks, and libraries.

At the base level, platforms and SDKs provide the foundational tools needed for developing AR and VR applications. These platforms vary widely depending on the target device (mobile or headset) and the intended user experience.

For mobile devices, ARCore by Google and ARKit by Apple are leading SDKs that enable developers to create smartphone AR experiences. These SDKs use advanced algorithms for environmental understanding, allowing devices to detect surfaces, estimate lighting conditions, and understand the user's surroundings in real time. These capabilities are crucial for overlaying digital content in the real world in a contextually relevant and engaging way.

For more immersive experiences, dedicated MR headsets such as the Meta Quest and Apple Vision Pro offer their own SDKs which are designed to work with their own operating systems – Meta Horizon OS and visionOS, respectively. These tools provide developers with access to powerful MR features, such as high-fidelity tracking, room-scale experiences, and integrated hand tracking. Similarly, for AR, devices such as Microsoft's HoloLens and Magic Leap come with their own sets of development tools that allow for creating applications that blend digital content with the real world in complex ways.

Game engines such as Unity and Unreal Engine play a pivotal role in the development of AR and VR content. These engines provide robust tools for rendering 3D graphics, handling physics, and managing animations, making them ideal for creating immersive and interactive virtual environments. Unity is particularly popular in the AR/VR community due to its ease of use, extensive asset library, and strong support for both AR and VR platforms. Unity offers built-in support for a vast range of AR and VR devices, including iOS and Android smartphones and headsets such as Meta Quest and Apple Vision Pro. It also integrates with various AR SDKs, enabling advanced features such as object recognition and spatial mapping. Unreal Engine is known for its high-fidelity graphics and cinematic content creation capabilities. It is favored for applications that require photorealistic visuals and dynamic lighting, which are common in high-end VR simulations and interactive AR applications.

To aid in cross-device application development, developers can turn to a standard developed by the Khronos Group called OpenXR. By providing a common API, OpenXR facilitates the development of applications that can run on any hardware that supports the standard. Meta, Magic Leap, HTC, Bytedance, and more have adopted OpenXR. The adoption and improvement of this standard become increasingly important as the number of available AR and VR devices continues to grow.

Another important standard for AR/VR development is WebXR. WebXR is an important development in making AR/VR content more accessible through web browsers. This W3C (World Wide Web Consortium) standard enables immersive experiences directly within the browser. It allows users to access AR and VR content on a wide range of devices, including AR smartglasses, MR headsets, and mobile devices. While powerful, WebXR adoption varies across different browsers and devices, with some offering full support while others have limited or no compatibility.

Web developers can use a number of web development platforms with WebXR to develop browser-based content, including Mattercraft, PlayCanvas, and 8th Wall. Niantic's 8th Wall platform also offers an SDK that works across mobile devices and browsers to ensure that the developer's AR-enabled websites can be engaged with any user with a modern smartphone. In addition to widening the reach and accessibility of WebAR for developers, the 8th Wall SDK also brings AR features to the mobile browser beyond the capabilities of the WebXR standard, such as human AR and spatial mapping. As a platform, 8th Wall also offers its developers a complete set of tools to build immersive content, including an integrated development environment, source control, and hosting.

The development of immersive content on the web also requires the use of web 3D frameworks, such as three.js, A-Frame, and Babylon .js. These JavaScript libraries enable the creation of 3D graphics in the browser using WebGL (Web Graphics Library). WebGL is a JavaScript API that allows web developers to create 3D graphics within web browsers without the need for additional plugins. Building on that foundation, WebGPU is the next step, offering even more powerful and efficient graphics-processing capabilities for richer and more complex 3D experiences in the browser.

Whether through sophisticated game engines to build native applications or browser-optimized frameworks and libraries for creating on the web, developers have the necessary tools to create software that continues to push the boundaries of what's possible in AR and VR, shaping the future of how we interact with technology.

Sparking Spatial Strategies

Strike up strategic dialogue about AR's role in your business with these essential conversation starters:

- **In the boardroom:** How can we implement AR/VR strategies into our business plans to ensure our organization gains insights and does not fall behind in this next wave of computing?
- **For your team meeting:** With companies such as Apple and Meta pushing into spatial computing with devices such as the Apple Vision Pro and Meta Quest, how do you think our customers' daily lives might change in the next few years?
- **Around the water cooler:** Did you know spatial computing started back in the 1980s in geospatial mapping? It's amazing to see how it's now morphing into AR and VR. What do you think the next big leap in spatial computing will be?

Share this on your socials: Spatial computing has evolved from a niche GIS term in the '80s to a broad tech umbrella encompassing AR, VR, and more. It's shaping our interaction with the digital and physical worlds and promising revolutionary applications across industries. #thenextdimensionbook

CHAPTER 3

Your 3D Wake-Up Call

My virtual surroundings looked almost (but not quite) real.
Everything inside the OASIS was beautifully rendered in three
dimensions. Unless you pulled focus and stopped to examine
your surroundings more closely, it was easy to forget that
everything you were seeing was computer-generated.

— Ready Player One *by Ernest Cline*[1]

Chapter Cheat Sheet Powered by AI

I asked an AI to read this chapter and create a cheat sheet. If you only
have five minutes to spare, here are the three must-know insights to
help you level up your spatial computing knowledge.

♦ **Investment in 3D:** As AR and VR become more prevalent, businesses must develop a strategy to integrate 3D
content across various platforms, including virtual worlds,
AR/VR experiences, and traditional 2D content such as
e-commerce and games. This approach leverages investments in 3D assets for broader applications, enhancing user
engagement and ROI.

♦ **A New Device Ecosystem:** A new ecosystem of spatial computing devices, including AR wearables, self-driving vehicles,
and robots, presents fresh business opportunities. Companies

must adapt by rethinking customer interactions, reshaping offerings, and evaluating business models to capitalize on these evolving technologies.

♦ **Keeping Pace with Innovation:** While embracing emerging technologies, businesses should adopt a pragmatic approach by assessing the technological maturity and market readiness of different spatial computing categories. This strategic pacing aligns with consumer adoption rates, ensuring that business transformations are timely and effective.

Want to talk to an AI about this book? Scan the QR code or visit ai.thenextdimension book.com in your browser to access The Next Dimension Book GPT.

Scan Me

A New Device Ecosystem

Technology is now ready to bring our computing experience into 3D space. This presents a new imperative for businesses and brands to update their strategies to stay relevant. Businesses will need to rethink customer touchpoints, reshape products and services, and evaluate business models as a brand-new set of hardware options becomes available to consumers. From self-driving vehicles and robots to AR/VR headsets and other wearables, there are a myriad of new devices being introduced to consumers under the umbrella of spatial computing. Each of these presents new opportunities that businesses will need to consider.

It is important to remember that we are just at the beginning of this shift in computing, so these advancements will take some time to realize their full potential. It is best to take a pragmatic approach when implementing these into your strategy, assessing where each spatial computing device category is in its readiness for your target audience. This will ensure that your plans are well paced along the adoption curve and help ensure that your goals are rooted in what is possible at each point along the hardware journey. It is also important to keep in mind that these new devices will exist alongside each other as well as with the existing device ecosystem already in play, including computers, smartphones, smart TVs, and other IoT devices. In this way, business strategies must account for the opportunities these new device categories generate on their own and consider how these devices work with and change the dynamic of existing devices as part of a new consumer device constellation.

While all spatial computing device categories are nascent, AR and VR are among the most ready opportunities for businesses today. With AR available on smartphones and MR headsets at a relatively affordable price point, the opportunity for businesses to reach consumers is sizable and growing. Development and creation tools are readily available for businesses to use to ramp up their own internal teams or with a growing ecosystem of creators, agencies, and freelancers who possess the skills and experience to create content. Most importantly, consumers have already started to use AR and VR on a frequent basis, with over 90 million monthly users of AR and nearly 70 million VR users in 2023, according to a report from eMarketer.[2]

It All Starts with 3D

While there is a stark difference between AR and VR experiences, the basis for both is 3D. All immersive content takes up space, whether it is a full simulation you move around in or virtual elements you engage with in your own physical environment. To do this, content needs to have depth. While 2D elements, such as video and images, can be used in immersive experiences, AR and VR experiences mostly require 3D assets to feel real and evoke a sense of presence.

However, 3D media isn't just important for enabling AR and VR content but is also useful in 2D content such as desktop and mobile gaming or e-commerce product pages. This is an important consideration as much of the investment in 3D asset creation and skill generation for AR and VR can also be used in content opportunities that arguably have even greater immediate reach and vice versa. Devising a 3D content strategy for your business that considers all distribution opportunities will help justify the investment. Consider the use of 3D in gaming, virtual worlds, websites, apps, and social networks, and even use these assets for video and photo shoots such as TV commercials or print ads. Building and leveraging a catalog of 3D assets across multiple touchpoints will enable your business to see the total return on investment in this new media.

While there are many generative AI solutions being worked on to help make 3D content creation easier, more efficient, and democratized, at this time, 3D content creation requires specialized skills. It is important that your business invest in hiring or upskilling your team with expertise in this area or develop a network of partners for production. Crafted using specialized 3D modeling software such as Blender or Autodesk Maya, 3D models are a foundational element in the design of immersive content. These models are often animated to bring dynamic movement into the scene – characters run, machinery operates, and trees sway – creating a world that feels alive and responsive. In addition to 3D modeling, 3D assets can also be created by scanning real-world objects, people, and environments using technologies such as photogrammetry, neural radiance fields (also called NeRFs), and gaussian splatting. While commercial projects may wish to work with professional solutions that use specialized equipment to scan and create content, we are quickly seeing 3D scanning be democratized with apps that use your smartphone to capture, such as Polycam and Scaniverse.

In addition to 3D assets, immersive content creators also need to think about the experience's spatial logic and add other sensory elements, such as haptics and spatial audio. The physics engine in immersive content simulates realistic interactions between objects, which we take for granted in our physical real world. This engine ensures that objects behave as expected by harnessing the laws of physics, such as gravity and other forces. The physics engine can be designed to mimic the physics we are used to in our everyday reality, such as a ball rolling down a slope, debris scattering from an explosion, or the subtle sway of a bridge underweight. Or it can be designed to alter these forces to be out of this world, where a ball might float upward, defying gravity, an explosion could freeze in mid-air, turning it into a slowly expanding sculpture of light and energy, and a bridge could ripple like a wave, undulating continuously without ever collapsing.

Equally important to the realism of immersive content is its sound design. Strategic use of audio effects, background music, and, notably, spatial audio enriches AR and VR atmospheres. Spatial audio techniques allow sounds to be placed anywhere in a three-dimensional space, providing the listener with a more lifelike auditory experience.

This enriches the ambiance and provides vital cues about the environment or off-screen events. Sound can influence the emotional tone, heighten tension, or offer relief, guiding participants' emotional responses and enriching their overall engagement.

As you look to upskill your team or work with partners, you will want to consider 3D content creation capabilities that focus on asset creation and the ability to develop elements that bring a 3D scene to life – from animation and physics to spatial sound. Ramping up your teams with 3D specialized skills and keeping an eye on emerging AI-enabled solutions, including generative 3D media and smartphone scanning solutions, are essential ways to ready your business for spatial computing.

Spatializing 2D Content

While creating fully immersive content utilizes the full potential of AR and VR, adding 3D elements to existing 2D content can breathe new life into traditional media and be a great way to ease into immersive content for your business. Whether adding a 3D model viewer to product pages on your e-commerce site or embracing a 3D animation in your website hero banner, this multidimensional content can significantly enhance your visual storytelling and lead to deeper user engagement.

Unlike 2D, where interactions are limited to a flat plane, 3D elements allow users to explore content in all directions. This spatial freedom makes content more lifelike and relatable, which can increase the impact and retention of information. In this way, the depth and realism that 3D adds can turn a simple viewing experience into a memorable journey, creating a stronger emotional bond with the content. For example, adding 3D replicas of products as part of the product page carousel on your e-commerce site can provide customers with a realistic preview of products. The addition of 3D on your 2D site enables shoppers to view products from all angles by rotating and spinning them around and even potentially resizing the product so that they can get up close to the details.

3D can also be a great fallback for mobile AR in cases where users may not wish to turn their cameras on. Preparing for this scenario can allow users to access a version of your immersive content rather than presenting them with an error message. Alternatively, your roll-out of an AR experience may begin with 3D, which can immediately engage a user with less friction. You can then show immediate value, which can be enriched by transitioning to the whole AR mode.

Finally, bringing your 2D content, such as videos, into MR for use in a headset can be a quick win. Consider taking this to the next level by adding 3D elements around it. For example, characters from your video can sit beside the floating screen and watch it with you. Users can find themselves sitting inside the environment from one of the film's scenes as the backdrop for the viewing experience. This mixed media approach can be an effective way to get your existing content in a headset to learn more about this opportunity and its audience.

Gaming and the Metaverse

Another great way to dip your toes into immersive content and harden your team's 3D skills is through gaming and the emerging concept of the metaverse. According to McKinsey & Company, "The metaverse is the emerging 3-D-enabled digital space that uses virtual reality, augmented reality, and other advanced internet and semiconductor technology to allow people to have lifelike personal and business experiences online."[3] Today's platforms act as essential proving grounds and developmental stepping stones for the future of AR and VR content. They can provide crucial insights and foundational know-how for the approaching spatial computing era.

Gaming, specifically games in virtual worlds such as Roblox and Fortnite, can be viewed as early representations of the metaverse. Experiences in virtual worlds share very similar qualities to AR/VR content, such as the need for real-time interactions, 3D assets, and world-building. For businesses and development teams, engaging with today's gaming and virtual worlds is not just about participation; it represents a strategic investment in enhancing skills and understanding market dynamics they can take into tomorrow. As these teams refine content creation, deployment, and management within current metaverse platforms, they also accumulate valuable business intelligence. This includes insights into user behavior and preferences in virtual settings, vital for designing user-centric experiences in fully immersive environments.

The shift to spatial computing requires a deep understanding of creating content with space at the center. Businesses active in current virtual worlds are leading the way, not only by using 3D technologies but also by setting standards for user engagement and content relevance. As we move toward the full potential of spatial computing, the experiences and lessons from today's gaming and virtual environments on 2D screens will be invaluable.

The State of AR Today

AR is as much a technology of today as it is the medium of tomorrow. While MR headsets are just beginning their journey to consumer adoption and smartglasses are mainly proving value in transforming the enterprise, the most significant opportunity for AR lies in the hands of billions of users around the world in the smartphone.[4]

The portable supercomputer we have been carrying around for over a decade has gradually become a powerful AR machine. Year after year, these devices have received significant upgrades in chipsets, processors, cameras, displays, and sensors. Each iteration enables more sophisticated AR experiences, giving new functions to a familiar device. In addition to hardware advancements, the evolution of mobile operating systems that support sensor fusion, integrating data from various sensors, and the support for new 5G connectivity, which reduces latency and increases the speed at which data is processed, creates a fertile playground for AR.

Today, there are three main categories of mobile AR to consider as opportunities for your business: social AR, web AR, and native application AR. Each presents different AR capabilities and is a very different distribution channel for your AR experience, so it must be considered carefully when devising your AR plans.

SOCIAL AR

Social AR is the most well-known and utilized type of AR for businesses. This is primarily because of its large, addressable audience already active with camera-enabled content. All the most popular social networks have AR tools that enable brands, agencies, and creators to develop filters and lenses published directly within the social network. For Snapchat, that is Lens Studio. For TikTok, that is

Effect House. Meta Spark Studio is used for Instagram, Facebook, and Messenger. All these tools equip creators with what they need to develop AR effects that let social media augment the content on their social feeds. How users utilize these AR effects within each social network is nuanced. Snapchat, the OG of social AR, has its lenses, which are typically 10-second effects meant to augment quick videos. Instagram and Facebook have filters originally optimized to augment photos in these feeds. TikTok has effects intended to be used as a UGC (user-generated content) video editing tool for creating short-form, 30-second videos. In this way, think about making a lens for Snapchatters that encourages friends to share a quick video to continue their streak, a filter that enhances a photo so that it gets people to stop scrolling in their feed, and an effect that creates a trend that TikTokkers can use to create videos that get on your For You Page (FYP). While these are not hard and fast rules, understanding the different expectations of AR for each social network can be critical to the success of a social AR campaign. In addition to the nuanced use of AR, each of these social networks also presents different opportunities related to the demographics of its addressable audience.

The creator community is a critical community on social networks relevant to AR. The social AR creator community is quite large, and brands and marketers are familiar with tapping into this ecosystem to create compelling marketing content with them. As AR creation tools are accessible and free, any social media user can become a creator, which is why the number of creators is growing. Social AR creators are critical partners to marketers. They partner with marketers to create AR content and inspire marketers to show them the bounds of social AR, all while deploying AR content to the networks that are helping millions become AR users. In this way, AR creators have become a new type of influencer, and many AR creators on these networks have amassed large followers due to their creative capability to harness these tools.

Snapchat launched its Lens Studio in 2017[5] after acquiring Looksery in 2015.[6] As a technology company that believes "the camera presents the greatest opportunity to improve the way people live and communicate," Snapchat has become synonymous to many with AR.[7] This is partly due to Snap's central role in introducing and adopting AR in the mainstream. Snap has reported that over 300 million users engage with Lenses daily on average.[8] The Snap website also states that over 300,000 creators have created over 3.5 million Lenses that have been viewed more than nine trillion times.[9]

Meta Spark Studio AR filters can be published on Facebook, Messenger, and Instagram. Meta has reported that over 400,000 creators have created more than 1.2 million AR effects using its platform, which have generated more than a billion views.[10] The Meta website also states that over 750 million users use mobile AR experiences monthly.[11] Despite its scale, Meta announced in August 2024 that its Meta Spark platform and content will no longer be available effective January 2025.[12]

With over a billion users in its global community, AR content on TikTok has the potential to go viral quickly.[13] TikTok's Effect House is the most recent social AR content studio to become available, reaching general availability in 2022.[14] TikTok reports that it has over 400,000 members on its Effect House discord and that Effects created by the community have inspired more than 21 billion videos, garnering over 8.6 trillion views globally.[15]

WebAR

Web-based AR, often called WebAR, allows developers and creators to move beyond social media's walled gardens by harnessing the browser's power, freedom, and flexibility. Web browsing has become a core part of our daily digital lives, so leveraging this user behavior lowers the friction for AR adoption. Frictionless AR is also afforded by the fact that no app is required to access web-based AR. This fundamental element of WebAR resonates strongly with marketers at a time when smartphone app fatigue is a real problem. The shift toward browser-based AR solutions empowers marketers to transcend the confined ecosystems of app stores and social media platforms, tapping into the unrestricted expanse of five billion WebAR-capable smartphones.[16] While WebAR offers unparalleled reach, it does not provide an immediate addressable audience. Instead, an AR-enabled website must be integrated as part of the marketing mix – included as a URL destination in newsletters, text message blasts, or websites or as a QR code on billboards, magazine pages, or packaging.

Various platforms are available to create WebAR content, all leveraging advancements in 3D graphics in web browsers. Two of the most common are Zappar's Zapworks and Niantic's 8th Wall platform, which offer tools and AR technology that enable content to work across iOS and Android smartphones. Niantic reports that the 8th Wall platform has been used to publish over 100,000 web apps, with over 2,500 commercial experiences for top brands across industry verticals.[17] Developers can also opt to create web AR content using the evolving WebXR browser standard, which is being spearheaded by the W3C and leverages the native XR capabilities of the device on which it is running.

NATIVE APP AR

The last of the three major mobile AR categories, native app AR, refers to the creation of downloadable smartphone apps available in the Google Play Store or Apple App Store. Native applications benefit from seamlessly integrating with the device's hardware capabilities, which may be more robust in some cases than what is available in the browser. Apple's ARKit and Google's ARCore are AR frameworks instrumental in developing native application AR. Several third-party SDKs also build on these frameworks and bring additional spatial awareness capabilities, such as Niantic's Lightship ARDK, which offers long-distance meshing, semantic spatial understanding, and a centimeter-level precise visual positioning system (VPS). Vuforia, Immersal, and EasyAR are just a few other notable SDKs also available to enhance the AR capabilities within a smartphone app.

To build these native applications, developers turn to popular game platforms such as Unreal Engine and Unity or integrated development environments from Google and Apple such as Android Studio or Xcode. Unity is one of the most popular platforms for AR app development. The company has invested heavily in providing the right tools to native app developers to create applications, such as Unity's AR Foundation, a cross-platform framework enabling developers to create AR experiences for Android and iOS devices.

These three categories of smartphone AR are not in competition with one another. When building out your AR plans, native app, social, and web can be an "and" and not an "or." To make the right decision, you will want to choose a platform based on what will allow you to reach the right audience and enable your team to develop the experience you envision for your users within the time and budget you have allowed. In some cases, developing your AR experience for multiple platforms may make sense to broaden the reach. This is where the investment in 3D assets can come in handy, although some optimization may be needed to utilize them on the various platforms.

The Market Readiness for AR

Consumers have been carrying smartphones in their pockets for over a decade and are ready to do new things with them. Our relationship with our smartphones is changing. Nothing encapsulates this as much as when millions of consumers put their phones in cardboard boxes and strapped them to their faces to try virtual reality for the first time, as we saw back in 2015. While we are early in adopting headset AR and VR, mobile AR has significant traction in the market.

According to a report by ARtillery Intelligence, the global mobile AR annual revenue is projected to grow from $10.5 billion in 2023 to $21.5 billion in 2028, representing a compound annual growth rate of 15.4%.[18] This report noted that marketing and commerce are the leading revenue categories, accounting for $4.71 billion in 2023, driven by AR's ability to provide immersive product demonstrations that boost conversion rates.

The growing number of AR-compatible devices further supports AR's scalability. With advancements in smartphone technology, more devices now come equipped with AR capabilities. AR Insider estimates that 3.21 billion WebAR-compatible units, 2.91 billion Meta Spark units, and 1.66 billion compatible units with Google's ARCore make up the growing AR install base.[19] This large installed base of AR-enabled smartphones is a primary driver of AR revenue growth.

Consumer engagement with AR is also on the rise. Statista estimates that there are 912 million active users across various AR methods, including visual search and mobile AR use on platforms such as Meta, Snapchat, and TikTok.[20] Furthermore, a survey conducted by Thrive Analytics and ARtillery Intelligence revealed that 32% of US adult consumers have used mobile AR, with 46% of these users engaging with AR at least weekly and 74% monthly.[21] These findings underscore the significant role that frequent interaction with AR technology plays in driving continued revenue and market growth.

Demographically, younger adults, mainly Gen Z and millennials, are in charge of embracing AR. According to a Harris Poll, "One in three (32%) Millennials currently uses AR technology (compared to 23% of Gen Z, 14% of Gen X, 6% of Baby Boomers)."[22] "Gen Z and Millennials emerge as the leading adopters of AR/VR technology, with higher ownership levels at 18% and 12% respectively," according to a survey by AddictiveTips.[23] However, while younger demographics may be the first to adopt AR/VR technologies, that same survey found that "82% of respondents from all age groups expressed their enthusiasm for embracing the potential of this advanced AR/VR technology for entertainment purposes."

Societal Considerations

As society grows more accustomed to AR as a part of everyday life, businesses need to consider some key issues when planning their AR strategies. Privacy concerns are crucial because AR can collect a lot of personal data, and it's essential to keep that information safe and respect users' privacy. Legal issues also need attention, from protecting creative content to ensuring product safety to staying on the right side of the law. Ethical considerations are also vital, such as making sure people know and agree with what's happening when they use AR. Plus, there are health aspects to consider, such as the impact on users' eyesight and mental health. Addressing these issues will help businesses use AR in a safe and respectful way for everyone.

PRIVACY AND DATA SECURITY

As spatial computing technologies rely on sensing the world around them through sensors, including cameras, privacy and data security are at the top of mind. AR technologies require the use of visual and location data to function effectively. This raises significant concerns about user privacy and the security of the data collected. How AR companies manage, use, and protect this data is a critical issue with implications for personal privacy and potential surveillance. Many

AR platforms are designed with privacy in mind and have architected their sensing capabilities and data storage policies to protect user privacy. However, as a business, it will be vital for you to understand the privacy policies of the platforms used in your AR solutions to ensure that they meet your requirements. You will also want to design your applications with privacy as a key tenet, including implementing requests for permission to gain sensor access or data collection and being explicit about what and why sensors and data are required.

LEGAL AND ETHICAL CONCERNS

Depending on your use of AR, your legal team may also want to be involved to ensure that your use of AR necessitates strict adherence to existing laws and proactively engages with emerging regulations. AR can create complex situations involving intellectual property. AR experiences that overlay digital content onto physical space, such as commercial property and existing OOH (out-of-home) advertising, objects, and copyrighted or trademarked materials without permission, could lead to legal challenges. In addition, keeping your users safe will also need to be at the forefront of your mind, especially when using AR in public spaces, as distractions caused by AR could lead to accidents. Regulating where and how AR can be safely used, especially in vehicles or outdoors, as part of the design of your AR solutions will be critical.

Another perspective to consider as you build AR into your plans is potential ethical concerns in using this technology. Here, user consent is paramount. It will be essential to design applications that ask its users to be cautious of capturing individuals who may be unknowingly captured when the AR experience is active. This ensures they know what data the app collects and how it is stored. AR solutions need to make consent clear and straightforward. This means giving users simple, easy-to-understand choices about what data they share and how it will be used. Users should be able to offer their permission actively, not just by default or through complicated settings.

As AR can alter how we perceive reality, especially as the technology gets even more powerful and immersive, it may have an even more significant influence on the decisions and behaviors of the user. It is crucial to design solutions with this in mind to ensure your user has complete awareness and maintain their autonomy. Users should have control over whether they participate in augmented environments and be free to make their own choices. When AR affects how we see and interact with the world without fully understanding it, we can feel as if we're not entirely in control of our decisions. Those creating and using AR technology need to make sure people know when and how they're entering these augmented environments and give them the choice to opt in or out.

AR often requires high-performing hardware, whether the latest smartphone or a newly launched headset, which can create a digital divide as this hardware may not be accessible for all people. This uneven access to AR technologies can exacerbate existing social inequalities and see only specific segments of the population benefit from AR applications. Additionally, there's a need to ensure that AR technologies are accessible to people with disabilities, which involves designing inclusive AR systems that accommodate diverse needs.

PHYSICAL AND PSYCHOLOGICAL HEALTH

Businesses should also be aware of potential health and psychological concerns associated with these new technologies. As more people use these devices regularly, the health impact of prolonged use of AR technology, particularly on vision and spatial awareness, is an increasing concern. As AR requires users to look through a screen, this close interaction may strain the eyes, mainly when used for long periods, potentially leading to issues such as eye discomfort, blurred vision, and headaches.

Another aspect to consider is spatial awareness and physical safety. AR can alter our perceptions by changing or obscuring the natural environment with digital elements. For instance, if someone is walking and using AR to navigate, they might be less aware of physical obstacles, leading to a higher risk of accidents. This alteration of perception can also have more profound implications, such as affecting one's ability to judge distances or recognize hazards immediately, which is crucial in everyday activities. Given these concerns, users and developers need to consider the physical implications of AR. Users should be mindful of the time spent using AR and take regular breaks to reduce eye strain. Developers can encourage these user behaviors by implementing design principles that minimize visual overload and encourage safe usage patterns for their AR experiences.

There are also potential psychological effects to consider, such as the blurring of the line between real and augmented experiences, which can affect mental health and well-being. This can be especially important for face effects that modify a user's appearance. These effects may impact self-esteem as they may portray unrealistic beauty standards and alter one's perception of self. Frequent use of AR filters might lead individuals to feel less satisfied or more critical of their natural appearance, diminishing their confidence and worsening their mental health.

When new technologies such as AR emerge, concerns about privacy, legal issues, ethical dilemmas, and health impacts often appear more daunting. The frameworks for managing these risks are not fully developed in the early stages, leading to heightened anxiety about potential abuses and harms. However, as these technologies become more widespread, society begins to adapt. New norms, agreements, and societal contracts are established while laws and regulations evolve to address these concerns more effectively. Over time, as understanding deepens and protective measures are put in place, these concerns tend to diminish, allowing for safer and more confident use of the technology.

The Year Is 2035

Due to its reach and scale, the smartphone will remain the most significant platform for AR. However, the landscape of AR is set to transform dramatically in the coming decade as we advance into the age of spatial computing. Several trends will broaden the scope of AR during this period. Still, the most powerful will likely be the convergence of AI and AR, the growth of MR technologies, and the introduction of smartglasses.

AI-ENABLED CONTENT CREATION

Generative AI (GenAI) is well on its way to being a major game changer for content creation, and it has significant implications for creating AR experiences. Generative media solutions that enable users to create high-quality 2D images and video with the ease of a text prompt can be used to create textures for 3D assets in an AR scene, which can customize assets such as the clothing on an avatar or add 2D media such as photos and videos to objects in space. Many solutions are in the works to unlock generative 3D media, enabling users to create 3D assets. As in the case of text and 2D media solutions, users will enter a prompt to generate the 3D mesh of a model and, in some cases, create front and back textures for this model and even generate full rigs and animations to bring it to life. Generative media solutions can also be used to create 360° skyboxes to create virtual worlds in minutes. These solutions are in the early days today but are already in a good enough state to start to create models for prototyping purposes.

While GenAI is proving to be a powerful way to create assets, it is also demonstrating its value in assisting developers to code. Co-pilot solutions are partnering with developers to automate certain coding tasks, suggest improvements, and provide real-time feedback and solutions. AI co-pilots are being trained on libraries, frameworks, and even entire codebases to auto-complete lines of code, suggest entire blocks, and offer debugging assistance while working within the development environment. Just like generative media solutions, co-pilots are still in their early stages. Still, many are already proving to enhance productivity by reducing the time developers spend on routing coding tasks and improving code quality by reducing the likelihood of errors.

Eventually, generative AI may reach a point where it will enable world-building, generating code and assets with a single prompt. One day we may tell an AI what we want to see to create full games and AR/VR experiences. Imagine wearing a headset and speaking into existence the experience you want to see in front of you. Soon, the meaning of the development acronym WYSIWYG will likely move from "what you see is what you get" to "what you say is what you get."

MIXED REALITY MATURITY

MR headsets are certainly a turning point for AR. These devices aim to deliver on the promise of AR by blending the physical and the digital in a way that mimics how we experience our everyday lives. While today's devices are enabling hands-free, wide field-of-view MR content that can be engaged with intuitive and natural ways using our hands and eyes, we are only just at the beginning of this device category's journey.

There are several different things to watch in this area to keep your MR strategies ahead of the curve. The first, of course, is in hardware. MR devices are expected to get smaller, faster, and more powerful with each major cycle. This may include displays that boast higher resolution and offer an expanded field of view, which offers even more realistic and immersive visuals. More powerful cameras and sensors give the device greater spatial awareness, including tracking the user and the world, to bring both more into the MR experience. More efficient processing capabilities and longer battery life will enable users to experience MR without frequent recharging interruptions. As the technical specifications improve, so may the form factor of these devices, which most likely will be more light-weight and comfortable to wear for extended periods with designs that may look more and more like eyewear and less like gadgets. This may encourage MR to be used more often and even begun to be used outdoors, carried and used like laptops at coffee shops, friends' houses, parks and other common places.

As the hardware advances so too will the operating systems. Headset operating systems will continue to get more powerful and efficient, making use of new hardware components and benefiting greatly from advancements in AI. As the headset space matures, we may see greater integrations and interoperability between devices, which may be key to multiuser and social features. We may also see user interfaces begin to be standardized, which will facilitate easier navigation and interaction across different platforms and devices. We may even see that the integration of adaptive and contextual technologies which will allow operating systems to tailor experiences to individual user needs, behaviors, and environments, enhancing usability and immersion.

As MR technologies continue to evolve, the need for standards and interoperability in development platforms becomes increasingly critical. Currently, developers must navigate a fragmented landscape with varying standards and tools specific to each device. Over time, we will likely witness a significant shift toward platform convergence. This will enable developers to build once and deploy across multiple systems, reducing both time and cost. Converged platforms will offer robust tool sets that are versatile across hardware types, fostering innovation and creativity by lowering entry barriers.

Alongside the convergence of developer platforms, app stores are expected to mature significantly. New digital marketplaces may appear, while existing ones may evolve to better cater to immersive experiences by offering features specifically designed for MR and VR content. These may include new discovery opportunities that use AI and AR/VR technologies, such as advanced search capabilities, more personalized recommendations, and reimagined product merchandising.

Monetization strategies within these ecosystems may also mature. We should see these expand beyond traditional app purchase and subscription models to include more diverse revenue streams, such as in-experience transactions and tiered access levels. Advertising within MR may evolve to be more integrated and less intrusive, utilizing the environment itself to create compelling, context-aware campaigns that add value to the user experience, such as object-level ad bidding and networks that serve immersive content. For businesses and brands, this means a more dynamic environment in which to engage with customers.

With more standardized platforms and richer app ecosystems, businesses can more easily enter the MR and VR spaces to provide unique, immersive experiences. Whether for marketing, direct sales of virtual and physical goods, virtual events, or a new form of customer service, the opportunities for brand engagement in virtual spaces are bound to grow. The increased focus on discovery mechanisms within app stores will also enable brands to target and reach the right audiences more effectively than ever before.

SMARTER SMARTGLASSES

While MR headsets continue to mature, keep an eye on the other eyewear opportunity emerging for consumers: smartglasses. Many consider smartglasses the holy grail of AR and expect them to be the ultimate device that will finally cause us to leave our smartphones behind. However, it is important to understand the journey this device category is on to gauge opportunities for your business.

The most important thing to understand in the smartglasses category is that there are a variety of devices that offer features that exist across a spectrum of capabilities. Connected eyewear sits at one end of the spectrum where lightweight, fashionable devices are available for consumers today but with the trade-off of not yet being capable of true all-day, everyday AR. While enterprise AR headworn devices offer fully sophisticated AR, their machines are too large, too inefficient, and somewhat limited, especially in field-of-view, for prime-time mainstream use. We may see this device category eventually move more into the middle, where consumer eyewear gets more powerful, and enterprise machines get to a state where you could imagine bringing them home to try with the family.

We need only look to previous waves of computing to understand where we are today and potentially how long the road ahead is. This could be quite insightful for your business as you engage in longer-term planning for your organization.

Today's MR devices are very much like the emergence of the early personal computers back in the 1980s. These devices were large and limited compared to today's standards. Early VR and MR devices are following a similar path. Just like the PC, we will most likely see the inevitable miniaturization of these devices as they get even more powerful. This laptop moment will free MR devices from the confines of the home or office, giving them more portability to different locations in the outside world, whether this be to take it to a friend's place, a coffee shop, or enjoy it outside at a park. It is not quite a mobile replacement, but it has enough flexibility to unlock brand-new use cases.

At the same time, you can view today's connected eyewear for consumers, like the feature phones of the late '90s. They somewhat resemble their eventual endpoint of smartglasses as much as the feature phone did for the smartphone. They were extremely limited in capabilities and hardware specs at the start, but this evolved over time. In this way, you can imagine the smartglasses we do have today, Magic Leap and HoloLens, are like early PDAs, such as the Apple Newton, which predated the smartphone. They resemble much more in functionality the holy grail, an all-day, everyday pair of AR glasses we can imagine consumers wearing in the future but are not yet fully there.

Eventually, we may reach a point of convergence in smartglasses which will give birth to an iPhone moment, positioning this device as the smartphone replacement it is expected to become. In the meantime, businesses will have multiple opportunities along this device journey to benefit from learning and realize real return on investment (ROI) from applications and solutions they may develop.

Sparking Spatial Strategies

Strike up strategic dialogue about AR's role in your business with these essential conversation starters:

- **In the boardroom:** What skills do we need to develop within our team to begin to specialize in 3D?
- **For your team meeting:** What are the potential risks we should anticipate when thinking about using these new technologies as part of our business plans, and how can we mitigate them?
- **Around the water cooler:** Which new device from the emerging spatial computing ecosystem are you most excited about and why?

Share this on your socials: Investing in a 3D content strategy now can not only unlock opportunities in gaming, virtual worlds, and mobile AR today but also provide your business with the skills and insights for more immersive AR and VR content tomorrow #thenextdimensionbook

CHAPTER 4

Marketing in an Augmented World

We're always looking for opportunities from a marketing standpoint to see where new technologies or emerging technologies can help us tell the stories.
> — George Felix, *CMO at Pizza Hut, from an interview with Business Insider*[1]

Chapter Cheat Sheet Powered by AI

I asked an AI to read this chapter and create a cheat sheet. If you only have five minutes to spare, here are the three must-know insights to help you level up your spatial computing knowledge.

- **Widespread Adoption and Impact:** Companies are already investing in AR, with many brands and multiple campaigns using this technology. The growing interest in AR by brands echoes the rising user base of this technology worldwide.
- **Competitive Advantage and Differentiation:** AR is recognized for providing brands with a competitive edge by enabling personalized, memorable marketing experiences. This differentiation comes from AR's ability to integrate real-world elements, making marketing efforts more engaging and uniquely tailored to each consumer.

♦ **Early Adoption Benefits:** Early adopters of AR technology benefit from a competitive advantage by future-proofing their marketing strategies. As AR evolves, brands that are early participants can develop expertise and build consumer trust, positioning them favorably as the technology becomes mainstream in marketing.

Want to talk to an AI about this book? Scan the QR code or visit ai.thenextdimension book.com in your browser to access The Next Dimension Book GPT.

Scan Me

You Can't Spell "Brand" without the "A" and "R"

Marketers are traditionally one of the first to adopt new technologies. Technologies such as AR let brands cut through the noise by demonstrating innovation and creativity. A report by PwC found that 34% of companies are already investing in AR and are seeing it deliver value for specific use cases.[2] While AR can be used as a competitive advantage for companies solely on innovation, the use of AR is not just for novelty. AR's unique ability to personalize marketing content by using people and places as part of the experience enhances its meaning and impact, resulting in measurable success.

Indeed, AR offers brands novel ways to engage with consumers and to measure this engagement. These insights give marketers a fresh perspective on their audience and enable them to make marketing decisions by looking at a unique dataset. Emerging technology always starts shiny and new for consumers and brands alike, but as it matures, customer expectations change, asking businesses to harness these tools in more sophisticated ways. Brands that get started early will have a leg up, which is why starting as early as possible with new technologies is fundamental to future-proofing your business.

This is the thinking of many marketers today. According to a report from Hubspot, 14% of marketers are already employing AR and VR as part of their marketing mix, with 49% planning to increase their investment.[3] Marketers' growing interest in AR matches the growth trend in expected AR users. A report by Statista estimated there would be 1.73 billion active AR user devices in 2024 worldwide.[4] This global adoption is a key driver behind the increasing use of AR by marketers, as it presents a more attractive audience size and a more significant possible return on investment.

While AR is still new to many marketers, the use of AR to engage consumers with brand content goes as far back as the early 2000s, with technological roots that go back even further. In 2009, LEGO pioneered an in-store AR demonstration for a selection of its play sets.[5] Powered by an early AR SDK, Metaio, shoppers held up a LEGO toy box to a webcam in a kiosk, and the display showed a 3D model of the assembled LEGO set on the screen. Also that same year, Paramount Pictures used AR to promote its film *Transformers: Revenge of the Fallen*. Users visited the We Are Autobots website on their PC, where they activated their webcam to transform their face into Transformers characters Optimus Prime or Bumblebee on their monitor.[6] This web-enabled activation was created by the creative agency Picture Production Company in partnership with the digital agency Total Immersion. The DVD and Blu-ray release of the same film also used AR, this time activated from the packaging.[7] Fans pointed the packaging at the webcam of their PC to play holographic games and witness Transformer characters appear in 3D on top of the box.

This early use of AR technology was groundbreaking. It showcased AR's potential for engaging consumer experiences and set the stage for future brand innovations in AR. However, these early examples relied on PCs, specialized kiosks, and unique AR markers that took up precious space in marketing materials. This added friction for brands to adopt and consumers to utilize. But that was then, and this is now. Adopting and using AR has never been easier, all thanks to the widespread presence of smartphones with robust capabilities that make them mobile AR machines. With nearly eight billion people worldwide expected to have smartphone subscriptions by 2028, according to Statista, the total addressable market for AR is expansive.[8] This is illustrated by brands across nearly every industry regularly tapping into AR's power for marketing today. Some of the world's most recognized brands, such as Nike, Coca-Cola, Honda, and Netflix, join thousands of examples of AR marketing content to promote their products and brands.[9] LEGO alone has launched dozens of AR marketing efforts since its in-store AR kiosk in 2009.[10] AR LEGO experiences have engaged millions of users worldwide, from AR scavenger hunts to AR-activated toy sets.[11]

Jumping the Immersive Innovation Chasm

AR has slowly but steadily made its way into the marketing mix for many brands, but it remains a part of their innovation spend for most. This is not unusual as all emerging technologies follow a similar pattern of starting with innovation before leaping to a more stable part of the marketing plan. This is not to say that AR is not ready for use today, nor that it isn't delivering value. Instead, it speaks to the nascency of the technology and how early it is in its journey. The path to becoming a staple in the marketing budget will require a number of things, including a more scalable cost for AR content creation, consistent and standard measurement, and more optimal devices available at scale. It will also be aided by the sharing of proof points and case studies from the industry and promising results from experiments and pilots by the brand itself.

One of the reasons why marketers are taking a cautious approach to AR today is the relatively high development costs and the need for specialized expertise to create high-quality AR experiences. While many AR platforms and tools are free, most of the budget stems from a need to create 3D assets and animations, which are fundamental ingredients of any AR experience. As 3D is a brand-new medium for many marketers, it drives a need to find specialized agencies or team members who can create these assets. These resources have harnessed tools catering to various aspects of the 3D workflow, such as modeling, texturing, rigging, animation, and rendering, using tools such as Maya, Blender, Substance, and Cinema4D. They also have experience creating accurate product replicas and translating campaign concepts into 3D. In addition to the 3D specialization, there is also a need to work with agencies and freelancers who can take these assets and use them to develop the AR experience. Costs will come down as more people ramp up on the tools and choose to specialize in 3D, including team members who work directly for the brands and businesses currently outsourcing this business to agencies. Budgets will also benefit from a broader investment in 3D, where assets and art are planned for multiple parts of a campaign, including 2D, such as TV and websites, and new immersive opportunities, such as AR and VR.

Additionally, as AR is still an emerging technology, its full potential and long-term ROI are yet to be fully understood, leading to hesitation in allocating substantial mainstream marketing budgets. While proof points and case studies of AR's measurable impact on marketing exist, there is a need for more storytelling around ROI to help bolster confidence in its use. The reason we don't see many success stories about AR out there isn't due to a lack of achievements but more because companies are careful about what they share publicly. Seeking out data-driven case studies by keeping abreast of new reports and news articles in publications featuring immersive technology in marketing is key. In addition, ensuring that measurement is a key element of your business's experiments and pilots will help you collect valuable insights from your use of AR. This data will be invaluable for refining your use of AR as part of your marketing plans. It will also help you build a business case for its eventual move to your mainstay marketing budget.

Businesses may be more apt to tell data-driven stories once AR marketing moves toward more consistent and standardized measurement methods. Today, marketers are taking a bespoke approach to defining success for AR marketing campaigns, often relying on analytic systems created for 2D digital media. While there are some consistent metrics, such as views and shares, there has yet to be wide-sweeping agreement on the new hero metrics for AR as a medium for marketing. Standardization will also help bolster confidence in AR's ROI, enabling marketers to compare apples to apples between their campaigns while benchmarking against case studies and data points made publicly available.

Finally, while mobile AR offers reach and scale, the mobile form factor is holding AR back from its true potential. While today's smartphones are becoming more powerful AR machines with every upgrade cycle, the handheld nature of the device and a screen size that offers a small field of view for AR experiences limits what is possible with AR. These issues resolve with consumer-ready headworn wearables, beginning with MR headsets and eventually followed by AR smartglasses. These devices offer a more natural and compelling way to engage with immersive media. While the headset category is just getting started in the consumer sphere, IDC expects AR/VR headsets to reach just over 35 million units by 2028.[12] To put this in context, this is just around the same shipment numbers as the iPhone

3GS in 2009.[13] It is just a matter of time before headsets are common-place in consumer homes.

As AR technology continues to evolve and become more acces-sible, its adoption will expand beyond the innovation niche, as we have seen other innovative technologies do in the past. It wasn't long ago that mobile and social technologies emerged and have undoubt-edly become fixtures in marketing plans. As brands become more comfortable with their capabilities and witness the tangible benefits of immersive experiences, AR is poised to become a staple in mar-keting strategies, moving beyond its current experimental status to become a critical element in the marketing mix. In the meantime, the journey toward ubiquity is essential for marketers. Those brands and businesses that adopt AR early will gain essential learnings, including forming the necessary teams and partnerships and earning consumer trust and equity in using this new technology.

Proving Value Along the Marketing Funnel

AR delivers impact across the marketing funnel while transforming the traditional marketing path of a consumer. Brands today use AR as an immersive way to engage consumers at every stage of their jour-ney. As a new technology, it may be assumed that AR is used solely to stand out in a crowded space for consumers. This is true, but there have been many examples shared by brands that show AR is also moving the needle at every step of the marketing path. From aware-ness to consideration and through the decision-making process, AR is proving to be novel and effective in engaging and demonstrating value across the marketing funnel.

AWARENESS AND INTEREST

Social AR dominates the top of the funnel. AR filters and lenses have become a staple in our social feeds, turning faces, places, and things into powerful brand moments. As social AR benefits from an immediate addressable audience, marketers can tap into the billions of users on platforms such as TikTok, Instagram, and Snapchat, making it a perfect tool to increase brand visibility and capture a consumer's attention. Brands have been using social AR for nearly a decade. Over time, they have quickly become a staple in marketing campaigns, especially for those targeting the millennial or Gen Z audience. Filters and lenses lend themselves to achieving the typical goal of a top-of-funnel campaign of attracting and engaging a broad audience. They also offer marketers the ability to measure metrics typical for this stage, such as impressions, views, and shares. In fact, "four out of five brands that used AR lenses and filters improved their brand awareness metrics," according to a report by Snap and Ipsos.[14]

AR helps posts stand out in the infinite scrolling feed by transforming the ordinary into the extraordinary. It also encourages users to become creators by allowing them to apply the filter to their content, using it as a content creation tool. While the filter may be the same for all users, how an individual user applies the AR to their video or photo will always be unique, and, in this way, the filter keeps the output of a branded social AR activation fresh and new. If a branded filter does its job right, it will inspire many social media users to contribute their unique spin with AR, which could cause your brand to go viral. This way, you can view today's filter creators as a new form of social media influencers. The filters that creators launch, either on their own or in partnership with a brand, can shape trends and the content created by social media users. Many creators on platforms such as Instagram have large followings, so followers are the first to know of new filters they can try. If your goal is brand awareness and virality with a social AR campaign, choosing a creator with a large following can be a significant upside, as having it shared across both the brand page and the creator page could increase its usage and, therefore, get you closer to your campaign goals.

CONSIDERATION AND CONVERSION
Moving along the funnel, AR also plays a major role in how consumers evaluate their options during the consideration stage. Here, blending interactive and immersive AR experiences with traditional marketing strategies helps customers better understand and visualize how products fit into their lives. AR experiences that place virtual cars in driveways, couches in living rooms, or even makeup experiences that allow consumers to see the right shade on their lips enable a hands-on approach to product evaluation.

This merging of the digital with the physical is often called "phygital." Phygital strategies play a pivotal role in the consideration stage by giving the virtual online experience some tangibility by bringing digital content into the user's space using AR. A phygital experience can highlight product benefits and differentiators in immersive and memorable ways. They can also afford consumers a level of personalization that might not be possible with more traditional marketing tactics by demonstrating products and adding campaign elements in the consumer's space. Additionally, AR can significantly reduce the barrier to entry for trying new products. By allowing customers to experience products virtually, AR reduces the friction associated with adopting new or unfamiliar products, facilitating quicker and more confident purchasing decisions. According to a report by Snap and Ipsos, "82% of brands claim the number of returns a customer makes will be reduced by AR."[15]

Brands can harness AR to personalize marketing at scale, allowing them to tailor experiences to individual preferences, which enhances relevance and appeal. AR facilitates a higher level of product interaction and engagement, allowing customers to explore features, variations, and details in a way that static images or videos cannot match. This depth of experience enriches the customer's understanding and appreciation of the product, which can lead to higher conversion rates. AR's ability to personalize marketing builds trust between consumers and brands quickly, which is instrumental in the conversion stage. In fact, Snap reported that AR experiences lead to a 94% higher conversion rate.[16]

Trust is an essential factor at the conversion stage of the funnel, and AR enables this through its interactivity. AR's interactive nature engages consumers in an ongoing dialogue. This consistent engagement fosters trust, which is compounded at every step. This results in a meaningful relationship with the consumer that carves out a natural path through the consideration stage toward decision-making. All of this results in an increase in the likelihood of conversion. In fact, "82% of brands who use AR state it helps to drive sales, acquire new customers, and drive performance metrics," according to a report by Snap and Ipsos.[17]

BRAND LOYALTY AND ADVOCACY

This relationship continues beyond the conversion stage, as AR can be used to foster brand loyalty. A report by Snap and Ipsos highlighted that "69% of brands utilizing AR say it improved loyalty or customer experience."[18] After purchase, AR can enhance the product experience through interactive guides and tutorials. AR can overlay information on a product or even place a holographic product representative in a customer's space to offer a product education experience that can feel very hands-on and, in some cases, VIP. AR can also unlock personalized experiences and rewards for customers that can encourage new use cases or forge new brand touchpoints. This continuous engagement keeps the brand relevant and creates a stickiness with the product. In both cases, the immersive and personalized nature of AR experiences creates a deep connection between the brand and its customers. This personal touch makes customers feel valued, encouraging repeat business and long-term loyalty.

As AR experiences can be shared on social media, customers can use it to become brand advocates. When users share their unique AR experiences, they increase brand visibility and endorse the brand to their network, amplifying trust and credibility. This peer-to-peer recommendation is invaluable in building a loyal customer base and attracting new customers who trust the opinions of their friends and family over traditional advertising. The novel and immersive nature of AR experiences encourage repeated interactions, transforming one-time buyers into loyal customers and brand ambassadors. This makes AR not just a tool for conversion but also a strategic asset in building and maintaining customer loyalty.

Collapsing and Twisting the Marketing Funnel

Just as AR proves it can be applied across the marketing funnel to deliver value, it also demonstrates that it is completely reinventing the traditional funnel altogether. This evolution has begun with mobile AR and is expected to accelerate as headset AR proliferates. This reinvention is fascinating for marketers and is something the marketing community will play a significant hand in shaping over the next decade.

While we wait for headset adoption to rise, we can see into the future by looking at how mobile AR is changing the marketing funnel today, and it is doing so in two significant ways: collapsing and twisting it.

The typical marketing funnel is a progressive set of steps consumers must follow to convert. While AR can enhance the impact at each of these steps, it also causes consumers to veer from this path. In many ways, it collapses the funnel into a dynamic, immersive experience that finds consumers simultaneously moving through multiple stages all at once. AR blurs the lines between the different stages, causing consumers to fall through the stages at a velocity that increases the chance of conversion. AR marketing efforts use the physical real world of the consumer as a canvas to move them effortlessly from discovering a product to visualizing it in their environment to making a purchase decision, all within a single, continuous flow. This unified consumer experience reduces the friction and gaps between each stage, bringing a sense of ease to the experience and reducing the risk of abandonment. It keeps users in a funnel where the stages are so tightly connected that they feel like one.

As AR requires consumers to participate actively in marketing, this heightened engagement changes the flow of the typical path. Consumers are no longer being pushed through a funnel but rather pull themselves forward as part of an experience they feel is theirs. For an AR marketing activation, consumers are in control when the camera is activated, co-creating the marketing experience with the brand and its environment. Engaging consumers as a director of the marketing experience moves them quickly into more advanced stages of the marketing funnel due to a sense of ownership. With consumers in the driver's seat, they no longer need to be led through a funnel but steer their course with intent and consideration right from the get-go. The immediacy and interactivity of AR move consumers more directly toward a purchase decision, shortening the time to get to the end of the funnel.

This sense of ownership is heightened by the hyper-personalization of AR marketing activations, which tailors the consumer journey to meet individual needs and preferences. AR's use of a person's space or face immediately makes it unique to the consumer and, therefore, feels as if it was created just for them. In addition, the real-time data analytics possible in AR can customize experiences at an unprecedented scale. This personalization transcends traditional demographic targeting, focusing instead on behaviors and context, which makes every interaction feel unique and directly relevant to the user. As a result, the marketing funnel becomes less linear and more responsive. Consumers can now leapfrog stages, propelled by personalized prompts and experiences that resonate deeply with their immediate needs and interests. This applies every time they engage with an AR marketing activation, which will change and suit their needs depending on where they are, when they are engaging with it, and who they are with. Every AR experience you launch as part of your marketing will deliver infinite variations poised to resonate specifically with the consumer who activated it. This dynamic, interactive, and efficient nature of AR reshapes the consumer-brand relationship and, in turn, restructures the funnel.

AR also twists the linear progression of the funnel stages, turning it into something more cyclical. AR creates a continuous loop of engagement, where the consumer does not end with the purchase. Post-purchase AR experiences ensure ongoing engagement, turning customers into brand advocates and repeating the cycle of the marketing funnel. These AR experiences can provide product education, walkthroughs, or continuing entertainment and fun. These enhance the product experience through interactive features, leading to higher satisfaction, loyalty, and advocacy. As advocates, consumers who share the AR experience generate valuable earned media for the brand, bringing new consumers into the cycle.

The New "P" in Marketing

Integrating AR into the marketing mix marks a significant evolution in consumer engagement. It introduces a new fifth element, presence, to the traditional 4 Ps of Marketing model of product, price, place, and promotion. AR enables presence by bringing digital campaign elements into a user's space, making them feel tangible and real. This technology shifts the marketing paradigm from solely relying on visual and textual content to offering multidimensional experiences that co-exist with a consumer. Presence is not merely about visibility – it involves creating an interactive relationship where consumers can engage with the brand in significant and compelling ways.

Incorporating presence into the marketing mix revolutionizes consumer engagement strategies. It shifts the focus from merely persuading consumers to select a product based on price or features to creating memorable experiences that cultivate a deeper emotional bond with the brand. This experiential focus can profoundly influence consumer behavior, fostering loyalty and increasing the likelihood of conversion and advocacy.

Presence does not function in isolation but synergizes with the traditional four Ps to forge a more dynamic marketing strategy. AR can enrich the product experience by providing extra information, demonstrations, or customization options, making the product more appealing and tailored to individual consumer needs. Interactive experiences allow companies to justify their pricing by demonstrating the product's value in a more comprehensive and engaging way. AR diminishes the importance of a physical location, enabling consumers to interact with products and campaign elements from anywhere they are. Additionally, AR offers creative ways to promote products through interactive advertisements or virtual events, making promotional content more engaging and memorable.

The integration of presence within the marketing mix enhances traditional elements while evolving the way brands connect with their consumers. This unlocks new opportunities for engagement and brand differentiation for marketers.

Generation AR

The use of AR in brand marketing is especially attractive to younger generations, including Gen Z, the generation born between 1997 and 2012, which now makes up more than 20% of the US population.[19] A Snap survey found that 92% of Gen Z consumers want to use AR.[20] It is AR's ability to make marketing experiences feel bespoke that resonates with this generation. "60% of Gen Z consumers said the use of AR made the marketing experience more personal, and over half said they would pay more attention to marketing with AR."[21] AR is also enabling this generation to build trust with brands through its interactive and immersive dialogue capabilities. "One in two Gen Z feel it is important for brands to build connections with them," according to another report by Snapchat.[22]

As mobile is the primary device for younger generations and is the device most available today for consumers to engage with AR, there exists the perfect opportunity for brands to use this technology to reach this demographic. According to a report by Statista, "97% of US adults aged 18 to 49 own a smartphone."[23] Younger generations are spending a lot of time on their devices. In fact, according to a report by Zippia, Gen Z spends the most time staring at screens, at an average of 7 hours and 18 minutes per day.[24] It is no wonder that this generation is called the "digital natives."[25]

However, Gen Z is not the only generation interested in AR. Their older counterparts, the millennials, are also engaging with this new technology. A Harris Poll found that "32% of Millennials use AR compared to 14% of Gen X and 6% of Baby Boomers."[26] The youngest of the generations, Gen Alpha, or those born between 2010 and the mid-2020s, will be the first to grow up with technologies such as AR, VR, and AI, including access to consumer-ready MR headsets.

Whereas today, the use of mobile AR in marketing will strike a chord with millennial and Gen Z audiences, tomorrow, Gen Alpha, followed by Gen Beta, will expect AR-enabled experiences in headsets. With 75% of the US workforce expected to be represented by millennials by 2025, now is the time to start integrating AR as part of your marketing strategies.[27]

Sparking Spatial Strategies

Strike up strategic dialogue about AR's role in your business with these essential conversation starters:

- **In the boardroom:** How can we utilize AR to differentiate our brand and join the companies already investing in this technology to give them a competitive edge?
- **For your team meeting:** How can we integrate AR to enhance our current marketing campaigns, and what specific outcomes should we aim for?
- **Around the water cooler:** LEGO and Paramount Pictures were pioneers of AR in the early 2000s. Can you think of any other brands that are early AR adopters?

Share this on your socials: AR is shaping the future of marketing! In 2024, there is expected to be 1.73 billion active devices engaged with AR, offering brands a massive audience to captivate and convert. Is your brand ready to leverage AR's unique, immersive experiences? #thenextdimensionbook

CHAPTER 5

Redefining Mobile Marketing

AR has a major role in the future of marketing and commerce, from virtual try-ons to immersive digital experiences.

— Sanja Partalo, *Executive Vice President, Strategic Development & Partnerships at WPP*[1]

Chapter Cheat Sheet Powered by AI

I asked an AI to read this chapter and create a cheat sheet. If you only have five minutes to spare, here are the three must-know insights to help you level up your spatial computing knowledge.

- ◆ **AR in Marketing:** AR is powerful in modern marketing, creating immersive and engaging brand experiences. It revitalizes traditional methods by allowing interactive product visualizations and experiences, enhancing online and offline engagement.
- ◆ **Consumer Participation:** AR transforms consumers into active participants in brand narratives. Through platforms such as WebAR, consumers can become characters in interactive stories, boosting their connection to the brand and enhancing social sharing, as brands such as Netflix and Warner Bros. demonstrate.

◆ **Physical and Virtual Integration:** AR brings the virtual world into the physical space, enabling consumers to interact with brand elements in their environment. This increases engagement and memorability, as seen with innovations such as interactive portals to other worlds and AR-enhanced product packaging.

Want to talk to an AI about this book? Scan the QR code or visit ai.thenextdimension book.com in your browser to access The Next Dimension Book GPT.

Scan Me

Integrating AR as Part of Your Marketing Mix

Integrating AR with traditional and digital marketing channels is essential in creating cohesive and immersive brand experiences. As consumer demand for personalized and engaging brand interactions rises, blending AR with established marketing strategies is a great way to engage audiences across multiple touchpoints and demographics.

AR has started to become a vital part of the marketing mix for many brands, revitalizing and adding depth to current marketing methods. AR complements rather than replaces existing marketing approaches, combining offline with online strategies. In this way, it will make use of the expertise and learnings your business has acquired in marketing with traditional channels while challenging your team to see these channels from a different perspective.

Product packaging, for instance, becomes a direct gateway to augmented brand engagement. By scanning QR codes on packaging with a smartphone camera, consumers can unlock AR content such as instructional visuals, product stories, and interactive games. This enriches the product experience, fosters repeated interactions, and strengthens brand connections as consumers engage with a brand-new use of a product. Additionally, AR-enabled packaging can trigger online discussions from consumers sharing videos of the packaging being brought to life with AR. This can extend brand exposure and engagement beyond the initial purchase.

Traditional marketing materials such as catalogs, brochures, and print magazines can be rejuvenated through AR. Like packaging, incorporating QR codes as part of the printed material can be used to trigger an AR experience that uses images on the page. Depending on the technology used, the AR content can stay anchored to the page or use the printed material as a starting point as consumers watch AR content jump off the page and into the world around them. This modernizes classic print marketing by merging the physical with the digital.

In a similar way, AR can also transform public transport and outdoor advertising. AR content on posters in subways or bus stops or within the vehicles themselves turns commuting into an interactive brand experience. Outdoor AR installations in urban spaces, including billboards and murals on buildings, can encourage public interaction and create larger-than-life brand experiences.

In-store experiences also benefit from AR, with AR-enabled mirrors or kiosks enabling virtual try-ons. AR activations triggered by in-store signage can gamify the store, transforming it into an interactive adventure. AR can also be used to help navigate consumers to areas within a mall or individual stores, acting as a way-finding service assisting consumers in either a practical or fun manner, depending on the campaign.

In a very similar manner, AR can elevate brand presence and audience interaction at events and trade shows through immersive experiences incorporated into booths or displays, making brand presentations and product demos more interactive and memorable. If designed to do so, AR can also bring the booth experience to attendees not at the event. This is particularly useful for hybrid events with a virtual audience or as content for in-person attendees to use when they return to the office after the event.

Audiences can be invited to scan QR codes or text a number to receive web links during ads that feature AR content on broadcast media such as TV and radio. The augmented reality can bring content featured on these channels out from the screen or speaker into the consumer's physical space. This not only provides an opportunity for new and extended engagement with campaign content, but it also provides measurable digital data.

Digital marketing channels are naturally suited for AR, enhancing digital user engagement and yielding insights into consumer behavior on the very devices required to activate this immersive content. AR transforms emails from static to dynamic by encouraging recipients to click a link to interact with AR directly from the inbox, which brings campaign content off the screen. Similarly, buttons and links on websites and apps can be used to trigger AR experiences directly in the app or browser. This is made especially easy when users are engaging with websites and apps directly on their smartphones. This includes the distribution of AR content through digital ads, making the AR experience the destination of a banner or video ad.

Of course, a natural place to leverage AR is on social media, where platforms are designed to create and distribute AR filters and lenses for brands. This content can be a fun, interactive way to connect with social media audiences and encourage user-generated content through the release of a branded effect with the aim for it to go viral. This can be helped by engaging social media influencers to use a branded lens or filter and share it on their feed as part of the campaign. Advertising networks within social networks can also be used to promote longer-form AR content the campaign may have, such as an AR app or AR-enabled website.

Make Consumers the Main Character

AR can invite consumers into the world of your brand or product and transform them into a main character. Enabling consumers to assume a vital role in your marketing story creates a deep relationship with your brand or product almost immediately. It also allows consumers to interact with your brand as a co-creator. Leveraging AR filters, effects, and lenses, consumers can see themselves as part of the experience you have created for them. The content they create as a character in your world can be shared with friends and family through messaging and social networks.

To celebrate the launch of its new series *Cursed*, Netflix teamed up with digital creative agency Powster to create a WebAR experience that gave users a chance to enter the world of the show and become a main character.[2] The web AR app included three experiences designed to ascertain if a user's magical powers were good or evil to show them what character in the series they would be. Users took a quiz where each response activated an interactive AR challenge. Using the rear-facing camera on their smartphone, they augmented their world, harnessing lightning, growing or destroying massive vines, and wielding the sword of power. After completing the challenges, their character was revealed, and they were able to see their new selves through an AR filter using the front-facing camera on their phone. Users could then record themselves using the face effect and share it on their social feeds.

This interactive WebAR experience, powered by Niantic's 8th Wall platform, was one part of an overall digital campaign that also included an online portal with exclusive video content.[3] The AR experience was a compelling way for users to quickly create a relationship, which was important, seeing that this was a brand-new show on Netflix. AR was also a more interactive and memorable way to introduce characters and abilities featured in the show than traditional means such as text and video. The addition of a social sharing element was key as it introduced a highly personal way for more users to be introduced to the show as social media users stopped to watch videos of their friends and family as the show's AR-enabled characters in their social feed.

Using AR to turn people into characters on screen is also something Warner Bros. employed.

Warner Bros. worked with Snapchat to use AR to transform Snapchat users into characters from the movie *Dune: Part Two*.[4] Using Snapchat's AR lens capability, Snapchat users became Fremen, one of the fictional groups of people in the Dune universe, and found themselves riding a sandworm as their new character. This lens was part of an overall campaign on Snapchat, which also featured a video ad running inside the app with a direct link to purchase tickets on the official movie site.

Warner Bros. worked with Snapchat in a similar way for the *Barbie* movie.[5] The Barbie lens invited Snapchat users to dress up like Barbie or Ken using some of the fashion from the film. It gave users the option to mix and match a variety of outfits and accessories and personalize their backgrounds. For US-based Snapchat users, Warner Bros. also launched a location-based lens that took famous landmarks, such as the TCL Chinese Theater in Los Angeles and the US Capitol Building in Washington, DC, and made them appear as bright pink and pastel versions that would have fit in the world of Barbie.

In both examples, Warner Bros. used AR to transform consumers into characters from their films. Using AR to enable consumers to become a part of the world being marketed creates a deep relationship with the brand almost immediately. Consumers not only learn more about the product being sold, in this case, a film, but they can also visualize themselves literally with it, which helps them fall quicker through the marketing funnel. In addition, as filters and lenses are meant to capture yourself and share a moment with your friends, a campaign that includes it has the upside of encouraging user-generated content and turning the user into a brand advocate. In turn, content created and shared by consumers who use your AR effect will resonate even more with the viewers of this content as it would have been personalized with someone they know.

Open a Portal to Your Brand World

AR can bring a consumer into the world of your marketing content, inviting them to interact with your brand elements in a brand-new way. This transforms the consumer from a passive viewer to an active participant, enabling a two-way relationship between the consumer and the brand. Portals are a great way to do this. Portals open doorways into virtual worlds that consumers can explore in 360°. These virtual worlds can be based on real places around the globe, locations from another time, or entirely fictional destinations. Portals are an effective way to fully immerse consumers in your campaign, leading to significant engagement time and the creation of meaningful memories with your brand.

Anheuser-Busch InBev teamed up with WebAR agency Aircards to create an AR-enabled portal for a Michelob ULTRA Pure Gold marketing campaign.[6] The browser-based AR experience asked consumers to place a sizeable virtual tent in their physical space. Once placed, they could walk into the tent, and inside was a virtual version of a campsite at Yosemite National Park. They could then move around with 360° of freedom just as if they were really there, exploring the virtual campsite from different angles and taking in the views of the mountains. Inside the campsite was a campfire and park bench where a cold pack of Michelob ULTRA Pure Gold and some food invited consumers to get up close with the product. Hotspots around the virtual environment educated the consumer about Michelob ULTRA Pure Gold as well as the brand's commitment to national park preservation. In addition, consumers could tap on persistent buttons in the experience to purchase the product online.

The Michelob camping portal is an excellent example of how you can transport consumers from their physical, real-world location to a virtual destination that immerses them in essential qualities of your brand and campaign. This use of AR brings a powerful type of experiential marketing to your marketing mix, allowing consumers to move about a brand space from the comfort of their own environment.

Cadbury and Coles employed the same AR tactic – transporting consumers to a real-life destination using the camping portal community – to invite users into a fictitious world crafted out of paper. Created by creative technology studio Zebrar in partnership with agency Traffik, this web-based AR experience was launched around the Easter holiday to engage consumers with a virtual Easter egg hunt.[7] Using their smartphone, consumers place a life-size Cadbury chocolate egg in their physical space and then follow the bunny paw prints into the egg to explore a world made of paper. Once inside, this 360° portal experience immersed consumers in a fantasy land with fairy tale moments such as a chocolate Humpty falling from a treehouse and breaking apart to reveal chocolate beans inside.[8] Consumers were challenged to find as many eggs as possible to be entered for a chance to win an instant prize and be added to a draw for an even bigger win.

AR can invite your audience into your brand content by bringing an experiential marketing experience to them no matter where they are. Consumers have agency and freedom to explore the virtual environment as they wish, which can result in meaningful engagement time and brand recall.

Bring Content into the Consumers' World

AR can enable consumers to enter your brand world. It can also be used to bring your campaign content into the consumer's physical space. This is compelling, especially when paired with traditional marketing content such as TV commercials and print ads, where AR can enable elements from the flat campaign to pop off the page or escape the TV screen and exist in the real world, extending the campaign.

Brazilian financial services company Banco Bradesco used AR to bring its beloved fireflies, originally featured in a 2020 commercial entitled "Shine in Your Own Way," into viewers' homes.[9] The three-minute animated short film, created by Publicis and produced by Zombie Studios, features Luna, a firefly that does not light up and suffers for being different. The TV spot focused on themes of diversity and inclusion, which are the bank's core values.[10]

During an episode of *The Voice Brasil* TV show, the commercial featured a QR code that invited viewers to scan with their smartphones to trigger an AR experience.[11] The WebAR experience, which was created by Buu Digital using Niantic's 8th Wall WebAR technology, brought fireflies featured in the animated commercial into the living rooms of viewers. Viewers watched as the same characters on screen flew around their own physical space. They also watched as swarms of fireflies danced and came together to create fantastical images in the air around them. According to information from Buu Digital found on the 8th Wall website, over 260,000 people simultaneously activated the experience during the three-minute commercial, with more than half of this traffic generated in the first seconds of the commercial airing.[12] Buu Digital also shared that, in total, the experience saw over 671,000 visits, which had viewers engaging with the characters from the brand hours after the commercial had ended.[13]

As part of marketing its latest series, *House of Dragon*, the HBO Max Innovation team partnered with technology creative studio The Mill to launch an AR mobile app called House of the Dragon: DracARys.[14] The app gave users the chance to get up close with the dragons from the show. HBO was eager to use AR's ability to bring virtual content into the world with characters from the show. "With DracARys we wanted to explore what it would mean for the dragons of Westeros to exist in our world, an idea that very much has AR at its core. This app was born from an initiative to combine emerging technologies with promoting 'House of the Dragon' to pursue something novel and interesting for fans and potential fans to explore," HBO said on the app marketing page on its official website.[15]

The app gives users the chance to raise their own dragon. After entering an AR portal to a cave in Westeros, the land featured in the series, users choose an egg that will eventually hatch to become their dragon. The dragon appears in the user's physical space once hatched. According to the HBO app marketing page, each dragon is procedurally designed, so no two dragons are the same.[16] Once the dragon is born, users can train and help their dragon grow up by interacting with it as if it were there with them in the real world, including using voice commands. Each dragon is unique to the user in design and behavior because of how the user develops and trains their beast. Users feed their dragons with meals generated based on the user's environment by foraging for food in different spaces such as the beach or park. Once the dragon reaches adulthood, they can fly so other app users can see in the sky. Users can always call their dragons back to the ground using a voice command or when they throw food down on the ground. According to The Mill, the app, launched at San Diego Comic-Con, saw over 78,000 downloads in its first launch week.[17]

HBO Max and The Mill utilized Niantic's Lightship SDK to build the app, which brought robust spatial awareness to the AR experience and added a greater sense of realism. This technology enabled virtual dragons to react and affect the environment around them and added depth and occlusion to the experience, which made the dragon feel more as if it were really present in your physical environment.

Using AR to give consumers a chance to get up close and personal with characters and concepts they typically only see behind the screen can heighten their relationship with the brand. As AR engages consumers in their space it creates an intimate atmosphere to explore and engage with brand content.

Awaken Your Product So It Can Sell

AR can help your product stand out from others on the shelf. It can also enable your product to sell itself, literally. Consumers can scan a QR code to open an AR-enabled website and then point the smartphone camera at the label to provide product information and education in an immersive and engaging way.

Leading wine importer Frederick Wildman & Sons did just this with two of its fine Italian wines: Santi Ventale and Nino Negri Quadrio. The winemaker used WebAR to offer consumers a virtual wine tour, bringing the winemaking experience you would typically only get when visiting the vineyard to every bottle.[18] The experience featured holographic tour guides, designers, and Italian wine lovers Pia and Davide Baroncini, who were volumetrically captured live on a stage and turned into 3D avatars. Once engaged with the AR experience, users saw the tiny digital versions of Pia and Davide in the space in front of them. Their digital twins would then lead a virtual wine-tasting experience discussing wine notes and pairings and teaching consumers how to see, smell correctly, and taste wine.

"There is an untold story behind every bottle of wine, and we are excited that this AR program will make the passion, history, and technique behind these wines more tangible and accessible for everyone who experiences them," said Amanda Paul-Garnier, director of Italian Fine Wines for Frederick Wildman in a press release for the launch of this experience.[19]

The AR-enabled website was unlocked by scanning a QR code on the neck of the bottle with your smartphone camera. Consumers then activated the tasting tour by scanning the bottle, and the whole experience occurred within the browser. Creative agency Tactic created this experience using Niantic's 8th Wall platform, leveraging its frictionless image target AR capability. Activating the AR experience from the label on the bottle kept the product at the center of the experience.

Using volumetric video and AR, Frederick Wildman & Sons found a way to scale the sommelier experience, typically something a wine drinker may only encounter at a winery or a special event. The AR experience elevated product education by enabling consumers to learn about the wine in an extremely intimate and novel way.

Nike used AR to transform the top of its shoe boxes into a vehicle for storytelling as part of its Move to Zero campaign.[20] Working with innovative production studio UNIT9, specially marked shipping boxes came to life with a 3D experience to help raise awareness of Nike's commitment to sustainability.[21] The boxes featured a QR code, which, when scanned with a smartphone camera, enabled consumers to activate the AR on the top of the box. By pointing their phones at the top of the box and viewing it through its screen, consumers saw an animated 3D experience pop up, telling the story of Nike's journey to zero carbon and zero waste.

With AR, the top of the box became a virtual habitat complete with a forest, windmills, and a logistics plant, all of which represented parts of Nike's sustainability advancements in its distribution process and packaging. The forest and trees illustrated Nike's commitment to planting more trees, and the logistics plant with solar panels and surrounding windmills related to Nike's focus on clean energy.[22]

Nike's AR-enabled packaging is a perfect example of using this technology to tell a story while keeping the product at the center. Learning about Nike's sustainability commitment through animations on top of a shoe box was a more exciting way to digest this information. Still, it kept the Nike product in sight while consumers learned more.

Connecting your packaging with AR can be like bottling up a spokesperson for your brand and product. It can be an extremely helpful way for consumers to get to know your product while instore and further their relationship with it when they get home. While delivering a new way to convey product education is something you can easily achieve with AR, it can also be seen as adding to the value of the product if done in the right manner.

Add a Talking Twist to Your Packaging

Connecting your packaging with AR can also enable your product to talk to consumers. AR can animate a character featured on your packaging to speak to your consumer. This can be taken further by developing an experience designed around branching narratives or using GenAI. This allows for a two-way conversation that engages consumers with your brand mascot or spokesperson as if they were in the same room together. This use of AR can be novel. Bringing a bottle or box to life can feel magical and inspire a consumer to want to share the experience with those in the room or on social media.

Chronic Cellars created a first-of-its-kind AI sommelier experience, bringing to life the character on its label to let consumers have a two-way conversation.[23] Working with leading immersive agency Rock Paper Reality, the winery combined AR and AI to give the skeleton featured on the front of the bottle, known as Purple Paradise, the ability to chat. Rock Paper Reality partnered with Inworld AI to use it GenAI solution which enables characters to have endless conversations with consumers, all within the limits configured in the system to ensure that the skeleton remains in the world or on brand. This results in a genuinely personal and immersive experience where the skeleton can answer questions and hold a conversation. After triggering the WebAR experience by scanning the QR code on the bottle, consumers can talk to Purple Paradise, whose primary role is a sommelier. While chatting, they can find more detailed information about Chronic Cellars' extensive wine portfolio, get wine recommendations, learn about tasting notes, and more.

The AI-enabled experience was not the first time Chronic Cellars used AR with Purple Paradise. Before this campaign, the bottle was brought to life with WebAR technology to engage consumers in a two-minute interactive game experience. When a user scans a QR code on the bottle and points their smartphone at the bottle label, it allows users to look inside the bottle and see Purple Paradise as an animated, talking 3D character. They then engaged with the skeleton in a game of over and under with a pair of virtual dice. According to a case study published by the agency behind this experience, Rock Paper Reality, consumers spent an average duration time of three minutes and 26 seconds with an average game return rate of 25%.[24]

Both Chronic Cellars campaigns are great examples of the power of AR to bring packaging to life and engage consumers in an interactive experience. Combining GenAI and AR takes this to a whole new level as characters can be brought into the same space as users with AR and be equipped to have seemingly endless conversations with consumers, which increases the realism and enhances the personalization of a campaign.

Australian wine company Treasury Wine Estates is no stranger to AR. Working with creative production studio Tactic, it has made its 19 Crimes Wines a pioneering wine brand that has used AR to bring its label to life. In 2017, it launched an AR-enabled mobile application called Living Wine Labels, where consumers could use their smartphone cameras to watch the historical figures featured on its bottles become animated to tell their life stories.[25] The app saw millions of downloads and increased the volume of cases of wine sold by about 40%, according to a PTC Vuforia case study.[26]

"We know that it's often difficult for consumers to select wine from a crowded shelf," Michelle Terry, TWE's chief marketing officer, told Andrew Kaplan in an interview for SevenFity Daily. "We wanted to find a way to add an experiential element to selecting and purchasing wine – and make our brands stand out beyond the traditional neck tags and shelf wobblers. This technology has been even more successful than we anticipated, bringing new consumers into the category as well as appealing to tech enthusiasts and wine lovers. It's a great example of how we're thinking differently about marketing wine."[27]

In 2020, 19 Crimes collaborated with Snoop Dogg on Snoop Cali Red, featuring an AR experience as part of the wine brand's Living Wine Labels. In this WebAR experience, users pointed their smartphone cameras at the bottle when visiting the AR-enabled website to watch the bottom of the bottle unlock a platform where a hologram of Snoop Dogg appears.[28] Consumers can then ask Snoop Dogg questions and receive an answer from him. In 2022, 19 Crimes debuted Snoop Dogg Cali Gold, where it again paired an AR experience with the bottle, this time a browser-based experience that brought the picture of Snoop Dogg on the bottle to life.[29] The CGI virtual avatar would talk to consumers in AR when activated.[30]

As consumers were getting used to 19 Crimes as an AR-activated wine, the winemaker debuted a brand-new way to engage with their bottles and AR with a talking experience between two bottles in 2023. As part of its "Snoop & Martha 2-Pack," 19 Crimes debuted a WebAR experience also created by Tactic, which enabled a bottle of Snoop Dogg Cali to talk to a bottle of Martha's Chard. The experience brings to life Snoop and Martha on the bottle, where they banter back and forth in a dialogue.[31]

AR-enabled packaging can give your product a voice, enabling it to dialogue with the consumer and even with other products you may offer. This can lend itself to significant engagement time with your consumer, and the magic of seeing it come to life and talk can inspire social sharing with your product at the center of the media created.

Let Your Packaging Entertain Your Consumer

Using AR, your product packaging can become an interactive game or a stage for a holographic performance, transforming it into an opportunity to entertain and delight your consumer. These experiences can act as incentives to purchase. They also encourage consumers to spend a considerable amount of time with your product, including sharing the experience with others in the room or to capture and share it on social media.

As part of its Newstalgia campaign, which aimed to bring back a nostalgic feel of Pizza Hut in the 1980s, Pizza Hut teamed up with BANDAI NAMCO Entertainment Inc. to turn select pizza boxes into an interactive PAC-MAN game. Millions of specially marked pizza boxes featured an image of the classic arcade game, reminiscent of the PAC-MAN tabletop cabinets often found in Pizza Hut locations at this time.[32] Consumers were encouraged to use their smartphones to scan the QR code next to a picture of a coin slot and then point their phones at the top of the box to bring the game to life using web-based AR. Once activated, the consumers could play a full 3D PAC-MAN game on top of the box. This experience was created by Tool of North America in collaboration with GSD&M and utilized Niantic's 8th Wall WebAR technology, which made it extremely accessible to users.

"There aren't many brands with more iconic elements than us, whether it's the red cups, checkered tablecloths, connection to pop culture and entertainment – like PAC-MAN – or our iconic Pan Pizza," said George Felix, Pizza Hut's chief marketing officer, in a press release on the company's website.[33] As we look to connect with a new generation of pizza lovers, we are tapping into those things that make Pizza Hut great in a modern and relevant way."

Coca-Cola turned its latest zero-sugar soda, Coca-Cola Starlight, into a stage fit for a star.[34] Consumers who scanned a bottle or can of the new Starlight beverage activated a holographic concert of Ava Max, including a performance of three of her hits – "Kings & Queens," "Sweet But Psycho," and "EveryTime I Cry." The web-based AR experience, created for Coca-Cola Creations by Tool of North America in collaboration with Virtue, used volumetric video capture of Ava Max by Metastage to bring a hologram of the singer into the consumers' physical space. The AR "Concert on a Coca-Cola" was set in a fantastical outer space setting, complete with a light show and backup dancers.[35]

"We love Ava's creativity," said Oana Vlad, The Coca-Cola Company's senior director, Global Brand Strategy in a press release on the company's website.[36] "She's bold and bright, and embodies the experimentation we hope to embrace through Coca-Cola Creations. And the fact that she's a lover of both Coca-Cola and space made her a natural fit."

Burger King also used its packaging to trigger a musical performance with AR. The fast food company debuted a new song from rapper Tinie Tempah as part of an AR activation, which saw the rapper perform as a tiny version of himself.[37] Touted as "the world's smallest gig," Burger King consumers in the UK scanned a QR code to trigger the AR experience, which saw a tiny Tinie perform his single "Whoppa" on a Whopper burger. BBH created the campaign in collaboration with bully! entertainment who partnered with Dimension Studios to capture Tinie's performance on a volumetric video capture stage.

According to a case study of this campaign on the 8th Wall website, "The campaign achieved whopping results with 10.8 million social impressions driven by influencer activity and 220 pieces of media coverage from across the globe."[38]

Gamify the In-Store Experience

AR can turn an ordinary trip to a retail location into an extraordinary gamified experience. These experiences can help increase dwell time in the store and encourage shoppers to explore the store. In addition to making a mundane moment extraordinary, they can also help lead shoppers to a specific product, which can increase sales.

LEGO teamed up with innovative agency Trigger XR to take shoppers on an in-store AR ghost hunt.[39] Shoppers activated the WebAR game by scanning a QR code in select LEGO retail stores with smartphone cameras. This brought up the AR experience directly in the mobile browser, requiring no app to download. Shoppers were challenged to an interactive tap-to-shoot game, searching for ghosts floating around in the store. Faced with a challenge to stun and capture all the ghosts, the AR experience encouraged them to walk around various parts of the store. After catching all the ghosts, shoppers were invited to go hands-on with LEGO's AR-enabled Hidden Side product line in-store. They could also go directly to the LEGO website to learn more about the play sets and download the Hidden Side mobile app.

Using the Web to engage shoppers in an AR experience was a savvy idea by LEGO. It not only introduced a brand-new way for shoppers to explore and engage with the LEGO store, but it also gave shoppers a low-lift and frictionless way to be introduced to

AR technology, a hero feature of LEGO's Hidden Side product line, helping promote sales. As a reward for capturing all the ghosts, there was a chance to play with the Hidden Side play set in-store. The AR experience made good use of the retail space and bridged the digital experience with the physical in connecting it directly with continued play with the actual product.

Minecraft Quest is another excellent example of an in-store AR marketing activation. Created by Intergalactic Agency in partnership with Merchantwise, Microsoft, and Big W stores across Australia, this web-based AR scavenger hunt invited shoppers into the world of Minecraft.[40] Shoppers used their smartphones to hunt for specially marked point-of-sales signs throughout the Big W stores. Shoppers were encouraged to explore the store to find these markers and scan them with their smartphones. Doing so opened an AR portal inside the signage, which connected them to the world of Minecraft – inside, shoppers searched for hidden gems to collect all five unique gems. Collecting all the gems granted them a special Minecraft prize pack, which could be redeemed at the customer service desk. According to a blog post on the 8th Wall website, the technology powering the experience, the game was played over 12,500 times during its one-month run.[41]

This was Intergalactic Agency, Microsoft, and Big W's second iteration of an in-store AR scavenger hunt. It also launched a similar experience in retail locations where store signage featured Minecraft characters, which shoppers virtually collected when scanned. Upon scanning each character, they earned a $5 discount code for online Minecraft product purchases. As reported by the agency on the 8th Wall website, this scavenger hunt saw over 5,000 shoppers complete the challenge. It was also noted that this challenge increased SKU sales by 250%. The success of this first in-store AR scavenger hunt was sure to have played a role in encouraging the brand to use it again in a future campaign.[42]

Scavenger hunts encourage traversal in a retail location, which leads to an increase in time spent in retail and, as we have seen from these examples, leads to sales. However, not all in-retail AR needs to take on this structure. McDonald's Sweden partnered with NORD DDB and Stockholm-based agency DVA to create an AR experience to replace real balloons with virtual ones.[43] The WebAR experience challenged restaurant goers to pop as many McDonald's branded digital balloons as possible while enjoying a meal.

The experience added a sense of joy and wonder to the restaurant experience and demonstrated McDonald's commitment to reducing single-use plastics and waste. "By replacing our balloons with a digital AR game, we are giving more people the opportunity to have even more fun since the game can be played from anywhere. While at the same time doing something important for our planet," Staffan Ekstam, director of Marketing at McDonald's Sweden, told *Adobo Magazine*.[44]

From opening portals to new worlds to filling up the space with virtual objects, AR is a powerful way to bring a marketing activation to life in a retail location. Engaging users with AR in-store can transform an ordinary shopping experience into something extraordinary. This can help you achieve your campaign goals and create a lasting memory for consumers enabled by your brand.

Measuring Success with AR

Understanding and measuring the impact of AR campaigns is critical for businesses aiming to leverage this technology in a durable manner. As an experience medium, AR requires us to rethink how we gauge success for marketing activities. The key lies in the word "experience".

Measuring AR should be like assessing a life experience: just as we reflect on life by asking key questions about what we've seen, felt, and gained, we can apply the same approach to AR users. These insights help brands and businesses identify the key metrics that matter when evaluating AR in marketing.

Dwell Time: "How long did you stay?"

Just like when you visit a new city, time spent in AR is all about immersion. AR asks users to step away from the real world and dive fully into the augmented one. The more time they spend in this new reality, the better. But here's the trick: you've got to grab their attention fast and keep it with engaging, meaningful interactions. If you want them to stick around, don't make them wait!

Engagement: "What did you get up to?"

In AR, users aren't just spectators – they're part of the action. Whether they're trying on a virtual pair of sunglasses or exploring a digital world, AR requires them to interact. Think of it like exploring a new city – you can't just stand still. It's essential that your AR experience gets people moving and engaging in ways that tie back to your goals. Remember, AR isn't linear like a webpage, so users have more freedom to explore. It's your job to make sure they follow the paths that matter most to you.

Recall: "What stood out?"

Experiences are built on memories, and AR experiences are no different. With the level of immersion AR offers, people are likely to remember it vividly – so you want to make sure they remember the right things. Every detail you craft into the experience will shape how it's recalled. To measure this, keep an ear to social media mentions or follow up with users to see what stuck with them the most.

Sentiment: "Did you have a good time?"

At the end of the day, people remember how something made them feel. AR is no exception. If users leave your AR experience feeling excited, joyful, or inspired, that's gold. To tap into this, design experiences that evoke strong emotions and stick with users even after they step back into reality. An in-app rating system or a quick post-experience survey can help capture how your AR adventure resonated with them.

Of course, every AR experience should start with clear goals in mind. Once those are set, it's all about measuring, refining, and ensuring your audience is having an impactful and memorable experience.

Sparking Spatial Strategies

Strike up strategic dialogue about AR's role in your business with these essential conversation starters:

- **In the boardroom:** How can integrating AR into our existing marketing strategies enhance our brand's visibility and consumer engagement, and what potential ROI metrics should we consider?
- **For your team meeting:** What AR features could we incorporate into our next campaign to boost consumer interaction

and encourage deeper brand connection? Can we brainstorm ideas that align with our current marketing objectives?

◆ **Around the water cooler:** What did you think about using AR for interactive storytelling in marketing? Have you seen any good examples of this from brands?

Share this on your socials: AR isn't just a technology – it's transforming marketing by turning people's spaces into experiential destinations, creating lasting connections between brands and consumers. #thenextdimensionbook

CHAPTER 6

Marketing in the Era of Spatial Computing

I'm incredibly excited by AR because I can see uses for it everywhere. I can see uses for it in education, in consumers, in entertainment, in sports. I can see it in every business that I know anything about.

— Tim Cook, *CEO of Apple, said at an event hosted by the University of Oxford*[1]

Chapter Cheat Sheet Powered by AI

I asked an AI to read this chapter and create a cheat sheet. If you only have five minutes to spare, here are the three must-know insights to help you level up your spatial computing knowledge.

♦ **Rapid Growth in MR Headsets:** Major players such as Meta and Apple are driving the market with affordable models, increasing accessibility, and creating opportunities for brands and marketers.

♦ **Early MR Marketing Examples:** Brands such as Gucci and NBCUniversal are launching innovative MR marketing campaigns, leveraging immersive experiences to enhance consumer engagement and experiment with MR marketing strategies.

◆ **Cross-Platform Compatibility in MR Marketing:** MR headsets are essential in marketing but to expand the opportunity, marketers must think about making immersive content available across a variety of devices including mobile.

Want to talk to an AI about this book? Scan the QR code or visit ai.thenextdimension book.com in your browser to access The Next Dimension Book GPT.

Scan Me

AR Headworn Wearables Are Already Here

Today, the smartphone is the dominant device in a consumer's life. This will likely continue to be true for at least the next decade. At the same time, the headworn wearable device category has arrived and will continue to evolve and grow in adoption. This emerging category poses a viable opportunity for businesses today, but this will only compound over time. Some organizations are already experimenting with these wearable devices, generating brand awareness through PR and gaining valuable consumer insights and learnings as early adopters of these technologies. While various types of headworn wearables are available for purchase today, it is in the mixed reality headset category that brands have the most opportunity to reach consumers. Headworn devices, such as those from Meta and Apple, are ready for meaningful MR content creation and present the most significant opportunity for user adoption.

As the next generation of VR devices, MR headsets are riding a technology and adoption wave that started for recent consumer VR nearly a decade earlier. The VR device category's step change is the color passthrough capability, which allows VR devices to double as AR headsets through MR. The mixed reality headset category is currently dominated by two major players, Meta and Apple, with their devices Meta Quest and Apple Vision Pro. Meta's MR headset is an evolution of a VR headset, Oculus Rift, acquired by the company in 2014.[2] Apple Vision Pro is Apple's debut in the MR headset race, which started in 2023. It is also expected that an MR device from Samsung, in partnership with Qualcomm and Google, will join the category.[3] Additional Horizon OS–enabled devices from Xbox, ASUS, and Lenovo were also announced by Meta to be in the works.[4] With most of the major tech giants in the race, the MR headset is quickly solidifying its status as a legitimate consumer device category. For marketers, the proliferation of more headsets is critical. It bolsters confidence in the technology's long-term viability and substantially broadens its reach potential. The larger the audience that is wearing headsets regularly, the larger the value proposition for marketers.

An IDC report forecasts that 2024 would see over 9 million headsets shipped, with this number growing to over 30 million by 2028.[5] IDC points to MR as the growth accelerant for the AR/VR headset category: "Apple's launch of the Vision Pro grabbed a lot of headlines and has raised awareness for AR and VR, and although it's priced out of reach for most, it is helping raise the bar for competitors," said Jitesh Ubrani, IDC's research manager of Mobility and Consumer Device Trackers in an IDC press release. "Along with Apple, many companies such as Meta and others have already begun their journey, transitioning from VR to Mixed Reality, ultimately laying the groundwork for true AR experiences."[6]

With the Meta Quest device having seen multiple generations, it is no surprise that this headset is estimated to have the largest market share. According to a report from Statista, Meta was the leading headset vendor in 2023, with 72% of the market based on shipments in the fourth quarter. Sony followed Meta, whose headset accounted for around 15% of shipments. In another report, Statista forecasts that Apple Vision Pro shipments could go from 350,000 in its launch year of 2024 to nearly 1.5 million in the following year.[7]

With the opportunity at a sizable state, businesses and brands want to create content for these headsets. In fact, according to a 2024 report from Sortlist, which surveyed 1,000 businesses on their interest in Apple Vision Pro, "68% of businesses are ready to bet big on Apple's new spatial computer."[8] This same survey found that "50% of business owners plan on investing in marketing using the Apple Vision Pro, while 18% have already begun to do so."[9] Sortlist also found that the primary industries investing in immersive experiences for Apple Vision Pro are "e-commerce (79%), fashion (77%), and healthcare (72%)," with "virtual product demos" the most popular content type.[10]

Business interest is supported not just by the availability of technology but also by consumer interest. The Gen Z and millennial generations are already gravitating toward headset use. A Deloitte report highlighted that "40% have used VR technology in some way – from gaming to attending a concert or sporting event, or for work or school."[11] For those that have already adopted headsets and have them at home, their regular use is on the rise. A survey by Piper Sandler reports that "the weekly use of virtual reality devices increased from 10 to 13% compared to the fall of 2023."[12]

Headset use with the Gen Z and millennial generations should be "unsurprising when considering that half of Gen Zs and millennials surveyed believe online experiences are meaningful replacements for in-person experiences."[13] The same Deloitte study states that "close to 50% of Gen Zs and Millennials say they spend more time interacting with others on social media than in real life; 40% say they spend more time socializing in video games than in real life."[14] Deloitte's report draws a straight line from the behavior of Gen Z today to how this lends itself well to the digital reality headsets offer as it states, "For younger generations, especially digital-native Gen Zs, there seems to be little delineation between 'online life' and 'real life', and they are already looking to integrate the two."[15]

Developers are also resonating with the MR opportunity, with hundreds of MR apps already available for Meta and Apple headsets around the time of their launch, and this number is growing. According to a post from the Meta newsroom, "within months of the Meta Quest 3 launch, seven of the top 20 apps are mixed reality apps, and there are already hundreds of mixed reality apps in the store where most users have tried mixed reality features."[16] Around the Apple Vision Pro launch, Apple announced from its newsroom that over 600 apps had been developed specifically for the device, including apps from Lowe's, LEGO, J.Crew, Wayfair, MLB, and NBA.[17]

Meet the MR Marketing Pioneers

Companies have already begun tapping into the immersive power of MR headsets, propelling their brands into the next dimension. These innovators are not only leading the charge on what is possible for marketing in MR but are also benefiting from valuable early learnings from having in-market content engaged by users.

SNICKERS BRINGS FOOTBALL AND FORTUNES INTO YOUR LIVING ROOM
One of the first marketing experiences launched for Apple Vision Pro was for Snickers as part of its "Rookie Mistake" campaign.[18] In

partnership with technology company Blippar and The Mars Agency, the Snickers brand launched an MR app for the Apple Vision Pro just in time for the Super Bowl LVIII. The experience gives headset wearers the ability to simulate kicking a field goal in their living room through a goalpost made of Snickers bars. After scoring, they interact with a virtual version of Pittsburgh Steelers' T. J. Watt, who is inside a fortune teller box acting as a "misfortune teller." Watt encourages users to share an embarrassing rookie mistake. After they tell their story, the fortune-telling box reveals a life-size Snickers vending machine where users enter a sweepstakes to win prizes directly in the app or click a link to be taken to the Snickers website to buy some candy bars. A similar experience is also available on the smartphone.[19]

This spatial computing experience by The Mars Agency was well timed. The campaign took advantage of being first to market, riding the wave of Apple Vision Pro news as the device just came out the week before the app launch. It also helped the campaign break through a noisy and competitive time for marketing, the Super Bowl. Leveraging innovative technology gave journalists and users something new. As the AR experience could be engaged both inside the headset and on a smartphone, it is an excellent example of cross-device thinking with your creativity. This helps your campaign pack a punch on the immersive headworn wearable as the campaign hero while enabling your content to engage with as many people as possible via the smartphone.

NBCUNIVERSAL OPENS A PORTAL TO A PANDA AND PEACE
NBCUniversal launched an Apple Vision Pro app, Kung Fu Panda: School of Chi, to promote its latest film, *Kung Fu Panda 4*.[20] Developed by Nexus Studios, this DreamWorks Animation app opens a portal to The Valley of Peace, the world featured in the movie. Inside the portal, the lead animated character, Po, guides users through meditation as part of a kung fu practice. Users follow Po's lead, copying his moves and learning meditative patterns by moving their hands and body while wearing the headset. Users are rewarded when they complete a series of movements by a fully grown cherry blossom tree, which spreads its branches far beyond the portal into the user's physical space. Along with the interactive experience, the app allows users to watch a 3D version of the *Kung Fu Panda 4*

trailer on a screen set in an immersive environment of The Valley of Peace, where they can also purchase movie tickets on Fandango.

NBCUniversal's app on Apple Vision Pro is a great fit, especially as *Kung Fu Panda 3* is also available as a 3D movie to watch on the device. It also leans into one of the primary use cases Apple is highlighting for the Apple Vision Pro, media consumption, which is sure to resonate with headset owners. NBCUniversal could have just launched the 3D movie trailer for its latest movie, but instead, it took this opportunity to debut an interactive portal experience to leverage more of the device's capabilities. This was a wise choice because it offered a brand-new look into a franchise that has existed since 2008.[21] For the first time, *Kung Fu Panda* fans can get up close with the film's lead character and share an experience together that could only be made possible in an MR headset. The app's body tracking gives Po a greater sense of presence as it feels as if he is watching and ensuring you are following his movements. Sometimes, he shakes his head when you aren't mimicking his hand gestures correctly. The moments in which Po's world starts to creep out from beyond the portal into the real physical world of the user intensify this new connection with the film. This is all designed to sell you tickets to the next movie in this series and make you an even bigger fan.

DIAGEO SERVES UP COCKTAILS AND CULTURE IN HEADSET

Diageo became the first beverage company to launch a marketing experience for Apple Vision Pro.[22] The premium beverage leader chose to showcase its luxury brand, Tequila Don Julio, in an immersive storytelling experience exclusive to Apple's new spatial computer. The app offers tequila fans an up-close view of the brand's heritage, the stories of its creators, and the intricate production process of the product – agave harvesting, piñas baking, distillation, and aging. The app, which Diageo's Innovation Team created in collaboration with leading XR agency Trigger XR, uses a mix of immersive video and 3D content in the user's space to help users explore the phases of tequila production and also features guided tastings, mixology tutorials, and celebrations of Mexico's contemporary cocktail culture. It also used the device's hand tracking to do things such as harvest pencas (the large, fleshy leaves) from a fully matured agave.

"Apple Vision Pro offers us a new opportunity to bring consumers closer to the vibrant world of modern Mexico and all that goes into making Tequila Don Julio an iconic brand," said Sophie Kelly, senior vice president of Global Tequila and Mezcal Categories at Diageo in a press release. "Spatial computing gives us a rich canvas to deliver the closest version of the physical world of Tequila Don Julio through digital content while allowing users to stay wherever they are in the world. What was once limited to visitor centers, distillery tours, and physical activations, we're now able to inspire and educate seamlessly with behind-the-scenes access to our award-winning portfolio."[23]

Diageo's MR experience used the Apple Vision Pro's high-resolution display and infinite canvas to show its content on a theater-sized screen and the ability to change the lighting in the user's space to create an intimate experience with the luxury brand. The mix of video and 3D content, including interactive moments, fully utilized the magic of MR. Along with a compelling user experience, Diageo also used the launch of this first-of-its-kind for spatial computing to highlight its commitment to innovation by raising the in-house Innovation Team it has established to future-proof Diageo brands by gaining key learnings on new platforms that will eventually become staples in the marketing mix.

GUCCI REIMAGINES THE FASHION DOCUMENTARY IN 3D

Luxury fashion brand Gucci also joined the early brands to launch an app for the Apple Vision Pro. Launched at the beginning of April 2024, the Gucci app engages users in an immersive adaptation of the documentary *Who Is Sabato De Sarno?* which follows creative director Sabato de Sarno preparing his debut collection in the Gucci Ancora show.[24] The documentary takes viewers through the weeks leading up to de Sarno's debut show in September 2023 in Italy.

The Gucci app for Apple Vision Pro offers a new and exciting way to engage users with video content. The app combines 2D video with immersive environments, 3D elements, and interactive moments introduced throughout the screening. This heightens the experience for the viewer in ways only possible in a headset. Viewers begin by watching the documentary on a theater-sized screen floating in their space. During certain moments of the film, 3D elements appear in the viewer's space, such as a massive 3D model of an airplane appearing above the screen during a travel sequence. A train track appears, and a large red train arrives in the viewer's space, timed perfectly with its entrance in the film. These moments bring aspects of the movie into the viewer's space. When the documentary introduces the original location for de Sarno's debut show in the city of Milan, the viewer's physical, real-world environment fades, and they find themselves watching the documentary in the alley depicted in the film, complete with de Sarno's dog walking down the street. These types of moments bring the viewer into the film. Finally, at various times throughout the documentary, the viewer can interact with 3D models of objects in the film they are currently viewing. Most of these points invite viewers to explore high-quality 3D models of Gucci apparel and accessories, such as the Gucci Horsebit platform loafer and Gucci Bamboo 1947 handbag.

The Gucci Apple Vision Pro experience is a masterclass in combining legacy 2D media with new spatial content – the new multimedia. This new meets old approach can only be achieved with a spatial computer. The documentary has a style, pace, and soundtrack that only improves when moments of immersion are added. Gucci has also taken a thoughtful approach to the interactive moments, ensuring viewers can choose when and how to engage with them. The interactive moments give viewers the option to get up close with 3D models relevant to their location in the film. The 3D models of Gucci accessories featured in the experience, such as the iconic Gucci Loafers or Jackie handbag, were extremely high quality, which was even more evident with Apple Vision Pro's high-resolution screen and when you manipulate the models, such as rotate or pinch and zoom, to get up even closer. Overall, the documentary experience took a very intelligent approach to immersion. When 3D elements were introduced, they were additive and enhanced the overall experience.

In a sea of e-commerce brand experiences at the launch of Apple Vision Pro, Gucci made the conscious decision to go in a different direction. According to a social post on LinkedIn from Micael Barilaro, Gucci VP of Brand Innovation Ventures, "While recent applications of the Apple Vision Pro have predominantly revolved around e-commerce, we recognized the importance of charting a distinct course that resonated with our brand ethos. Our focus lies in crafting curated, emotionally resonant experiences that place emphasis on meaningful engagement."[25]

HYUNDAI CARD'S DUAL-REALITY EVENT

Whereas the MR experiences highlighted so far are aimed at users at home, Hyundai Card, a credit card company under Hyundai Motor Group, made an MR experience that could only be experienced by users at an event activation. DaVinci Motel in Mixed Reality was a cultural festival hosted by Hyundai Card in 2023 in collaboration with Meta.[26] According to a case study on the Quantum Universe website, the agency that created the experience, the MR-activated event, was inspired by Leonardo da Vinci and '70s motels in California. The experience blended the real-world physical location of the Hyundai Card Music Library in Seoul with virtual content, transforming the building into a vintage DaVinci Motel. Event attendees virtually checked into the DaVinci Motel using the Meta Quest Pro. Attendees were presented with a virtual key to the DaVinci Motel and then were walked through the check-in process before engaging with the virtual characters staying at the motel. Attendees could also interact within the virtual world of the DaVinci Motel by leaving their signatures on LPs, refueling a virtual classic car, and more as part of the phygital experience.

Hyundai's DaVinci Motel campaign was a compelling brand activation that illustrates how to use mixed reality in your event marketing. As not everyone has an MR headset at home, creating an event experience that provides attendees with a headset ensures your content will be used. An MR-powered event activation can be a crowd-pleaser for attendees purely for the chance to try out devices they currently don't have at home. Hyundai Card's use of MR also demonstrates how MR-activated events give marketers more control over the user's environment, which gives the brand much more creative control over the experience. It enables MR content to be closely tied to a specific location, such as a building at the event, a booth, or a creative set constructed for the experiential marketing activation.

Key Principles in MR Headset Marketing

With headsets on the heads of consumers and brands with apps in the app store, now is the time to incorporate MR wearables into your marketing strategy. There are several important factors to remember while developing your plans to fully capitalize on the reach and effectiveness of your mixed reality marketing campaigns.

CREATE CONTENT THAT WORKS ACROSS HEADSETS

Considering a cross-platform strategy for your content will help you maximize the potential reach within the small but growing audience size for MR headsets. To assist with this, you will want to leverage tools designed to help you quickly create and deploy content to as many available headsets as possible. Standards such as OpenXR and WebXR are quite helpful here, as are platforms such as Unity and Niantic's 8th Wall, which have tools designed to make cross-platform applications and browser-based content more efficient.

While developing once and deploying to as many headsets as possible will maximize your reach, you will want to be sure your content utilizes the nuances of each device. This is the same whether you are building an app or a website. Failing to make the proper adjustments for each device could result in users feeling that the content wasn't explicitly designed for them, which could result in frustration, cause you to miss your goals, and potentially create a negative impact. It is essential to understand each headset's features, strengths, and weaknesses to make the right decisions for your content. A more tactical example today is Apple Vision Pro's support for eye and hand tracking as the primary interaction method for applications versus Meta Quest's focus on controllers with the option to use hands if preferred. Content designed for hand interactions may work just fine across device platforms, but if your content was developed only for controller use on the Quest, you will need to do some work to customize these interactions on Apple Vision Pro to use its hand-eye coordination.

CREATE CONTENT THAT WORKS ACROSS DEVICES

A cross-platform focus is just one aspect of your MR marketing strategy that can help you increase your reach and impact. The other area to consider is cross-device, considering devices beyond the headset. Specifically, marketers can tap into the immersive power of the headset and benefit from the massive reach of the smartphone or computer when creating content that connects users across different device platforms. Platforms such as Unity and Niantic's 8th Wall also have tools to make cross-device content more efficient. Niantic's 8th Wall platform features Metaversal Deployment, a pioneering capability designed to enable developers to build WebAR content once and deploy it across a new device ecosystem of smartphones, computers, and MR headsets. Content built with this feature can be accessible in 3D on computers, AR on smartphones, and VR or MR on headsets. This feature ensures that when a user visits your immersive site on any device, the right experience is provided, guaranteeing that your users will have a meaningful experience no matter how they access it.

When devising a cross-device content plan that spans headset and smartphone, you will want to decide what type of relationship the content will have across devices. Will your mobile content be a similar experience to what is available in the headset? Are you connecting mobile users to headset users in the same experience? Or are you creating a companion smartphone experience that extends the headset play to the outside world but differs from it?

Enabling mobile and headset users with a similar experience is an excellent solution for less complex content, as the level of immersion and user interaction dramatically differs between a headset and a mobile device. In this scenario, you will want to identify the critical path of your AR marketing content and create adaptations of the experience that are optimal for both handheld and headworn devices. The core of the experience may be the same on both devices, but the mobile experience will most likely have less fidelity than the headset due to its limited field of view and spatial capabilities. By making the right trade-offs, you should be left with a compelling experience that is easy to engage with smartphone and headset users.

This approach differs from developing content to connect mobile users with headset users in social play. In this scenario, the goal is to network users on different devices within the same experience. Here, you will want to consider where your users will be. Will they be in the same room, remote, or both? You will also need to design a companion experience that makes sense for the smartphone device form factor, which may be more 3D on 2D versus the more immersive spatial experience on the headset. In addition, consider what role the smartphone player will take in the experience. Will they enter the experience as a spectator only? Will they engage simultaneously as the actor in the experience or assume another role? Either way, a key focus on networking, co-localization, and other multiplayer features will be necessary to succeed.

Finally, you may choose to create a cross-device experience where mobile is used to extend the same experience beyond the living room. Here, mobile could let users take action in the physical real world to influence aspects of the headset experience, such as collecting objects or activating outdoor locations to unlock levels and aspects of immersive headset gameplay. Or vice versa.

CREATE CONTENT THAT MAKES USE OF SPACE

Location is everything when it comes to MR experiences, as it provides the context for your content. MR devices use their spatial awareness to map the user's space, enabling you to build environment-aware experiences with rich interactions with the user's physical surroundings. This includes placing persistent virtual content using spatial anchors and occluding content behind physical objects in the space to elevate realism. As the developer, you will dictate how much or how little of the user's space is necessary for the experience. These decisions will shape the overall user experience. For example, creating a room-scale experience that uses a user's full space will require users to get off the couch and move around.

Meanwhile, stationary experiences can be engaged using a smaller footprint while standing or seated in a single spot. For Apple Vision Pro, applications considered "Windows" or "Volumes" are optimal stationary experiences. These experiences float before the user and are designed to be easily engaged with while standing or sitting. At the same time, apps considered "Spaces" are more immersive experiences that use the entire space and, therefore, ask users to be more active in getting up and moving to explore virtual environments. When deciding on the content experience you will develop, you will want to consider space limitations, fatigue, and accessibility. It is critical to consider where your users will be and how you want to engage them. Ask yourself: Where will your users be? How will you make use of this space? And how do you intend for them to engage with the space around them?

As current MR headsets are designed for indoor use, your consumer will most likely be in a living room or bedroom, so creating apps with these environments in mind is a safe bet. Knowing this, you can start to make decisions on the types of objects you would find in this scene and consider how to use these as part of your experience. For example, tapping into the semantic spatial understanding capability of a headset will allow your content to react differently on a table versus the ground, such as sprouting flowers on tables and grass on the floor. Knowing the space will also help you design an experience that works with space limitations, considering the size of the room and the furniture in it. You may choose, for example, to use teleporting locomotion in your MR experience rather than ask your user to physically walk around their room or opt for an app that only requires users to engage with virtual content on a table or desk. Designing MR content with a clear perspective on the user and the user's space will help ensure it is successful.

CREATE CONTENT WITH VARYING LEVELS OF IMMERSION

MR headset content can also be created with varying levels of immersion, engaging users with 3D or 2D content to be effective and meaningful. Consider mixing media within your spatial experience, leveraging digital assets from other parts of your campaign, such as images and videos, alongside 3D models and animations. Using digital assets, you may have already created as part of an overall campaign can be a quick way to develop MR content and help keep creative development costs down. Viewing 2D video on a giant movie theater–sized panel in your own space can be entirely novel for headset users. While bringing 2D into 3D space is a significant first step, you can go beyond simply porting your content by connecting your 2D content to 3D elements, immersive environments, and interactive moments.

3D elements can appear beyond a 2D screen or panel and help emphasize certain moments in your video. We saw this in the Gucci experience, where a 3D model of a plane appeared behind the documentary when the film reached a point where the main character was traveling. Choosing the right moments to use 3D elements with your video is essential. These elements can either elevate a mundane moment or enhance an existing crescendo in your film. Either way, the mix of media feels magical. Bringing content from the video into the viewer's space immediately increases the intimacy with the content and transforms it into an even more exciting and memorable experience. It is also something that can only be achieved while experiencing the content on a spatial computer, which differentiates the experience from watching the same video on 2D screens.

This is also the same for immersive environments. While 3D elements bring things from the film into the viewer's space, immersive environments transport viewers into parts of your film by modifying their location. Immersive environments remove the viewer's physical location, transforming it into something completely different. Like 3D elements, immersive environments can emphasize certain moments in your video, transporting viewers to other places they see at various parts of the film. You can also choose to play the entire video within an immersive environment, which perhaps the viewer has a choice to select before watching.

Finally, you can give viewers more agency with 2D video content when combining it with interactive moments. Like 3D elements and immersive environments, you can time these interactive moments to spots in your video. This could allow viewers to get up close to a 3D model of a product featured in your video and view it from all angles. It could also let viewers play spatial mini-games designed to help them better understand concepts or go deeper into specific parts of the story. You can opt to have viewers be entirely in control of whether they wish to engage in interactive moments or elect to stop the video and engage them directly. Giving viewers the ability to watch your video as a passive participant or take more of an active role by engaging with the interactive moments can allow the same video to be experienced in various ways, which can increase repeat views.

Looking into the MR Crystal Ball

While the future is hard to predict, several trends are at play today that are most likely to continue shaping spatial computing opportunities well into the next decade or so. The key ones to pay attention to as marketers include the growing adoption and evolution of head-worn wearables, the ferocious velocity of AI already starting to eat the world, and the next step for the Internet, sometimes referred to as the spatial web or metaverse.

EMERGING WEARABLE TECHNOLOGY TRENDS

While AR headsets have already arrived, we are just at the start of our wearable technology journey, especially in the consumer sphere.

Early MR headsets will begin with indoor consumer use, but as these headworn devices evolve, they will slowly make their way out of the office and homes into the streets worldwide. This will likely happen first, like laptops, where goggles are carried around with us and put on for specific periods at places such as parks and cafés before going back in their case. But eventually, smartglasses will replace our phones as the all-day, everyday device in our lives. As marketers, it is important to keep an eye on the evolution and adoption of headworn wearable technology to ensure that you keep pace with your marketing plans and strategies along its journey.

Just as an evolution in form factor opens new use cases for marketers, so do new device features that marketers will be able to take advantage of as part of their campaign projects. Following-generation devices and the ongoing advancements in operating systems and developer tools will inevitably elevate the interactivity and immersion of AR experiences and unlock new types of content for marketers to create. Building campaigns and marketing properties with platforms and tools designed to keep you relevant across devices will be a key element of your future-proofing plans.

If you are a brand, you can easily rely on your digital agencies to select the right tools for the job. This is especially true during the innovation phase of new technology adoption, where businesses and brands have yet to invest in developing AR marketing initiatives in-house. As this category continues to evolve, brands and agencies will need teams dedicated to spatial computing to ensure their efforts are kept up to date. Innovation teams will always be charged with keeping at the forefront of new technology. As a team of futurists, they should be tapped into what is new and hone in on the timing and pace of technology. Eventually, as these new technologies prove ROI and scale, a natural hand-off will occur to digital marketing teams. With spatial computing requiring team members to think in the three dimensions, it may be possible that as this new era of computing progresses, it will first need a specialized team while the skills required to succeed, such as 3D modeling, AR and VR development, and spatial data analysis, become standard digital marketing capabilities.

As you start bringing AR development in-house to enhance existing marketing properties, such as your app and website, and eventually launch new spatial computing marketing centers, you will want to perform your due diligence in selecting the right platforms to invest in. This is a crucial step, as the right platform can accelerate your success and provide a long runway for future-proofing of your spatial computing strategies. Here, you will want to evaluate several things. Perhaps the most important is an AR platform's ability to integrate with your brand's digital infrastructure, including your existing apps, websites, and systems, such as your billing, CMS, and analytics. In addition, you will want to find a platform that enables cross-platform support, especially for the most popular devices and platforms that will afford you the most extensive reach possible. Platforms compatible with a growing ecosystem of partners, including third-party tools and solutions, are also a great fit, as they will help ensure you have a path to using the latest technologies even if they are not made available directly from the platform itself.

Evaluating performance and the ability to create experiences with a high level of interactivity and immersion is another dynamic critical for AR platforms. Ensuring your platform is well funded and supports similar businesses both in size and from within your industry are also important things to consider, as this may mitigate the risk of having to switch providers prematurely because they are not a good fit or shut down during your service period. If you are looking at a platform to help you tap into the right users, ensuring that the AR platform's user base aligns with your brand's target audience and considering factors such as age, location, and interests for tailored AR content will be key. A platform's commitment to maintaining a safe and respectful user environment, including adherence to AR content guidelines and privacy regulations to protect the brand's integrity and user data, will be a growing requirement, especially as the AR space matures. You will also want to look at the availability of specialized analytics tools within the platform to track engagement, user behavior, and conversion metrics specific to AR experiences.

While a focus on spatial computing platforms is key, the other thing marketers will need to keep on top of with the proliferation of AR headworn devices is the changing role of the smartphone. Today, the smartphone is the hero in our daily digital lives. As wearable technology evolves and is adopted, it will slowly become a sidekick. This transition will happen slowly, but it will be necessary for your team to keep an eye on picking up the signals and adjusting your investment and plans on mobile accordingly. We already see the smartphone as a wearable hub, offering it the computational power and connectivity required to function. We also know the smartphone plays a role in connecting users who don't have a headset with headset players. And finally, we see the smartphone as a companion outdoor device to indoor headsets, enabling the capture of spatial video and extending the experience beyond the living room. In these ways, the smartphone plays an even more critical role in our lives, reinforcing its use. This has the upside of creating more touchpoints with mobile phones, which, therefore, can assist your current mobile marketing strategies in succeeding. To tap into the relationship between the smartphone and headset, you will want to evaluate platforms that enable cross-platform and cross-device development. Platforms that can help you easily port content from one device category enable efficient ways to modify content to be compatible and suit the needs of each device and network user across devices in a high-performing way.

Finally, marketers must keep up with the generational use of spatial computing, including new and younger generations who will grow up as wearable natives. User demographics are essential to any marketing strategy, and a new dynamic for marketers will be keeping tabs on the growing adoption and use of spatial computing, specifically AR headworn devices, for each group. AR interest and adoption will be wide-sweeping across older and younger audiences. Still, like all new technologies, the younger generations will be more likely to integrate it as an essential part of their daily lives. This includes wearable natives, starting as early as Generation Beta (born 2025–2039), who will grow up using headworn wearables. The post–Gen Z generations will see similar patterns to the iPad generation, whose childhood was shaped dramatically using mobile technology available since birth. For these generations, headworn experiences will not only be ubiquitous, but there will also eventually be specific spatial computing apps and experiences designed to entertain, teach, and engage children across their formative years and beyond. The wearable native generation, MR headsets for Generation Beta and AR glasses for Generation Gamma, will be much savvier in their use of headworn wearables and, therefore, will demand more sophisticated experiences from businesses and brands. Marketers who cater to this wearable native generation by enacting marketing strategies that embrace interactive and immersive content using the latest spatial computing will have a leg up against their competition.

EMERGING AI TRENDS

The change in hardware from handheld to headworn is one of the significant trends marketers should watch over the next decade. AI is an underlying technology that has already demonstrated that it will change every facet of our digital lives. AI plays a significant role in spatial computing. It enables computers to make sense of the world by processing and making sense of large amounts of data gathered by sensors. It also changes how content is created by unlocking new scanning and rendering capabilities, such as gaussian splatting, and enabling everyday users to create 3D models, skyboxes, textures, and more with generative AI. Advancements in AI will also unlock more sophisticated AR and MR experiences with algorithms designed to give computers a greater sense of perception and awareness, such as geospatial systems and a wide range of classes that enable spatial semantic understanding. AI will also allow new devices to enter the market, such as AI-enabled wearables and autonomous vehicles, offering new consumer touchpoints for marketers and brands. The latter will be increasingly fertile environments for AR and VR content as cars that can operate independently of the people within them will free passengers up to enjoy new experiences, including immersive ones.

Just as your team will evaluate agencies and platforms for AR headworn devices, you will also want to do the same for AI. Agency and brand teams will want to cultivate a workforce proficient in AI, including the use of AI to supercharge development of AR and use AI as a feature within immersive experiences. Training current team members and hiring new talent with specialized skills in AI will ensure that the organization stays ahead of technological advancements and can swiftly adapt to the growing use of AI in AR-enabled marketing plans. Marketers will also want to choose platforms that supercharge development through the use of co-pilots, procedural development based on semantic segmentation, and even WYSIWIG (the new "what you say is what you get") functionality, which lets you create AR marketing assets using a descriptive prompt. Solutions that integrate AI as part of their AR tool set, such as GAN (generative adversarial network) filters, geospatial systems, and robust semantic classes that enable object detection, for example, should also be considered. These tools will allow your agency or team to create more sophisticated AR that feels more real and immersive. As advancements in AI emerge, these platforms should help keep your teams ahead of the curve, enhancing their skills and enabling them to create content that is relevant to the times.

One of the key aspects of AI is hyper-personalization. Marketers should expect that as each generation gains an increasing proficiency in AI, they will expect their marketing experience to be catered to them. Generation Beta (and following this, Generation Gamma) may never know a world in which marketing content wasn't explicitly targeted specifically and individually to them. These wearable natives will demand content that caters to their unique perspectives, preferences, and behaviors especially as they spend more time experiencing the world through a digital lens. In addition, as their default becomes always-on AR, creating interactive narratives and immersive experiences that encourage participation and co-creation.

EMERGING SPATIAL WEB TRENDS

Over the next decade, massive changes in hardware, software and connectivity will culminate in the ushering of a brand-new Internet. This is often called the spatial web, Web 3.0, or the metaverse. This third-generation Internet will be just as disruptive to marketing as its predecessors. Imagine, a decade from now, stepping into an online immersive digital universe where the lines between the physical and virtual worlds blur, offering an unparalleled opportunity for marketers to craft experiences that resonate deeply with users on a personal level.

The spatial web will render rich, interactive, and three-dimensional experiences that transcend traditional digital engagement in the browser. As we move away from flat websites to a collection of worlds, creating immersive brand experiences will become expected, as will the ability to easily traverse from one destination to another.

It is hard to imagine a browser web page to be, well, anything but a page. Still, we are already starting to see a glimpse of this spatial web today in headset browsers where a click into an immersive experience is possible to engage users with virtual content in their space or as a complete simulation.

Today, we see dedicated AR/VR websites linked from 2D pages the spatialization of 2D pages with 3D and AR components on the page. These are all great opportunities for brands and marketers to take advantage of. Eventually, we will leave the 2D web behind and shift fully into an immersive browsing experience. This will especially be needed when AR smartglasses become our daily devices, where content is more contextual and meant to live in the physical world. Here, a spatial web will be essential, enabling always-on experiences that are ready to provide AI and AR-enabled content depending on the situation and location you are in with no app download required.

Marketers and brands should start today evolving web strategies and properties using 3D technologies such as WebGL, for instance, adding 3D models to product pages or 3D interactive elements to hero banners on their sites. This can be taken a step further to embed AR in web pages so that smartphone users can place content into their space. They can also stay ahead of the curve by developing headset-ready web pages that fully immerse users in experiences that make use of the headset's spatial awareness. These early learnings will set marketers up well to keep pace with the emergence of the spatial web.

Sparking Spatial Strategies

Strike up strategic dialogue about AR's role in your business with these essential conversation starters:

- **In the boardroom:** Considering the rapid adoption of MR headsets and technological advancements, how should we allocate our R&D budget to capitalize on MR technology?
- **For your team meeting:** How does the current MR headset market landscape influence our upcoming marketing strategies and product development plans?

◆ **Around the water cooler:** Which MR marketing campaigns, like those from Gucci or NBCUniversal for Apple Vision Pro, have you found most engaging or innovative?

Share this on your socials: As MR headsets gain traction, driven by Meta and Apple, marketers are finding innovative ways to engage consumers, with shipments expected to hit 30 million by 2028. #thenextdimensionbook

CHAPTER 7

Advertising in the Next Dimension

Brands are increasingly utilizing AR in their media campaigns to connect with consumers in more meaningful and immersive ways.

— Zoe Soon, *VP of the IAB Experience Center*[1]

Chapter Cheat Sheet Powered by AI

I asked an AI to read this chapter and create a cheat sheet. If you only have five minutes to spare, here are the three must-know insights to help you level up your spatial computing knowledge.

- ◆ **AR ads offer unprecedented personalization:** By integrating consumers into the experience through spatial or facial interactions, AR ads create deeply personal and memorable connections, significantly increasing engagement and effectiveness.
- ◆ **AR enhances traditional media:** Augmenting static formats such as print ads and billboards with AR breathes new life into them, transforming them into interactive experiences that captivate audiences and boost brand recall.
- ◆ **Vast reach via smartphones:** With over five billion AR-capable smartphones globally, AR advertising allows brands to engage a massive audience through traditional ad enhancements and innovative digital formats.[2]

Want to talk to an AI about this book? Scan the QR code or visit ai.thenextdimension book.com in your browser to access The Next Dimension Book GPT.

Scan Me

Moving Beyond the Banner Ad

The average American sees around 4,000 to 10,000 ads per day but can only recall a handful.[3] Advertisers are on the hunt for effective ways to win consumers' attention and lead them down the marketing funnel. The landscape is becoming increasingly challenging with the slow death of the cookie, making it harder to target advertising accurately. Additionally, digital advertisers face obstacles such as ad fatigue, privacy concerns, and the rise of ad blockers, all of which complicate capturing and retaining consumer attention. The time for a new medium for advertising has never been better, and AR advertising is well poised to revolutionize how brands interact with consumers.

Advertisers are not new to AR. One of first AR ads appeared in Germany in 2008. Readers of German car magazines *Werben & Verkaufen* and *Autobild* were invited to scan a BMW Mini print ad with their computer camera, which then displayed a virtual car model on page.[4] By moving the page, users could see the model from different angles. Though low-tech by today's standards, this ad was groundbreaking, offering a glimpse into the potential of AR. Fast-forward to today, AR technology has advanced significantly, delivering richer, more interactive experiences that seamlessly blend the digital and physical worlds, benefiting greatly from the proliferation of the smartphone.

By transforming ads into captivating and interactive experiences, AR effectively addresses some of the major challenges digital advertisers face today. The innovative quality of AR allows advertisers to cut through the noise and grab a consumer's attention with something brand new. AR ads stand out in a sea of banner and video ads. As AR uses a consumer's space or face, AR advertising is intrinsically personal, integrating the consumer into the advertising experience. This increases its meaning and effectiveness. The immersive and engaging nature of AR provides interactive content that captures user interest, helping to combat ad fatigue. Finally, as AR ads are often embedded in apps, the risk of ad blocking is somewhat mitigated.

As advertising requires scale to be most effective, most AR advertising opportunities today involve smartphones. With over five billion AR-capable smartphones globally, this device allows advertisers to reach a vast audience with AR ads.[5] There are two primary avenues for smartphone AR advertising: enhancing traditional ads such as print magazines or billboards with AR and using AR as a novel format within digital advertising. Both methods engage consumers with AR experiences directly inside the advertising units. This differs from the use of AR in marketing, where traditional advertising directs traffic to a separate AR destination.

Enhancing traditional ads with AR breathes new life into static formats such as print and out-of-home advertising, making them interactive and engaging. For example, a print magazine ad can transform into a platform for models to be viewed from all angles or appear to come to life with video. Likewise, billboards can be augmented to become portals to another world, display real-time information, or even become the anchor for 3D animations. AR brings traditional analog advertising online by bridging the gap between printed and digital media. This enables printed media to act like digital media, making creative work richer and more interactive while equipping advertisers with more detailed and real-time data on consumer engagement. Consumers bring printed ads, such as those found in magazines, newspapers, bus shelters, or billboards, to life by viewing them through smartphone cameras. Using image recognition, the AR application identifies the ad and tracks the AR experience against it, anchoring the digital experience in the original printed advertisement. Depending on how it was developed, this type of experience can be accessed in a web browser, inside a social media app, or as a feature inside a brand app. As reach is critical for advertising, web AR and social AR filters and lenses are the most effective as they add the least friction to this advertising experience. Consumers typically access the paired AR activation through a QR code included as part of the design of the printed ad.

Incorporating AR into digital advertising introduces a new level of interaction directly within ad units running inside apps, social

media, or websites. These AR ads draw attention and encourage prolonged engagement, boosting brand recall and user interaction while
keeping users within the original digital destination. AR-enabled digital ads use the same networks that serve display, video, or social ads.
By targeting mobile devices, these ads are presented to consumers
who are already well-situated to engage with AR. AR ads ask consumers to enable their smartphone camera, allowing the experience
to augment the consumer's space or face. Like AR-enabled print ads,
AR digital ads can use several technologies, including browser-based
and native ads, such as those found in social networking applications. Snapchat, Instagram, TikTok, and YouTube are just a few
examples of social applications that offer AR advertising within their
networks. Other opportunities include in-game advertising, such as
Niantic's Rewarded AR Ads in popular location-based AR games such
as Pokémon GO.[6]

Whether the consumer engages with AR as part of a print ad or
online through a digital network, the level of interaction AR ads offer
boosts the memorability of advertisements. Ads move beyond click-
ing and viewing to something engaging and experiential. These ads
can also drive high conversion rates, especially in cases where AR
is used to help consumers better understand and visualize products
before purchasing. AR ads can be highly personalized by incorporating the user and their space as part of the ad itself and by tapping
into available user data such as location, shopping behavior, and
preferences. This customization makes ads feel less intrusive and
more appealing, enhancing user satisfaction and fostering a positive
brand relationship. This can all result in content that is more relevant
and engaging to everyone.

As technology evolves, the potential for AR in advertising is
expanding. AR can offer new ways for brands to connect with consumers by turning every ad interaction into a unique and engaging
experience. This can revolutionize how products are marketed and
the overall consumer journey, making ads more interactive, personalized, and even fun. The pioneering BMW Mini ad in 2008 was just
the beginning of this transformative journey. Today, brands have the
tools to create highly engaging, personalized, and memorable advertising experiences that capture attention and drive deeper consumer
engagement and loyalty.

A Massive Opportunity for Advertisers

Advertising is one of the most lucrative sectors for AR, and its potential is growing rapidly. The AR advertising market was projected to generate $1.2 billion in revenue in the US alone in 2024, according to Statista.[7] Globally, Statista estimated revenue for AR advertising was expected to reach $5.2 billion during the same period.[8] This market is not only significant in its current size but also in its growth trajectory. The same report from Statista indicates, "It is projected to experience a compound annual growth of 9.73%, leading to a market volume of $7.5 billion by 2028," citing the United States and China as leading the way in immersive advertising, setting the stage for how brands interact with consumers.[9]

Brands have explored mobile AR advertising for several years, especially on platforms such as Snapchat and Instagram. The rise in mobile advertising spend, estimated to reach $402 billion globally in 2024, according to Data.ai, has bolstered this interest significantly.[10] Mobile advertising has seen exponential growth, driven by the advanced capabilities of these devices and the increased time people spend on their smartphones. A Pew Research Center survey found that "Americans spend an average of four hours looking at their mobile devices daily and checking them at least 144 times daily."[11] Companies across various industries have experimented with AR ads, from high-end fashion brands such as Gucci[12] to everyday brands such as Lunchables.[13] Some brands have launched multiple AR campaigns, each one building on the learnings and successes of the previous ones.

Interest in AR ads is also on the rise. A survey from Vibrant Media polled agency executives found that "more than two-thirds (67%) of agencies want to see more AR and VR in digital advertising campaigns."[14] This interest is not just a passing trend but is rooted in the tangible benefits that AR ads offer. Many brands report significant value generated from AR ads. For instance, a study from Snap, in partnership with IPSOS, found that "four out of five brands that use AR lenses/filters improved their brand awareness."[15] The same study found that "86% of brands who use AR state it helps to drive sales, acquire new customers and drive performance metrics," not to mention the "74% of brands who use AR say it improves loyalty or customer experience."[16]

One of the key drivers behind the surge in AR advertising is the shifting media consumption habits of younger generations. Millennials and Gen Z are increasingly seeking out experiences that blend the digital and physical worlds. This demographic is not just passively consuming content; they crave interactivity and personalization. A Snapchat survey conducted by Global Crowd DNA revealed that "60% of Gen Z consumers said that AR experiences feel more personal, and over half would be more likely to pay attention to an ad that uses AR."[17] This immersive and interactive advertising preference aligns with broader consumer trends. An Accenture report found that "more than half of consumers would better remember brands that regularly engaged them with immersive technologies."[18]

Advertisers who have used AR have reported early signals that AR-enabled ads can be more effective than traditional options. An Emodo survey found that "74% of people indicated that AR ads captured their interest or attention more than non-AR ads, and 68% agreed that these ads reflected positively on the brand."[19] Consumers also suggested they want more AR ads, with "70% of respondents indicating they want to see more AR ads in the future."[20]

The collaboration between technology providers and brands is propelling the growth of AR advertising. Partnerships with platforms such as Snapchat, Instagram, and TikTok have enabled brands to leverage advanced AR tools and reach a broad audience. These social media giants continue to invest heavily in AR capabilities, rolling out new features that make it easier for brands to create and share AR content. In addition, we are beginning to see digital ad platforms add AR as a new type of advertising to their capabilities, such as Emodo, Ericsson's advertising arm, and global advertising technology player Teads.[21]

As AR technology becomes more sophisticated, we will likely see even more moves in the advertising industry to take advantage of this new format. The AR advertising market is poised for significant growth in the coming years. AR advertising offers unique advantages over traditional advertising formats. Brands that embrace AR advertising will be well positioned to capture consumers' attention, particularly younger audiences who value immersive and interactive experiences.

AR Ads That Go Snap, Insta, and Tok

Advertisers are most likely to be familiar with AR advertising in social media applications such as Snapchat, TikTok, and Instagram, as this is the most active category today. These networks present both a mass audience with which to engage and a new way to engage them through AR. Their social capabilities lend themselves well to AR use, a tool to create content and share their experience. In this way, social AR is most effective in achieving top-of-funnel success, although it isn't relegated to just moving the needle at this stage of the funnel.

SNAPCHAT

Snapchat has made significant strides in AR advertising, leveraging its platform's popularity among Gen Z and millennials to create engaging and interactive ad experiences. According to Snap, "Over 70% of the people who download Snapchat engage with AR during their first day using the app."[22] And according to Snap CEO Evan Spiegel, "On average, over 300 million people engage with AR every single day on Snapchat [playing] with AR Lenses billions of times per day on average and [the] AR creator community has built millions of Lenses."[23] Brands have been tapping into Snapchat's creator community, which now boasts 350,000 developers who use Lens Studio to create engaging lenses that can run as ads within the social media app.[24]

Several brands have successfully leveraged Snapchat's AR capabilities to create AR ads that drive impressive results. Christian Dior used Snapchat's foot-tracking AR feature to let Snapchatters try on six pairs of sneakers virtually.[25] This lens was promoted within the Snapchat carousel and Snap's ad network, allowing ads to appear in various places in the app. Snapchatters activated the lens and pointed their smartphone camera at their feet to see a high-quality digital replica of a pair of B27 sneakers on their feet. They could then share pictures or videos of their experience with their friends or tap on the website to purchase the shoes on Dior's website. According to a case study on the Snapchat website, the AR lens was viewed 2.3 million times, generating a return on ad spend (ROAS) of 3.8x.[26] This grew to 6.2x ROAS when isolating the performance to only the AR lens in the carousel.[27]

Generating awareness for a new product using a Snapchat AR lens is something Volkswagen also benefited from in a campaign for its ID.3 electric vehicle.[28] The AR lens, created in partnership between agencies Re-Mind PHD and DDB, gave Snapchatters a chance to sit virtually in the driver's seat of one of Volkswagen's latest electric vehicles. The lens gave users a 360° view of the car's interior, allowing them to get close to the model's new features, such as seats, display panels, and more. Snapchatters could also get out of the vehicle to look at a digital replica of the vehicle in their own space and choose to customize it with the available colors.

"Offering an immersive experience of the new 100% electric ID.3 with Snapchat enabled us to give as many people as possible the chance to project themselves into this best-selling compact model. It's an innovative, high-quality experience that Volkswagen has tested for the first time in France. AR has enabled customers to get inside the ID.3 and start the purchasing decision process in a playful way that encourages interaction," said Jean Manuel Caparros-Crespo, head of Communication & Digital at Volkswagen, in a case study published on the official Snapchat website.[29]

According to the Snapchat case study, the campaign reached nearly 3.8 million Snapchatters, with users engaging with the AR lens for an average of 16.36 seconds.[30] Snapchat reported that the campaign was effective in awareness and recall, resulting in a "12-point improvement in awareness of the Volkswagen ID.3 model and a 6-point increase in the association with Volkswagen as an electric vehicle manufacturer."[31]

Another excellent example of a brand tapping into the power of Snapchat AR advertising is McDonald's. The restaurant chain took to Snapchat to use AR as part of a total app takeover in the UK for the 40th anniversary of the Chicken McNugget.[32] Snapchatters were invited to use the "McNuggetWorthy Scale" AR lens with friends to determine whether they were worthy of their McNuggets. This extremely social experience "played a key role in full-funnel activity, generating a + 8 point shift in ad awareness, +3 point shift in message awareness and + 4 point shift in action intent," according to a case study published on the Snapchat website.[33]

Across these brands, it is evident that AR advertising on Snapchat not only interactively engages users but helps achieve campaign goals across the funnel. This is especially true for top and mid-funnel activities such as awareness and intent. This is demonstrated by measuring AR ad effectiveness with brand lift studies, which show noticeable point shifts in areas that matter for brands. Users resonate with AR ads and are favorable to brands who are using it to engage them.

TIKTOK

TikTok has rapidly evolved into a dominant force in the social media landscape, and its innovative approach to advertising is a key part of this success. Its Effect House is a studio where brands, agencies, and creators can develop interactive AR effects facilitated by its Effect House Branded Effects program. Branded Effects can be bundled with various TikTok's standard ad formats, including in-feed ads, as part of a campaign within the social network. TikTok reports that Branded Effects can lead to results such as "a 9.65% increase in brand recall and a 14% increase in brand favorability."[34]

TikTok users resonate with brands showing up on their main social media feed, referred to as the "For You Page," or simply "FYP." According to a study by TikTok conducted by Flamingo, "79% of users agree TikTok is a place for brands to demonstrate personality and express themselves, and 73% of users feel a deeper connection to brands they interact with on TikTok compared to other platforms."[35] One of the primary benefits of TikTok's Branded Effects platform is its potential for virality. Users on TikTok are encouraged to create and share content featuring branded AR effects, leading to organic, user-generated content that can rapidly spread across the platform. TikTok has reported that effects made by Effect House's community of creators during the beta of its Effect House platform have resulted in more than 21 billion videos, which have amassed more than 8.6 trillion views globally.[36] This user-driven amplification significantly enhances the reach and impact of advertising campaigns, providing brands with a cost-effective way to achieve widespread visibility.

Several successful campaigns have already demonstrated the power of TikTok's Branded Effects. For example, M·A·C Cosmetics partnered with TikTok's Creative Lab to launch an AR effect that lets TikTokkers add words of affirmation and love while showing off M·A·C's Love Me Liquid Lipcolour shades in their video.[37] The effect was supported by an in-feed and TopView ad, and the brand engaged well-known creators on the platform to kickstart its use. The #LoveMeMode campaign reached over 1.8 million unique users and generated over 170,000 video views, with the ads receiving an overall engagement rate of 6.08%, according to a case study published on the official TikTok website.[38] "A brand lift study also showed a 3.7% lift in purchase intent," according to TikTok.[39]

"This is a pioneering partnership for the brand. A first in the category, it allows customers to have fun with self-expression and color in a social and mobile-first way that spans multiple platforms," said Fiona Sainty, vice president general manager of M·A·C UK & Ireland, in a case study published on TikTok's official website.[40]

Samsung Electronics turned to a TikTok AR effect campaign and ad distribution within TikTok to introduce a new health feature for its Galaxy Watch6 wearable device.[41] Like the M·A·C campaign, Samsung also seeded the success of its AR effect with the creator community. The gamified effect encouraged TikTokkers to get their heart rate up by getting up and moving around to "tag" as many hearts on the screen as possible. The experience ended with a high score, encouraging repeat use to try to get your heart rate up as high as possible. According to a case study published on the TikTok website, this campaign "significantly increased brand awareness of the Galaxy Watch6 series with 15.9K videos created in just 12 days."[42] The results of the brand lift study for this campaign showed an 8.5% increase in brand awareness for Samsung Electronics with an increase in brand awareness in the five countries where this campaign was targeted.[43]

Upper funnel success was also demonstrated with a TikTok AR effect ad campaign for global beverage giant PepsiCo's launch of its new Pepsi in Pakistan.[44] Tiktokkers were prompted to record a video of themselves sipping the new Pepsi while using a combination of colorful animations and branding elements, such as backgrounds and text, to represent the beverage tagline of "Stronger, Fizzier, Tastier." An ad buy and creator outreach supported the effect.

According to a case study published on the TikTok website, "the campaign surpassed all benchmarks within a two-week duration, receiving 8.96 billion video views on the Hashtag Challenge page and around 11 million pieces of user-generated content on the platform."[45] Another considerable metric TikTok highlighted from this campaign was the 2.2 million plays on the Branded Effect panel in TikTok, which they report was higher than regional benchmarks.[46] A brand lift study demonstrated strong results, with a "97% brand link ratio and 53% of users claiming the campaign made them want to buy the product."[47]

TikTok's powerful ability to inspire video trends blends itself nicely with AR effects that equip users with a new tool to create content. It is no surprise, then, to see case studies celebrating top-of-funnel success from brands that are tapping into this combination.

META (FACEBOOK AND INSTAGRAM)

Meta's utilization of AR ads on its platforms, particularly Instagram, has been a game changer in digital marketing. The stats speak for themselves: according to data published by Meta, "AR ads drive incremental ad recall among the 18- to 24-year-old demographic 87% of the time, far outperforming their non-AR counterparts."[48] AR ad performance in Meta apps can be seen in various campaigns across different brands and industries.

One notable example is the AR campaign by Coors Light.[49] The beverage brand leveraged Facebook and Instagram AR ads to create an interactive experience that resonated with its target audience. Molson Coors' in-house creative agency, Volt, worked with Meta Business Partner Simone to produce the AR filter. The effect was both a world experience and a selfie experience. It transported Meta app users to different places, such as a golf course, lake, or swimming pool, by tapping on the screen. Or flip the camera around to show them wearing Coors Light–branded summer apparel such as a visor. A brand lift study for the campaign "revealed a 6.7-point lift in purchase intent and a 6.2-point life in brand message association," according to a case study published on the official Facebook website.[50]

The Walt Disney Company France tapped into the potential of AR ads with a campaign to promote its new animated film *Wish*. The AR filter invited Facebook and Instagram users to sing the movie's lead song as part of a karaoke-style experience that featured some of the movie's animated characters. Users were encouraged to record themselves singing using the AR filter and share it on social media. According to a case study published on the Facebook website, a brand lift study for this AR ad campaign resulted in a "27-point lift in ad recall and a 13-point lift in brand awareness."[51] The same case study also highlighted a "29% lower cost per ad recall for the AR ads along with video ads compared to just video ads alone."

In the automotive sector, luxury vehicle company INFINITI Canada utilized Meta's AR ads offering to give users a virtual tour of their latest models.[52] The interactive ads on Instagram and Facebook let users sit inside a car and explore the features and details of its interior. Created by INIFITI's creative agency, Publicis Q, the 360° AR experience featured hotspots that provide more interior detail and a call to action, leading to the INFINITI website. The results from a brand lift study published on the Facebook website found a "1.2-point lift in favorability after seeing the AR ads, and 40% of all incremental favorability generated during the campaign period was from AR ads."[53] The case study also reported a "25% lower cost per impression with AR ads compared to the average."[54]

Film studio Focus Features used AR ads on Facebook and Instagram, which resulted in a 2.6-point lift in action intent to see its latest film, according to a Facebook case study.[55] The AR filter allowed users to choose scenes from the film *Asteroid City* and use them as a virtual background for selfies. According to the Facebook case study, the AR ad campaign "resulted in a 5% incremental share of ticket purchases measured by a conversion lift study."[56]

Focus Feature's agency, EssenceMediacom, helped with the initial concept and managed the campaign, and AR creator Isabelle Udo (founder of VideOrbit Studio) created the AR filters. In a video featured as part of the case study, Isabelle Udo talks about how important it was to capture the film's aesthetic in the filters to immerse filter users in the world of the film and help them feel as if they were a part of the story.

"We found that building immersive AR experiences motivated audiences to see *Asteroid City* during its launch weekend, as there was a direct correlation to higher action intent and reported action after people saw the AR ads. Plus, bringing AR experiences to launch events enabled us to maximize our engagement footprint and create a model we can replicate in the future," said Rachel Berman, VP of Digital Marketing at Focus Features, in the published case study on Facebook's official website.[57]

These examples illustrate how Meta's AR ads on Facebook and Instagram are achieving campaign goals across the marketing funnel, including converting to purchase. Most interesting are the findings that show that AR ads can be more effective than traditional options, reducing the cost per impression. This underscores the power and effectiveness of AR in advertising to get consumer attention and engage them in a meaningful way.

AR Ads Outside the Walled Garden

While most AR advertising activity today occurs within social media applications, we are seeing new opportunities emerging outside these walled gardens. AR is beginning to be used as a new ad format in advertising platforms that run ads across brand properties. Early pioneers such as Teads, Emodo, and Niantic have all seen positive success signals from early offerings.

NIANTIC

Niantic, the company best known for its location-based AR games such as Pokémon GO, is pioneering the field of AR advertising with its Rewarded AR Ads.[58] This ad product is discovered inside the game and opens up the smartphone camera to engage players in AR experiences that use the space around them. Rewarded AR ads integrate seamlessly into the gaming experience, offering players incentives for engaging with ads while providing brands an immersive option to engage and interact with them.

One of the first campaigns to use this new ad format from Niantic was Circle K.[59] This pilot campaign engaged Pokémon GO players with an AR world experience that let them place a larger-than-life-size 3D Circle K coffee cup in their physical space to watch an animation. Players were introduced to this experience through an in-game balloon, which appeared while playing. After interacting with the AR coffee cup, the ad encouraged players to get real coffee at a nearby Circle K store. According to an official news post on Niantic's website, "The Rewarded AR ad campaign resulted in an average engagement rate of 76% and an average completion rate of 95% for the experience."[60]

"Rewarded AR integrates Circle K into this wildly popular gaming environment with timely and relevant offers that enhance brand awareness and loyalty, and we've been very pleased with the results so far," said Margaret Barron, the vice president of Global Marketing for Circle K in a Niantic news post.[61]

As Niantic's games are rooted in location and augmented reality, using AR for advertising feels quite natural within the gaming environment. This resonates with players. According to results from a study by Niantic, "Roughly 80% of players indicate that AR Ads are a good idea."

Lunchables became the first brand to commercially launch a Rewarded AR ad for a campaign for its Lunchables Playables brand.[62] Pokémon GO players discovered the ad via an in-game balloon. They then activated the AR experience and were invited to build six unique items out of Lunchables ingredients, such as a scooter, helicopter, and boat.[63] This world AR experience saw these items come together as 3D models in the user's space, resulting in a whimsical and fun way to play with the well-known product.

"We're constantly seeking new, innovative ways to grow our brand and when it comes to reaching our parents and kids, we see huge potential in AR advertising," said Kraft Heinz Associate Brand Manager, Brand Communications, Christina Brown in a news release from Niantic. "It's exciting to be the first brand partnering with Niantic on a Rewarded AR Ads campaign allowing us to engage with our target audience in a unique and unexpected way to help us grow brand awareness and affinity while encouraging rewards program participation."[64]

TEADS

Global advertising platform Teads has leveraged AR to offer highly engaging and innovative advertising campaigns. Teads partners with AR technology companies such as Aryel to enable AR and 3D ad units within their ad network of publisher websites.[65]

One notable campaign between Aryel and Teads was for Marcolin's GUESS eyewear.[66] This campaign allowed users to virtually try on different eyewear models using AR technology. The interactive nature of the AR try-on significantly boosted customer engagement. According to a case study on the Teads website, the campaign achieved a "44% higher Virtual Try-On (VTO) Engagement Rate compared to Teads' benchmark and a 13.3% higher 3D Engagement Rate."[67] The campaign ran in five countries and saw users spend an average of 19 seconds engaging with the ads.[68] The results in Italy were especially strong. According to the case study, "The engagement rate for the virtual try-on surpassed the benchmark by 60%, indicating an extraordinary interest in virtual product experimentation. Additionally, the average dwell time was significantly higher, exceeding the benchmark by +16.6%."[69]

Another successful example of AR ad formats from Teads is the Lacoste Christmas campaign, executed in partnership with Coty.[70] This festive campaign featured a unique AR experience where users could engage in a winter-themed treasure hunt. According to a case study by Teads on its website, "The campaign led to a 35% increase in brand consideration and a 51% increase in ad recall."[71]

Finally, Teads joined forces with beauty AI and AR technology company Perfect Corp. to enable AR virtual try-on ads for Christian Dior.[72] The ad campaign, which ran in four markets, allowed consumers to try on earrings using Perfect Corp.'s AR technology. The experience was distributed as a web ad on publishers' websites. This is an important detail as it kept users on the publisher's website and didn't require any app to download, which made it easy for users to engage with it. As highlighted in an article published on Marketing Dive, "Christian Dior saw a 43% increase in advertising recall and a 62% increase in brand linkage compared to traditional video formats used by the brand, according to results from the effort conducted with Kantar Profiles. Engagement with the advertisement saw growth, including a 12% rise in users who indicated that they were eager to share their experience and a 36% lift in purchase intent."[73]

Tead's AR ad format allows advertisers to use AR ads outside social networks and alongside publisher content. These examples show that this new ad format is effective, and in some cases, even more effective than traditional advertising formats such as video. It also showcases the use of browser-based AR, as Tead's offering uses advertising networks that exist today on websites.

EMODO

Emodo has also started differentiating its ad offerings with immersive AR to reimage consumer engagement. A subsidiary of Ericsson, Emodo announced it had launched the first 5G-powered AR ad for

The Broadway League.[74] The AR experience, which appears in the user's space as a snow globe, transports users to New York City's Times Square, where they can engage with content from 17 Broadway musicals and plays. According to a news release by Emodo, "5G ads are delivered up to 20x faster than ads on 4G, allowing brands to create more complex, immersive audio and visual content that wouldn't otherwise work – and consumers are ready for it."[75]

New immersive ad formats are the charge of a new Emodo Creative Labs team. Emodo states on its website that it is introducing experiential formats such as AR, 3D, and 360° ads that will run programmatically on its network. According to Emodo, "pilot campaigns ads in these formats delivered up to 4x the average engagement of standard mobile ads. Users repeatedly showed a high propensity to engage for up to 5 minutes with the branded content."[76]

Like Teads, Emodo brings the power of AR ads outside of the walled gardens of social media enabling these ads to run on its own network or publishers. This widens the opportunity for AR to prove its value as an advertising medium in more places. This was the case for The Broadway League campaign, which Emodo reported saw nearly three minutes of engagement from the 92% of users who saw the ad and engaged with the experience.[77]

Augmenting Billboards and Bus Shelters

Out-of-home advertising is a staple in many marketing strategies, offering a way to reach large audiences in public spaces. AR enhances traditional OOH ads, making them more engaging, interactive, and memorable. By integrating AR, advertisers can turn static billboards, bus shelters, and other public displays into immersive and interactive experiences that engage the audience in ways previously unimaginable.

One of the most infamous uses of AR and bus shelters was Burger King's AR campaign, which took a creative approach by allowing users to "burn" competitors' ads.[78] Users in Brazil could use the Burger King app and point their phone cameras at a rival's billboard and tap on the screen to watch the physical ad blaze with virtual fire and reveal a Burger King ad instead. This playful and provocative use of AR engaged users and encouraged them to interact with competitor advertising, turning a potential distraction into a brand interaction. Agency David São Paulo developed the campaign for Burger King Brazil. The campaign required users to watch the complete digital burn to get a coupon for a free Whopper.

Using AR to engage and entertain users as they discover OOH advertising was also for Global, the Media & Entertainment Group, and Barclaycard, who brought to life billboards in the UK to promote the music series Capital Up Close with Barclaycard.[79] The billboard featured UK superstar Anne-Marie and a large QR code to scan with a smartphone camera. Once scanned, a holographic version of Anne-Marie appears, breaking through the physical billboard as she moves to the center of a virtual stage. The experience was browser-based and did not require users to download an app to engage. Dimension Studio made Anne-Marie's digital twin possible using volumetric video technology, making it feel as if it was her inside the AR experience.[80] According to a case study on the Visualise website, the creative agency behind the AR campaign, the outdoor experience was rolled out to 1,000 billboards in the UK.[81]

ABinBev also turned to WebAR to bring an outdoor ad into the next dimension. Working with WebAR agency Aircards, the global drinks company, turned an OOH campaign in San Diego for its BonV!V Spiked Seltzer into an immersive experience.[82] Activated by a QR code, the vending machine images in the mural ad came to life as a 3D interactive vending machine. Users could then select the can of BonV!V Spiked Seltzer they wanted and have it virtually dispensed in AR. Users who were tempted by the AR version of the product could use the maps integration or integration with Instacart to immediately purchase the real thing. According to a case study published on the 8th Wall website, this campaign resulted in a 58% click-through rate to find the nearest store and engaged users for an average of two minutes.[83]

3D billboards have grown in popularity in the OOH space unsurprisingly as we enter the spatial computing era. These billboards don't require any device to use various screens to make 3D content feel as if it exists, extending from the corner of buildings such as those in New York City's Times Square. A 3D billboard in LA combined this new technology with web-based AR to make the experience even more immersive. The LA Kings featured legend Dustin

Brown as part of this campaign, which featured a hologram version of Brown holding the Stanley Cup and celebrating inside the billboard.[84] The digital twin was made possible with volumetric technology from YOOM. The video ad ended with a large QR code that users scanned with their smartphone to activate a WebAR experience created by Flamingo Filter powered by 8th Wall technology.[85] The AR experience brought Dustin Brown out from the 3D billboard and into the world around the user. The same volumetric video of the player could be placed in a physical space where fans could pose to take a picture.

"We wanted to do something big to help honor Dustin's many contributions to the Kings and to the Los Angeles community, and upon seeing the 3D billboard for the first time you really experience that 'wow' moment, especially how the Stanley Cup is featured. It is a great way to help celebrate Dustin's career, and with the AR component a new way to engage with our fans," said LA Kings president and Hockey Hall of Famer Luc Robitaille in an AEG press release.[86]

AR is revolutionizing the OOH advertising landscape by transforming traditional billboards, bus shelters, and other outdoor signage into interactive, engaging experiences. Brands that embrace this technology can create memorable campaigns that capture attention and significantly extend the engagement time with their ad. In addition, marrying a digital aspect with the analog ad grants advertisers a brand-new set of measurement capabilities to gauge the effectiveness of their OOH campaign. As AR technology continues to evolve, the opportunities for innovative and effective OOH advertising will most certainly expand, making it an essential tool in the modern marketer's arsenal.

Make Your Ad Jump Off the Page

Print advertising using AR represents a fusion of traditional media and cutting-edge technology, creating engaging and interactive consumer experiences that leap off the page. This innovative approach revitalizes print ads by integrating digital content, enhancing user engagement, and extending time spent with campaign content.

Porsche used AR to turn a magazine print ad into a major reveal for its new all-electric Porsche Taycan.[87] Readers of publications, such as Vogue Arabia, Emirates Woman, GQ Middle-East, and Forbes, were invited to scan a QR code found on the print ad featuring a classic Porsche vehicle. Once scanned with the reader's smartphone camera, they were taken to the browser, where the WebAR experience was immediately activated. The reader would then point their smartphone camera back at the print ad and watch as the vehicle on the page transformed into the all-new electric Porsche Taycan. This experience was made possible by WebAR agency Aircards in partnership with Blue Logic and powered by Niantic's 8th Wall technology.

Purolator used WebAR to add dimension to its holiday campaign in Canada. Created by agencies Rodmell & Company and Sherpa Marketing, the AR experience was triggered by a QR code on a direct mail campaign to send holiday cheer.[88] When recipients of the promotional material scanned the QR code with their smartphone camera, a 3D animated snow globe appeared. As an image target AR experience, direct mail is essential to the experience as the image on the printed material triggers and tracks the AR content. This ensures that the promotional material is always at the center of the user experience. In addition to being able to pick up direct mail while holding their smartphone to see the snow globe from all angles, users could also tap on one of the cute characters on the screen to send a personal greeting to friends and family.

AR was used to transform advertising for Warner Bros.'s animated film *DC League of Super-Pets*, found on Amazon boxes.[89] Amazon's packaging featured the adorable super animals from the movie on the side of the box along with a QR code to scan for the browser-based AR experience. When a user scanned the QR code with a smartphone camera, the characters from the film appeared as though they burst through the box and into the user's home. Created by immersive digital agency Pretty Big Monster in collaboration with Future House Studios, 8th Wall's image target AR technology was used to trigger and track the AR experience from the box, ensuring that the ad and box were kept a key part of the experience. The experience felt extremely tangible as the digital experience showed the box with a hole used for two stars of the show to escape into the world around the user.

Like OOH, pairing AR with print is a great way to reimagine this traditional media format. It significantly increases the dwell time with your ad and gives your business access to valuable digital data that wouldn't otherwise be available. Bringing your ad to life with AR can also help connect your print spend to more parts of the funnel, including the bottom-of-funnel actions, as the destination behind the QR code in the image can be designed to connect to the point of purchase.

Key Principles for AR Ad Success

AR advertising is a game changer, allowing brands to create immersive and interactive experiences. There are five fundamental principles to remember to get the most out of AR. These principles can transform your advertising strategy into a dynamic and engaging experience for your audience.

HAVE A 3D FALLBACK OPTION

First off, always have a 3D fallback option. Not everyone has the latest and greatest device capable of handling high-end AR. You can reach a wider audience by offering a 3D version of your content. This ensures that people with older or less powerful devices still get to enjoy the experience, keeping them engaged and happy. Plus, it helps avoid frustration for users who might feel left out if they can't access the AR content.

Having a 3D fallback is crucial because it broadens your campaign's accessibility. Imagine a scenario where a user is excited to try out your AR experience, only to find that their device isn't compatible. This can lead to disappointment and a negative perception of your brand. By providing a 3D alternative, you're ensuring that these users still interact positively with your content. This inclusivity is about reaching a wider audience and maintaining a consistent brand experience that caters to everyone's capabilities.

TARGET THE RIGHT DEVICES

Next, make sure you're targeting devices that can support robust AR. This means knowing the hardware and software requirements for a high-performance AR experience. Focus on the most common devices your audience uses, such as iPhones with ARKit or Android phones with ARCore. Doing market research to understand which devices your target audience prefers can ensure your AR content runs smoothly and satisfies users.

Targeting robust devices involves understanding the technical landscape of AR. High-quality AR requires substantial processing power, good camera resolution, and advanced sensors. You can optimize your AR content to run seamlessly by identifying the devices that meet these criteria. This enhances user satisfaction and ensures your AR experiences are immersive and engaging. Moreover, staying updated with the latest AR developments and device capabilities allows you to push the boundaries of what your AR campaigns can achieve.

SET EXPECTATIONS AND PROVIDE INCENTIVES

Setting expectations and providing incentives is another crucial aspect. Users need to know what they're getting into and have a reason to engage with your AR content. Clear instructions on accessing and using the AR features are essential, as is offering previews or demos to build anticipation. Incentives such as discounts, exclusive content, or gamified rewards can entice users to participate. Encouraging social sharing by providing rewards for sharing their AR experiences can also amplify your campaign's reach. By setting clear expectations and giving attractive incentives, you'll see more users engaging with your AR content and enjoying the experience.

When setting expectations, it's essential to communicate clearly and effectively. Provide step-by-step instructions on how to access the AR experience. Use visual guides or short tutorial videos to help users understand the process. This can reduce the barrier to entry and make users more comfortable engaging in AR. Additionally, showcasing previews or demos gives users a glimpse of what to expect, building excitement and curiosity.

Incentives play a pivotal role in driving engagement. Think about what would motivate your audience to participate in your AR experience. Discounts and special offers are always popular, but consider adding a layer of gamification. This not only makes the experience more fun but also encourages repeat interactions. Social sharing incentives can further extend your campaign's reach. When users share their AR experiences on social media, they're engaging with your brand and promoting it to their network, creating a ripple effect of awareness and engagement.

FOCUS ON ENGAGEMENT

AR shines when focused on engagement activities. Interactive elements such as games, virtual try-ons, or AR tours can create a deeper connection between the user and your brand. Engagement should be at the heart of your AR advertising. Interactivity can create a more memorable and powerful experience, leading to greater impact across the marketing funnel and significantly expanding meaningful time spent with your campaign. Interactivity makes the experience more engaging and activates the user as a critical actor in your advertisement, collaborating with the campaign content which, in turn, makes it unique to them.

AR advertising thrives on its ability to turn passive viewers into active participants. By inviting users to engage directly with the content, brands can forge meaningful connections that extend beyond mere exposure. This active involvement not only enhances brand recall but also cultivates a sense of ownership and personalization among users. Moreover, the data generated from these interactions provides invaluable insights into consumer preferences and behaviors, enabling advertisers to refine their campaigns for better targeting and effectiveness.

PRIORITIZE USER EXPERIENCE AND ACCESSIBILITY

Accessibility is not a nice-to-have feature; it's a necessity. By making your AR experiences accessible to users with different abilities, you demonstrate inclusivity, broaden your reach, and build consumer loyalty and trust. Voice commands can be handy for users who have difficulty with touch-based interactions. Visual and auditory cues can help guide users with varying sensory preferences through the AR experience. Ensuring compatibility with assistive devices, such as screen readers, ensures that all users, regardless of physical abilities, can engage with your content.

Optimizing user experience is critical in AR because it directly enhances the overall campaign's success and how users feel about your campaign. An intuitive interface ensures that users can easily navigate the AR experience without feeling overwhelmed or confused.

Real-time feedback, such as visual cues or haptic responses, can enhance this experience by providing immediate and clear guidance. For instance, if a user needs to move their phone to a certain angle to see an AR effect, a gentle vibration or an on-screen arrow can make the process smoother and more intuitive.

By adhering to these principles, brands can create AR advertising campaigns that are not only innovative and engaging but also accessible and user-friendly. This approach ensures that AR's potential is fully realized, offering all users a seamless and enjoyable experience that fosters a deeper connection with the brand.

Measurement and the Importance of Standards

The importance of measurement in AR advertising cannot be overstated. In a rapidly growing industry, accurate and consistent measurement is vital for validating the effectiveness of AR campaigns and providing advertisers with the insights they need to optimize their strategies.

Measuring AR advertising involves several key metrics that differ from traditional digital advertising due to the interactive and immersive nature of AR experiences, including AR impressions, AR sessions, engagement metrics, and engagement time.

AR impressions are typically counted when the ad is loaded and the AR session is rendered.[90] This guarantees that the audience engagement is accurately recorded from the moment the AR experience initiates.

AR sessions are another critical metric, documenting the entire duration of the AR expereince – from the initiation of the AR session, including the opt-in camera usage, to the session's conclusion, when the camera is disabled or the ad is closed. This helps validate whether the user genuinely experiences an AR ad impression.[91]

AR ad engagement metrics delve deeper into user interaction, capturing the triggers within an AR experience, such as tapping, moving the camera, expressions, or environmental conditions.[92] These metrics focus on quantifying engagement within the AR experience.

Engagement time is a very important metric in AR advertising, as AR invites users to spend more time with brand content. Examining the time spent on interactions within the experience can enrich the duration of engagement.

For social AR ads, some of the additional metrics that may be important to your campaign include the number of times your effect was saved, or the number of times your effect was shared.

Brand lift studies are also very common with AR advertising. These studies aim to measure brand awareness, favorability, and intent to action through surveys and can be very helpful when trying to assess the impact of your AR ad spend.

While advertisers can measure their AR ad effectiveness today, the AR advertising industry faces significant challenges due to the need for standardized measurement guidelines. Without consistent standards, it's difficult to compare the effectiveness of AR campaigns across different platforms and formats, leading to fragmented and often unreliable data. This inconsistency can hinder advertisers' ability to make informed decisions about their AR ad investments and optimize their campaigns for better performance.

There is movement in this space. In 2024, the Interactive Advertising Bureau (IAB) and Media Rating Council (MRC) introduced AR measurement guidelines.[93] Developed with industry leaders such as Niantic, Snap, Uber, and GroupM, these guidelines aim to bring standardized measurement to all AR-focused campaigns.[94] By establishing clear definitions and metrics for AR ad delivery, engagement, and performance, these guidelines will help brands and agencies maximize their outcomes and ensure more reliable and comparable data across the industry.

The guidelines will cover essential aspects such as ad delivery verification, viewability measurement, and engagement and interaction. This comprehensive approach intends to give advertisers the guidance they need to gauge the effectiveness of their AR ads accurately. The impact of these standardized measurement guidelines will be profound. By ensuring that all AR campaigns are measured consistently and accurately, the guidelines will enhance the credibility of AR advertising and increase advertisers' confidence in investing in this innovative format. This, in turn, will drive further growth and innovation in the AR advertising industry, unlocking new opportunities for brands to engage with their audiences in immersive and meaningful ways.

MR Headsets—A New Frontier for Advertisers

Despite the rapid advancements in AR and MR technologies, advertising on headworn devices, such as MR headsets, has yet to become a common practice. Unlike their smartphone counterparts, which have seamlessly integrated AR ads into the user experience, MR headworn wearables remain largely untouched by this form of brand engagement. As highlighted in the previous chapter, we have seen these devices be used for marketing activations, but we have yet to see AR advertising. However, examining the advertising activities in VR and the metaverse may provide valuable insight into future MR advertising trends.

One form of advertising we have seen in VR is video ads. These ads appear as pre- or mid-roll content within VR apps or games, like traditional video. The immersive environment of VR enhances the impact of these ads, as users are fully engaged and less likely to be distracted. But for the most part, this tactic relies heavily on the existing advertising models and does little to advance them within this new computing paradigm.

Another prominent example of advertising in VR and virtual worlds is billboards. These billboards are strategically placed within virtual environments, akin to outdoor advertising in the real world. For instance, in popular worlds such as Roblox, users can encounter virtual billboards promoting various products and services.[95] These billboards can be static images or dynamic displays, allowing for creative and interactive advertising opportunities. By seamlessly integrating ads into the virtual landscape, advertisers can reach users naturally and unobtrusively.

Sponsored virtual worlds represent another innovative approach to VR and virtual worlds. Companies can create virtual environments that reflect their brand identity and values, offering users a unique and immersive branded experience. For example, a fashion brand might sponsor a virtual world where users can explore virtual stores, try on digital clothing, and interact with branded content. Virtual goods are also a form of advertising. They scale product placement opportunities and reimagine them in the spatial computing era.

Drawing parallels from these VR and metaverse examples, we can envision how similar advertising strategies might be employed in AR and MR headsets.

Spatial anchors could integrate video ads into the user's experience of the physical world. For instance, when a user views a particular location or object through their headset, a relevant video ad could be triggered and positioned in a user's space. This video could be more contextual, providing additional information or promotional content using what it understands about the user and their environment to serve up relevant or personalized content. Similarly, virtual billboards could be overlaid onto real-world locations, offering dynamic and interactive advertisements that blend seamlessly with the user's surroundings.

Sponsored virtual items could become part of reality. Imagine an MR headset user walking around their house enjoying branded objects, posters, and virtual clothing on friends and family members around them. The key to successful MR advertising will be ensuring that these experiences enhance the user's perception of their surroundings rather than detracting from them.

As MR technologies evolve and more headsets are adopted, advertising opportunities will follow. By looking at the successes and innovations in VR and the metaverse, we can anticipate a future where advertising in MR headsets becomes feasible and an integral part of the user experience. The challenge will be balancing advertisers' commercial interests with maintaining a seamless and enjoyable user experience, ensuring ads add value rather than create disruptions.

Advertising in a World with AR Glasses

Peering into the crystal ball when we find ourselves in a future where AR glasses have become ubiquitous, there will be new opportunities for advertisers. This new world may be rich with immersive advertising, seamlessly integrating digital brand content into the physical environment in ways that captivate and engage users like never before. However, this potential utopia has its pitfalls, and we must be vigilant to avoid turning our world into a dystopian nightmare, such as a world filled with banners and brand notifications reminiscent of critical designer and filmmaker Keiichi Matsuda's *Hyper-Reality*, where your entire field of view becomes ad space.[96]

Imagine walking down a bustling city street. As you glance at a traditional billboard, it suddenly comes to life. Through your AR glasses, you see a car commercial in 3D, the vehicle driving off the billboard and onto the street, weaving through virtual traffic before zooming off into the distance. This AR-enhanced billboard doesn't just show you the car; it allows you to interact with it. You can change its color, explore its features, and even see how it would look parked in your driveway, all in real time.

Inside stores, AR product placement has taken shopping to a new level. As you walk through the aisles, virtual shelves pop up beside the physical ones, showcasing products tailored to your preferences. Pick up a cereal box, and a holographic character appears, explaining its benefits and suggesting recipes. Nearby, a virtual shopping assistant offers personalized recommendations, highlighting special offers that align with your shopping habits.

In AR, location-based ads may become incredibly sophisticated. As you move through different areas, AR glasses will deliver hyper-localized advertisements based on your current location and past behaviors. Stroll past a coffee shop, and a holographic barista might appear, offering you a discount on your favorite brew. Walk by a cinema, and a 3D movie trailer might play out in front of you, complete with interactive elements and the ability to book tickets through your glasses.

However, while these scenarios highlight the potential for engaging and personalized advertising, we must heed the warnings of Matsuda's *Hyper-Reality*."[97] This video depicts a world saturated with intrusive and overwhelming advertisements, where the line between reality and virtual content is blurred into chaos. In this dystopian vision, users are bombarded with endless pop-ups, notifications, and promotional content, creating a sensory overload that diminishes the quality of life and personal autonomy.

To avoid this fate, it is crucial to implement ethical guidelines and regulations for AR advertising. Advertisers should prioritize user experience, ensuring that ads are non-intrusive, contextually relevant, and enhance rather than detract from the real world. Transparency and user control must be paramount, allowing individuals to manage the type and amount of advertising they are exposed to.

As AR technologies evolve and the lines between the digital and physical worlds blur, a new advertising landscape will emerge. The future promises a revolution in how we interact with brands, making advertisements more engaging, relevant, and seamlessly integrated into our daily lives. However, we must strive to create a balanced and user-centric future, avoiding the pitfalls of a world dominated by invasive advertising.

Sparking Spatial Strategies

Strike up strategic dialogue about AR's role in your business with these essential conversation starters:

+ **In the boardroom:** Considering the projected growth of the AR advertising market, how should we allocate our budget to maximize ROI and stay ahead of competitors?
+ **For your team meeting:** What are some innovative ways to integrate AR into our current advertising campaigns to increase user engagement?
+ **Around the water cooler:** How do you think AR ads will evolve in the next few years, especially with the rise of headsets?

Share this on your socials: AR is changing the advertising landscape by making ads more immersive and personalized. Brands can now create interactive experiences that significantly boost engagement and recall. This transformation is reshaping how consumers connect with and respond to advertising. #thenextdimensionbook

CHAPTER 8

Selling with Spatial Computing

If you zoom out a little bit, this is visual computing, and it's all driven by 3D content, which will show up in multiple different ways. It's going to take a few years, but we will get to the point where you cannot merchandize a product without it.

— Shrenik Sadalgi, *head of Next (Wayfair's in-house R&D lab) and chair of the Khronos Group's 3D Commerce Working Group*[1]

Chapter Cheat Sheet Powered by AI

I asked an AI to read this chapter and create a cheat sheet. If you only have five minutes to spare, here are the three must-know insights to help you level up your spatial computing knowledge.

- **Revolutionizing Shopping Experiences:** AR significantly enhances the online shopping experience by providing interactive and personalized experiences through virtual try-ons for fashion and makeup and virtual try-outs for furniture and home decor.

- **Increasing Consumer Confidence and Reducing Returns:** AR technology allows consumers to visualize products in their physical space, leading to more informed purchasing decisions, increasing shopping confidence, and reducing return rates.

◆ **Bridging Online and Physical Retail:** AR can enhance in-store navigation with AR way-finding solutions, extend inventory through AR mirrors, and turn retail stores into experiential destinations with location-based AR technology.

Want to talk to an AI about this book? Scan the QR code or visit ai.thenextdimension book.com in your browser to access The Next Dimension Book GPT.

Scan Me

AR Sales Opportunities Today

AR is transforming the sales landscape online and in physical stores. It provides a dynamic, interactive way for consumers to engage with products and brands. It also acts as a powerful assistive technology that gives sales employees superpowers.

In the e-commerce sector, AR has revolutionized how customers shop by making the online experience feel more like the physical retail experience through virtual try-on and try-out experiences. Virtual try-on enables shoppers to visualize products on themselves, using AR technologies that recognize humans, such as face tracking, hand tracking, foot tracking, and body tracking. These experiences enable consumers to select a product and then see it on themselves virtually, whether it be a pair of sneakers, a watch, or a combination of beauty products.

Virtual try-out experiences use a shopper's space to visualize products such as furniture and home decor. This AR application uses the back-facing camera on your smartphone and leverages AR technologies that recognize the world around you, such as world tracking or image target tracking. It lets shoppers see virtual replicas of furniture and products in their space by viewing them through their smartphones. By virtually placing products in their intended environment, consumers can assess size, color, and style compatibility with their existing decor, enhancing the overall shopping experience.

One of the most compelling uses of AR in sales is bringing the showroom to the consumer. Traditional showrooms are often limited by physical space and inventory. AR allows consumers to experience a virtual showroom from the comfort of their homes and explore the entire catalog. Car manufacturers have embraced this technology, enabling potential buyers to explore car models in 3D, customize features, and even sit and explore the vehicle's interior. This immersive experience helps bridge the gap between online browsing and the in-person showroom visit, making the buying process more convenient and engaging.

In physical retail spaces, AR is innovatively enhancing the shopping experience. AR mirrors are a prime example. These interactive mirrors in stores allow customers to try on clothing and makeup virtually. By standing in front of an AR-enabled screen, such as an iPad or modified digital screen, customers can see how different products look on themselves without physically applying them. This allows customers to try on even more products on the shelves, explore more personalized and customized options, and increase the fun and engagement in the store.

Digital screens in-store may also be used to enable virtual sales associates. Virtual salespeople are emerging as a futuristic yet practical application of AR in retail. These virtual assistants can provide product information, answer customer queries, and even guide shoppers through the store. Virtual salespeople can appear as 2D avatars on digital screens or use new technologies such as lightfield displays such as those from Looking Glass or volumetric displays such as those from Proto to make 3D virtual people feel more like holograms.

AR navigation is another compelling use case in physical retail spaces. Large retail spaces, such as malls, can be overwhelming to navigate. AR apps that enable way-finding can visually guide customers to specific stores or products, offer personalized recommendations, and provide additional product information.

AR is also used with the products themselves. AR-activated products are another way to engage consumers. Customers can unlock additional content, such as usage instructions, promotional videos, or games, by scanning a product with an AR app. This interactive content adds value to the product and boosts the customer experience. It also enables products to sell themselves and stand out from other products on the shelves.

Finally, AR is more than just a tool to enhance the consumer experience. AR gives sales team members superpowers that act as powerful assistive technology to enhance their ability to do their jobs. AR solutions are used for inventory management, merchandising, and as sales aids for in-store sales associates. AR solutions are also instrumental for post-sales support, equipping employees with new ways to help customers troubleshoot issues they may have with purchased products.

Consumer Demand and Early Insights

The AR sales market in commerce is experiencing rapid growth, with significant expansion expected in the coming years. The AR software market in e-commerce was valued at $74 billion in 2024 and is projected to grow to over $333 billion by 2028, according to a report from The Business Research Company.[2]

According to a McKinsey & Company survey, 48% of respondents said they're interested in using "metaverse" technologies such as AR and VR to shop in the next five years.[3] In fact, it is expected that one-third of the shoppers in the United States will have used AR when buying products online by 2025, according to a Statista report.[4] AR is fast becoming an expected part of the shopping experience. A Reydar survey found that 61% of shoppers prefer retailers with an AR experience, and 71% said they would shop more often if they used AR.[5]

Consumer adoption of AR, especially among Gen Z, is notable. According to a Snapchat survey, 92% of Gen Z consumers want to use AR for e-commerce.[6] "60% of Gen Z consumers said that AR experiences feel more personal, and over half of Gen Z would be more likely to pay attention to an ad that uses AR."[7] The survey also found that Gen Z is likelier to buy a product they first experienced in AR than their millennial and Gen X counterparts.[8]

Retailers are responding to this consumer demand. A report from SkyQuest Technology reveals, "While 24% of respondents have said they are using the technology in their business, another 26% have confirmed they are considering its use. The most common use case for AR is product visualization, with 41% of retailers saying they are using or considering using AR for this purpose. Other popular use cases include customer engagement (34%), marketing and advertising (32%), and store operations (30%)."[9]

Impressive statistics underscore the effectiveness of 3D and AR in driving sales. Shopify reported that its merchants who use 3D as part of their commerce experience saw an average 94% higher conversion rate.[10] A case study published by Shopify featuring Shopify Plus merchant Gunner Kennels reported that the use of AR to help consumers visualize dog crates and kennels reduced the return rate by 5%, increased the cart conversion rate by 3%, and increased the order conversion rate by 40%.[11]

L'Oréal, an early adopter of AR as part of its online shopping experience, reported a 150% increase in virtual try-ons in recent financial results.[12] The beauty company reports that they saw over 100 million sessions of virtual try-ons versus 40 million the previous year.[13] L'Oréal CEO Nicolas Hieronimus told analysts on the financial results call, "So, it's augmenting. It's becoming part of consumers' habit."[14]

Demand for virtual try-outs is also on the rise. A PYMNTS study found that "among the 95% of consumers who own or have in their homes at least one connected device, 38% said they are very or extremely interested in using virtual technology to see how items look in their room before buying them, and 6% are already doing this. Plus, 32% said they'd be similarly interested in the ability to use VR technology to buy retail products that are in a physical store from their home or office, and 4% already do this. These technologies blur the lines between the physical and digital worlds."[15]

The AR sales market is poised for substantial growth, driven by technological advancements and increasing consumer demand. Major brands and agencies are already reaping the benefits of AR, reporting higher engagement and sales. With Gen Z showing a strong preference for AR-enhanced shopping experiences, the future of AR in retail and e-commerce looks promising, offering numerous opportunities for brands to innovate and connect with their customers in more meaningful ways.

Transforming E-Commerce into AR-Commerce

AR has already become a staple in the online shopping experience. Many brands have integrated AR as a core feature on the e-commerce product pages online or inside apps. This "phygital" feature brings a physicality to the digital shopping experience, allowing consumers to try out products before they buy virtually. This not only makes the online shopping experience more interactive and tangible, but it also makes the shopping experience feel more personal as shoppers see products on their faces or in their spaces. All of this boosts a shopper's confidence and can increase purchases, which can also be correlated to a reduction in returns.

As retailers aim to reach as many consumers as possible online, the predominant device for AR in e-commerce today is the smartphone. Consumers use their smartphones to engage in AR while shopping online in two main ways: virtual try-on and virtual try-out. Virtual try-on augment a consumer's face, such as enhancing their look with makeup or adding a hat on their head or earrings on their ears for them to check out on their mobile screen. Virtual try-on acts as a digital mirror where consumers can see themselves with your product and try different combinations to help them through the buying process. On the other hand, virtual try-outs add items to the consumer's space by viewing the augmented space on the smartphone screen. This could be used to view furniture, such as a virtual couch in your living room, or to see a digital replica of a painting on your wall.

Enhancing e-commerce with AR has wide sweeping impact across the funnel. It not only makes the online shopping experience more interactive, fun, and engaging but also drives impact in increasing the likelihood for conversion and reducing returns. The data collected from these AR interactions provide valuable insights into consumer preferences and behavior, which can help brands refine their product offerings and marketing strategies. By analyzing how customers use AR features, brands can identify popular products, preferred styles, and potential improvement areas. This data-driven approach ensures that brands stay ahead of trends and continue to meet the evolving needs of their customers.

AR is not just a novelty in e-commerce but a transformative tool that enhances the shopping experience, incentivizes purchases, and opens new avenues for digital goods. Brands at the forefront of this revolution are showcasing AR's diverse applications and benefits in the online retail space. As technology continues to evolve, the adoption of AR in e-commerce is set to become even more widespread and will soon become commonplace for the online shopping experience.

VIRTUAL TRY-ONS

Virtual try-ons are the most commonly used form of AR in shopping today. This technology lets consumers preview how products look and fit before purchasing, enhancing the online shopping experience, increasing the chance of purchase, and reducing return rates. Various brands across industries have successfully integrated AR into their e-commerce platforms, providing valuable insights into the technology's potential.

Walmart and AR and AI beauty technology company Perfect Corp. have partnered to introduce AR makeup try-ons in the Walmart app.[16] This enables shoppers to use AR to try on blush, lip color, eyeshadow, and bronzer. Customers can try on more than 1,400 products from Walmart's brands including Almay, Black Radiance, CoverGirl, e.l.f. Cosmetics, Maybelline, NYX Professional Makeup, and Revlon.[17] Walmart highlighted that the benefit of this technology not only gives shoppers a personalized experience but it also eliminates the need for physical product samples, making it a more sustainable and environmentally friendly option.

"As a destination for beauty, we're committed to identifying new and emerging opportunities to inspire our customers and create more personalized, seamless, customer-centric shopping experiences. That's why I'm so excited that Walmart is launching Beauty Virtual Try-On, to offer customers a more engaging and convenient try-on experience on the Walmart app," remarked Creighton Kiper, vice president of Beauty at Walmart US in a press release.[18]

Avon also used Perfect Corp. technology to enable virtual try-on for its brand.[19] The beauty company launched AR virtual try-on for over 400 makeup products, including a wide range of lip, eye, and skin products. This feature in the Avon app lets shoppers try on a variety of different styles and products in seconds. According to data provided by Avon published on the Perfect Corp. website, AR virtual try-on has resulted in a 320% increase in conversion rate, a 94% increase in average number of products viewed, and a 33% increase in average order value.[20]

Luxury fashion brand Gucci has embraced AR for several products, including its sneakers. It used AR technology from Wanna to enhance its app with a virtual sneaker try-on feature that used Wanna's foot-tracking AR capability.[21] Inside the app, shoppers select the shoe they wish to try on virtually and then activate their smartphone camera to view a high-quality 3D model of the shoe on their feet via the smartphone screen. According to a case study on the Wanna website, some of the goals for Gucci in using AR in this way included boosting product activation for new releases, engaging Gen Z customers, and positioning the brand as an innovator in the digital space.[22] This same case study also reported that the sneaker try-on increased the number of new users by three times, boosted the average session time up to five times, and generated a conversion to store rate of >25%.[23] The Gucci app also lets shoppers try on Gucci watches on their wrists using Wanna AR technology.[24] Shoppers follow similar steps as the sneaker try-on inside the app to use AR to visualize how a Gucci watch would look like on their wrist. They can view the high-quality 3D model from all angles and take a picture of the watch on their wrist to share it with friends to get a second opinion.

JLab, a wireless audio products company, has created a virtual fitting room using 8th Wall's WebAR technology.[25] Shoppers can use a "try-on virtually" button on select product pages on the brand's e-commerce site and on BestBuy.com to try on different headphones and earbuds using AR.[26] Using their smartphone or computer camera, users can see how various audio products will look and fit, helping them choose the suitable model without needing to visit a physical store. This experience uses the face effects capability of Niantic's 8th Wall platform, which is hyper-optimized for the browser and works across smartphones, laptops, and computers.

Warby Parker also turned to face tracking for its AR use to allow customers to try on glasses through its app virtually.[27] This feature employs face-mapping technology to create a realistic preview of how different frames will look on the shopper's face. This app feature can also recommend the best width and measure your pupillary distance (PD). Warby Parker has also made shopping using AR easier by allowing customers to quickly add frames they find look good to their cart and taking a photo that you can share with friends and family to get their opinion.

VIRTUAL TRY-OUTS

Virtual try-outs allow customers to visualize products in their environment to see how they would fit into their lives. Like virtual try-ons, this feature can be added to e-commerce apps and websites to facilitate an easy way to try products. Virtual try-outs use the back-facing camera of the smartphone and leverage computer vision to sense the world around the shopper to properly place true-to-size products, such as furniture, lamps, home decor, and even automobiles, in the shopper's space. This technology enhances the shopping experience and reduces the uncertainty and risk associated with online shopping, leading to increased customer satisfaction and sales.

Walmart has been at the forefront of integrating AR into its mobile shopping capabilities. The Walmart app and website lets shoppers view furniture, TV, and home decor items in their physical spaces.[28] The AR virtual try-out experience features over 300 compatible items shoppers can "View in Your Home." The app also lets shoppers toggle to the item dimensions when placed in their space to help ensure that it fits. Shoppers can also change the selected item style by seeing the item in the different color options available. Walmart designed this new AR feature with accessibility in mind; the tech is equipped with gesture control and voice-based instructions and descriptions, giving users different interaction options.

In an interview for VentureBeat, Desirée Gosby, vice president of Emerging Technology at Walmart Global Tech, said, that "when customers interact with the suite of AR features, the company said that it sees improvements in conversion rates, reduction in return rates and improvements in add-to-cart rates."[29]

Amazon, another retail behemoth, has enhanced its online shopping experience by incorporating augmented reality and artificial intelligence technologies into its e-commerce site. Amazon's "View in your Room" AR feature allows customers to visualize products in their environment using smartphones.[30] Shoppers can select items from Amazon's extensive catalog and see how they would look in their homes before buying. This includes visualizing home furnishings, tabletop items such as lamps, home decor, and small appliances such as toaster ovens and coffee makers. Customers can also change the color of the products to help them with their selection by seeing different options in their space. A survey conducted by Amazon found that 94% of Amazon customers who used the AR feature would want to use it again.[31] Amazon has also reported that the "View in Your Room" feature has resulted in an average increase of 9% in sales and that AR has been shown to double the purchase conversion.[32]

Amazon has equipped its sellers with tools to help them easily add this AR feature to their product pages.[33] This includes scanning tools to turn your product into a 3D model, access to 3D content partners to hire to create 3D models in cases where 3D scanning is not suitable, and tools to upload and manage your 3D asset. Once your 3D model is approved, the 3D and AR features will be added to the product page for customers.

Saatchi Art has taken a unique approach to integrating AR into its e-commerce platform. The online art gallery partnered with the Rock Paper Reality agency to enhance its website with a WebAR feature allowing customers to visualize artwork in their space before purchasing.[34] Saatchi Art's "View in My Room" AR feature is enabled for over one million works of art found on Saatchi Art's online e-commerce site. Once activated, shoppers use their smartphone camera to place digital versions of the artwork onto their walls. This innovative approach provides art buyers with a realistic preview of how a piece of art will look in their home or office, making it easier to choose the perfect piece. According to a case study published on the 8th Wall website, "Consumers who purchased on SaatchiArt.com and used the View in My Room WebAR feature spent on average ~17% more than those that purchased without the use of WebAR. Consumers who used the View in My Room feature were 4x more likely to convert than those that did not use the AR feature."[35]

Saatchi Art worked with Rock Paper Reality to design and develop the AR feature with scalability across the entire site. To do this, each of the art pieces is dynamically scaled based on the artwork's metadata and then applied to a true-to-size 3D canvas. The 3D asset is then used with 8th Wall's WebAR technology to visualize it in the consumer's physical space. Generating the 3D artwork on the fly allows new items added to the online gallery to immediately use the AR feature.

IKEA has been a pioneer in using AR to enhance the furniture shopping experience. The Swedish furniture giant launched its IKEA Place app, allowing customers to place furniture in their homes using AR technology.[36] The app enables users to select from a wide range of IKEA products and see how they look and fit in their space, including seeing multiple items at once in your space. IKEA has continued innovating with its AR capabilities, introducing the Kreativ app, which lets customers scan their room to create a 3D replica and add IKEA products to it.[37] The app also enables you to erase existing furnishings to make room for new virtual models and give shoppers an even greater sense of what replacing their couch, for example, might look like. The app lets you save your layouts and quickly adds what you like to your shopping cart.

Using AR as a Physical Product Perk

AR is reshaping the retail landscape by linking digital experiences to physical products, enticing shoppers to purchase. This integration offers unique, interactive perks that elevate the value of physical goods, creating a compelling and new reason for consumers to buy.

One striking example of this is the collaboration between Minecraft and Crocs. The shoemaker and gaming platform launched an AR experience linked to limited edition Crocs.[38] The "Choose Your Mode" experience features two AR games triggered by scanning a charm on the special edition shoes, while non-owners could scan a QR code on the experience microsite. The AR experience featured a Minecraft building experience called "Crocs Creator" and an AR game called "Crocs Crossing." Both experiences could be accessed in the browser and required no app to download. The experience was created by Gravity Road in partnership with Powster and used Niantic's 8th Wall technology.[39] This gamified experience adds value to the purchase and taps into the customer's love for Minecraft, making the product more desirable and fun.

Nike's metaverse team, RTFKT, launched an AR-enabled hoodie, "RTFKT x Nike AR Genesis Hoodie."[40] The hoodie was made available as an NFT (non-fungible token) available on the web3 platform OpenSea. It was made available first to RTFKT's NFT community, Clone X, before the wider OpenSea community could "mint" (the term used to purchase an NFT and gain ownership on the blockchain). NFT holders could then "forge" the NFT to unlock the AR digital asset. The hoodie has an NFC (near-field communication) chip, triggering the Snapchat AR lens when it encounters a smartphone. When the lens is active, the hoodie will be shown with large digital wings placed on the back of the wearer. The AR lens can also be activated by scanning a QR code found on the front of the hoodie as part of the hoodie design. According to data on OpenSea, there are nearly 5,000 owners of the AR hoodie.[41]

The appeal of these AR-enhanced products lies in their ability to offer more than just a physical item. They provide an added inter-action layer and engagement that traditional products cannot. For instance, the Minecraft Crocs serve as functional footwear and a gate-way to exclusive digital content. This dual-purpose approach makes the product more attractive to consumers, particularly brand fans of the associated digital content. The AR experiences connected to these products often offer exclusive content or functionalities that cannot be accessed otherwise. This exclusivity can drive demand and create a sense of urgency to purchase. For example, the AR hoodie from RTFKT and Nike offers unique digital effects that are only visible through the Snapchat app, making the hoodie a must-have for fans who want the whole experience. This strategy boosts initial sales and encourages brand loyalty, as customers are drawn to these products' exclusive, immersive experiences. AR-enhanced products can create a sense of community among consumers. For instance, fans of the Minecraft Crocs or the RTFKT AR hoodie can share their experiences on social media, showcasing the unique digital effects and engag-ing with other fans. This social aspect can amplify the reach of the product and create a buzz around the brand, driving more sales and increasing brand visibility.

The Rise of Virtual-Only Sales

The emergence of AR has unlocked new opportunities for purchas-ing virtual goods, a concept rapidly gaining traction. These virtual goods, which exist only in digital form, can be used exclusively in AR and VR environments, transforming how consumers interact with products and enhancing their digital experiences. Brands such as Gucci and platforms such as DRESSX are pioneering this innovative approach, showcasing the potential and appeal of virtual goods in the modern marketplace.

One notable example is Gucci's neon-color Virtual 25 digital sneakers.[42] These sneakers, created in collaboration with the AR technology company Wanna, are not meant to be worn in the physi-cal world. Instead, they exist solely in the digital realm, where users can wear them in photos and videos on social media platforms facili-tated by AR. Buying the digital shoe from the Gucci app for $13 enables owners to virtually wear all 25 AR shoes in the collection as a filter using Wanna's foot tracking AR capability.[43] It also unlocks an in-game downloadable version that avatars can wear in virtual worlds such as Roblox and VRChat. This product represents a significant shift in how fashion is consumed and experienced. The Virtual 25 sneakers give consumers a unique way to express their style digitally, tapping into the growing trend of virtual self-expression.

DRESSX is a digital fashion company at the forefront of the virtual product trend. It is considered the largest retailer of digital fashion.[44] Its app DRESSX Metacloset features hundreds of virtual looks that can be selected and worn using its AR feature. Users can create photos and videos wearing the digital apparel and publish it to the app's feed. The AR-enabled media can also be shared directly with TikTok, Instagram, and Snapchat. Users can also subscribe to a Meta-looks subscription to be able to upload a photo of themselves and be sent back an edited photo with the digital look fully applied. The DRESSX Metacloset desktop app lets users take Skype, Google Meet, Zoom, and Microsoft Teams calls with the virtual apparel applied.[45] DRESSX has partnered with countless brands and technology partners such as adidas, Lacoste, GAP, American Eagle, Meta, and Roblox to create digital collections that can be used in virtual worlds, AR mirrors, or AR inside the DRESSX app.[46]

The rise of virtual goods is just the beginning. As headworn wearables become more prevalent, the use and demand for virtual goods are expected to grow exponentially. These devices will provide more immersive and seamless AR experiences, allowing users to integrate virtual items into their daily lives more naturally and intuitively. For instance, AR glasses could project virtual outfits onto the wearer, visible to others using AR devices, creating a shared digital experience that blends with the physical world.

Several factors are driving the virtual goods trend. Firstly, there is a growing interest in sustainability and reducing the environmental impact of consumerism. Virtual goods do not require physical resources to produce or ship and offer a more sustainable alternative to traditional products. Consumers conscious of their environmental footprint can enjoy fashion and other goods without contributing to waste and pollution.

Gen Z, the digital native generation, which values unique and customizable online experiences, is behind the demand for virtual goods. This demographic is accustomed to expressing themselves through digital avatars and social media profiles, making virtual fashion and accessories a natural extension of their identity. By offering virtual goods, brands can tap into this market and create new revenue streams while fostering deeper connections with their tech-savvy audience.

Finally, the growing use of virtual worlds as the new social network is also a key factor behind the demand for virtual goods. Players can purchase virtual items that enhance their in-game characters or environments, adding value and personalization to their gameplay. Users can adorn their digital personas with exclusive virtual accessories on social media, enhancing their online presence and interactions.

Turn Catalogs into Retail Experiences

AR transforms catalogs and lookbooks into interactive product showrooms. This technology allows consumers to engage with products in a dynamic and immersive way, enhancing their shopping experience and providing brands with innovative ways to showcase their offerings.

KHAITE, a luxury fashion brand, utilized AR to enhance its product lookbook for its spring-summer shoe collection.[47] KHAITE partnered with agency Rose Digital to develop a WebAR experience where shoppers could view detailed 3D models of shoes from the collection in AR. Customers scanned the QR code found on the lookbook to be taken to their browser. There they could select the shoe they wished to see up close in front of them from the carousel. Each shoe was scanned utilizing photogrammetry to create a 3D model that contained the accurate details of the fabric, materials, and texture. The shoes could be placed on any surface in the user's environment where they could scale, rotate, and walk around each of the pairs to check them out. According to a case study published on the 8th Wall website, "This resulted in a huge success for KHAITE as they saw a 4x increase in sales of the collection featured in WebAR. In addition, consumers spent on average over 4 minutes interacting with the WebAR experience."[48]

H&M leveraged AR for a print campaign promoting their latest collection with Simone Rocha.[49] Partnering with UNIT9, which used 8th Wall WebAR technology, the AR experience brought to life a physical lookbook.[50] The book featured actual actors, musicians, creatives, and models using volumetric video technology provided by Dimension Studios. When users scanned the AR marker found on each of the lookbook pages, the characters popped out of the book and performed, dancing, posting, and making music, all wearing items from the collection.

Multinational clothing retailer C&A brought its autumn/winter collection magazine to life with WebAR.[51] In fact, it committed wholly to using this technology by publishing a magazine that seemed empty until you scanned it with your smartphone to see and engage with the content. Magazine readers unlocked the content by scanning QR codes found throughout the 20 pages of the book. Some of the experiences included watching the cover come to life, visualizing the new collection in your living room, sketching your own addition to the collection, and watching it appear on the 3D model in AR in your own space.

"By combining a traditional medium with the very latest technology, we have created something very unique," said Sven Verresen, media, PR, and events specialist for C&A Belgium-Luxembourg, in a blog post on the 8th Wall website.[52] "The new collection for the fall perfectly reflects what C&A stands for today: inclusivity, sustainability and positivity. It's a reminder that fashion matters, that clothing has the power to make a statement."

Bloomingdale's celebrated its 150th anniversary with a unique AR-enabled catalog, which was sent out to over 400,000 households across the United States.[53] Users scanned a QR code that brought them to the WebAR experience. They could then select from the carousel the look they wanted to see in their physical space using AR. Once selected, a life-sized model could be placed in the space providing users with a fashion show in their living room. This browser-based experience was created by Rose Digital and powered by 8th Wall. According to a blog post on the 8th Wall website, "Users can also click to purchase their favorite styles directly inside the experience. This led to a +22% conversion rate to shop and a +38% engagement rate."[54]

Bring the Showroom to the Consumers

AR showrooms provide an interactive platform for customers to explore products in detail. The ability to customize and interact with virtual models increases engagement and retention, offering a more personalized shopping experience. By bringing the showroom to the consumer, AR eliminates the need for physical travel, making it easier for customers to access and explore products from the comfort of their homes.

One notable example of this is the BMW Virtual Viewer, an innovative WebAR tool that allows customers to explore BMW's range of Plug-in Hybrid Electric Vehicles (PHEVs) in the UK from their own homes.[55] This tool enables users to place life-sized, virtual models of BMW's PHEVs (such as the X5, X1, or 3 Series Touring) in their environments, whether it be their home, driveway, or garage. Customers can customize the cars by selecting colors, alloys, and interior features and interact with the vehicles by opening doors, turning on lights, and even playing the radio. Additionally, the AR experience includes an "x-ray view" to showcase the PHEV's transition between gasoline and electric modes.

Sophie Chiappe, brand communications manager at BMW UK, said in a press release: "At BMW we want to ensure that we introduce digital tools in a way that really help prospective customers along their decision journey when choosing a car, whilst ensuring it's fun and user friendly. This AR work has been designed to be engaging to use, from the navigation through to the built-in quizzes, and we're excited to launch it showcasing three of our plug-in hybrid cars and the technology they offer."[56]

The Virtual Viewer also incorporated hands-free voice navigation and a chatbot, enhancing user interaction and engagement. This feature allows users to explore the cars and ask questions just like they would at a physical dealership. This experience was created by creative agency FCB Inferno in partnership with Antiloop, CRAFT, Wavemaker, and ZONE digital and was powered by Niantic's 8th Wall technology.[57]

Augmenting the Retail Space

AR is revolutionizing retail by turning these everyday spaces into immersive, interactive shopping experiences.

AR navigation aids shoppers in finding products within stores by overlaying digital directions on their physical environment. This technology can guide customers to specific items, highlight special offers, and provide product information, enhancing convenience and satisfaction.

AR mirrors extend inventory by allowing customers to try on clothing and accessories virtually. AR mirrors are customized digital displays that include a camera, a screen, and require AR software. Shoppers can use these in-store devices to see how different outfits look on them in real time, mix and match items, and even share their looks on social media directly from the mirror, creating a seamless and engaging shopping experience. They can even try on products and customizations that may not physically be in the store.

AR also transforms retail locations into experiential destinations, driving foot traffic by offering unique, interactive experiences. Stores equipped with AR can host virtual events, games, and spectacles that attract and engage customers. These can be always-on experiences or available for a limited time, requiring shoppers to visit at certain times of the day. For example, AR scavenger hunts can make shopping fun and memorable, encouraging repeat visits, and gamify the in-store experience.

NAVIGATION AND WAY-FINDING

ARway.ai's AR navigation platform is transforming the retail experience in a 300,000-square-foot Megatek store by providing advanced, user-friendly navigation.[58] This system allows customers visiting the flagship store of this leading home improvement retailer in Albania to use their smartphone to access a comprehensive directory of products and locate where they can be found. Shoppers receive real-time product descriptions and are guided to specific items in the store using ARway's spatial computing solution, enabled by visual marker tracking with centimeter precision. The platform aims to help shoppers easily and quickly find what they need in the large retail environment.

The ARway.ai indoor navigation and way-finding platform uses AR to provide visual guides on the smartphone screen to help shoppers find their way around malls and other large retail environments. These real-time paths are lit up with digital arrows and signs, which can be customized and styled using the tools provided as part of its platform.

By integrating AR technology, ARway.ai addresses common challenges large retail stores face, such as product visibility and navigation complexity. Customers can effortlessly locate products, explore new items, and receive information about ongoing promotions and discounts. The interactive nature of AR also attracts tech-savvy customers, offering a unique and modern shopping experience that distinguishes brick-and-mortar stores from online retailers. This innovation is poised to revolutionize retail by blending physical and digital shopping environments, making the shopping journey more efficient, engaging, and personalized.

AR MIRRORS

Incorporating AR mirrors into retail environments has revolutionized the shopping experience by allowing shoppers to virtually try on clothing and makeup, extending inventory, and personalizing the shopping journey. This technology enhances customer satisfaction and drives sales and engagement by offering a seamless, interactive experience.

Retailers such as Macy's have embraced AR to provide virtual try-on experiences in-store. Relying on AR mirror provider Zero10, shoppers can visualize clothing items from the Disney Princess Shop in the flagship Disney store in New York City without physically trying them on.[59] When a shopper interacts with the AR-enabled mirror, the computer vision capability estimates the shopper's body shape and position to overlay the selected digital apparel on them. They can then see themselves wearing it on the large screen in front of them.

Coach's partnership with Zero10 for its Tabby bag illustrates how brands can use AR to create immersive retail window experiences.[60] Shoppers in New York could stand in front of the window featuring one of Zero10's AR mirrors to see themselves with a Tabby bag virtually. They can choose to see the bag in different colors. The AR mirror window experience also featured other AR effects, including glittery pink balloons that spelled TABBY in the air. Inside the Coach retail location was another AR mirror, enabling shoppers to try on more of Coach's collection.

Zero10 has reported that pilot projects of its AR mirrors have resulted in "a staggering 60% increase in try-ons and foot traffic" and "AR Windows enhanced store window attractiveness by an impressive 93.5%."[61]

LOCATION-BASED AR

AR revolutionizes retail by transforming stores into experiential destinations, driving significant traffic. By integrating AR technology, retailers can create immersive and interactive experiences that attract customers, differentiate their stores from online shopping, and boost foot traffic.

One example of AR's impact in retail is Selfridges, a renowned department store that utilized AR to enhance its in-store experience. Selfridges partnered with Rose Digital, which used 8th Wall technology to create the WebAR experience.[62] Customers who visited could scan QR codes placed around the store to see life-size models show off the latest collection. This experience turned the Selfridges store into a runway where visitors could watch an AR-enabled fashion show.

Paper Tree, a San Francisco–based origami shop located in Japantown, partnered with agency Rock Paper Reality to create a location-based AR activation.[63] The agency used Google's Geospatial Creator and Adobe Aero to develop the experience. The AR experience transforms Japantown into a magical world of origami. Users who visit the area around the Paper Tree store scan a QR code and then use their smartphone to see 3D origami birds, objects, and sculptures in the physical world around them.

Nike utilized AR in their Play New campaign, which featured an AR scavenger hunt designed to engage customers in a fun and interactive way.[64] Participants could scan one of five QR codes throughout the store to unlock AR mini-games, including mini golf and football. The web app kept track of the shopper's progress, and once they completed all five of the mini-games, they received a prize they could redeem from the store concierge. This WebAR experience was created by Dream Syndicate and BRDG and was installed for a limited time in Nike's flagship House of Innovation stores in NYC, LA, and Chicago.

Principles for AR Commerce

Brands are exploring ways to improve customer interactions and increase sales, integrating AR into their sales strategies. To do this effectively, there are a few principles brands should consider.

TOP-NOTCH QUALITY

The quality of assets plays a role in AR experiences. Having high-quality assets is vital to creating attractive representations of products for consumers. Low-resolution models can decrease user satisfaction and reduce engagement levels. AR assets must mirror the products as closely as possible by incorporating high-resolution textures, accurate colors, and realistic lighting effects. When consumers use AR to visualize products in their surroundings, they should feel assured that what they see matches what they will receive. While top-notch quality is essential, it's also important for assets to be optimized for performance to ensure operation on a range of devices, from high-end smartphones to more basic ones. Striking a balance between quality and performance will enable a user base to enjoy AR applications without encountering technical issues.

PERSONALIZATION AND CUSTOMIZATION

Personalization plays a role in using AR for commerce. Empowering customers to customize products based on their preferences should be a key value in your AR-enabled sales strategy. Brands should offer customization options such as changing colors, textures, and sizes or adding engravings or other embellishments. For instance, enabling a shopper to view a sofa in fabrics it is available in or purses with different metal clasps helps shoppers better visualize their customized options. This could be furthered by implementing user profiles that store preferences, providing a more tailored shopping journey that remembers a user's customizations. In addition, incorporating features that allow customers to experiment with configurations or enable various products to be visualized in AR together, such as hats and jewelry or chairs, tables, and lamps, can significantly assist in helping consumers make well-informed choices.

MANIPULATION OF SIZE AND SCALE

One outstanding benefit of AR is its capacity to manipulate scale, enabling consumers to visualize products of their size within their surroundings. Offering the ability to view products that are true to size helps shoppers grasp how an item will fit and complement their space. Contrarily, giving consumers the ability to play with scale to enlarge items so that they are larger than life can allow them to get up close to intricate details, deepening their appreciation and under-standing of the craftsmanship of a product.

USER-FRIENDLY INTERFACES

A user-friendly interface is crucial to ensure that AR applications are accessible and enjoyable for all users. Complicated or unwieldy inter-faces may discourage users from using AR features. Keeping the interface simple and intuitive is vital; users should be able to explore AR features without requiring guidance. Clear symbols, menus, and straightforward instructions can enhance the experience. Providing guided experiences can assist users in learning how to utilize AR features.

SOCIAL MEDIA INTEGRATION

Integrating social media functionalities can expand the reach and influence of AR interactions. Allowing individuals to share their AR engagements can spark word-of-mouth marketing. Empowering users to capture and post their AR moments on platforms can enhance vis-ibility and credibility. This also includes the ability to share videos, GIFs, and photos easily on popular messaging platforms to facilitate opinions from family and friends.

CONNECTING AR WITH POINTS OF SALE

The use of AR should be well integrated with the sales aspects of your e-commerce property. Find ways to connect your AR capability to favorites and lists to increase the likelihood of purchase. Where possible, the ability to add to cart or purchase directly from within the AR experience could also boost conversions and make the shopping experience more enjoyable for consumers. Integrating AR into loyalty programs can also improve how we measure success and engage with customers. Brands can reward users who interact with AR fea-tures, for example, earning points for trying out products or sharing their AR adventures on media. This encourages people to use AR and gives brands more insight into what consumers like and do.

Measuring AR-Driven Sales Performance

Measuring AR's impact on commerce requires brands to rethink their tracking of sales and essential metrics. To effectively gauge AR's impact in commerce, brands must monitor metrics that center on the unique capabilities of spatial computing.

TIME SPENT

Time and engagement play roles in AR experiences. Unlike shopping, where spending more time on a webpage could signal confusion or frustration, longer engagement periods in AR typically indicate positive interactions. The longer consumers engage with a product, the more likely they are to form an attachment to it, potentially leading to increased conversion rates. Brands should monitor the length of AR sessions, the number of interactions per session, and the level of engagement, such as zooming in on details or exploring views of a 3D model.

ENGAGEMENT METRICS

A notable benefit of integrating AR into commerce is its capacity to deliver personalized experiences. Brands can monitor personalization-related activities, such as how users modify product colors or textures, experiment with sizes, or explore specific combinations of 3D models. These engagements generate data that can guide product recommendations and trend projections. For example, if many customers personalize a product with a specific color, it might suggest a pattern that the brand can leverage for marketing. AR can offer insights for inventory management. Monitoring which products are frequently viewed and personalized in AR can help brands better predict demand and can optimize their inventory levels.

Companies should also keep an eye on how using AR influences customer loyalty. By examining how often customers make repeat purchases and their overall value over time, brands can determine whether AR is helping them build connections with their customers. If AR users stick around and spend money, it suggests that AR experiences make a difference in how customers feel about the brand.

CONVERSION RATE

Another key metric is the conversion rate stemming from AR experiences. This can be assessed by comparing purchase rates between users who interacted with AR features and those who did not. A higher conversion rate among AR users highlights the efficacy of

AR in boosting sales. Furthermore, observing engagement behaviors such as adding items to the cart, sharing their AR experience on social media, or revisiting the product page multiple times can offer insights into how AR influences purchase decisions.

SHARING

Social media metrics serve as another data source for evaluating AR in e-commerce. Brands should keep an eye on the reach and engagement of posts featuring AR, including likes, shares, and comments, and usage of branded AR filters or effects. Elevated levels of engagement indicate consumer interest and the use of filters and lenses amplify the exposure of products and services through organic sharing.

CUSTOMER FEEDBACK

Gathering customer feedback plays a role in evaluating the impact of AR technology in the world of commerce. Brands must encourage users to share their opinions by leaving reviews and rating their experiences with AR. This type of feedback provides insights for improvement and offers authentic testimonials that can be utilized in marketing efforts. Surveys are also effective in obtaining input on what users enjoyed or didn't like about their AR interactions and how these experiences influenced their buying decisions.

ANALYTICS

Integrating analytics into AR experiences on e-commerce platforms is vital for understanding performance. By combining tools that track user engagement within AR environments with typical e-commerce analytics, brands can fully view customer behavior and journey. Analytics in AR should consider key event tracking around the product, such as heat mapping to help illustrate the points of focus while evaluating products in space and monitoring personalization and customization choices.

Shopping in Mixed Reality

Despite MR headsets being relatively new to the market, brands have already started to utilize these devices to engage shoppers in new ways. Many brands used the launch of the Apple Vision Pro to demonstrate new ways to shop with applications that were available when the device debuted.

Lowe's introduced the Style Studio for the Apple Vision Pro.[65] This app lets customers design their dream kitchen in mixed reality. By donning the headset, users can walk through a virtual 3D rendition of a kitchen they designed, experimenting with different layouts, colors, and products from Lowe's extensive catalog. This immersive experience lets customers see how a kitchen backsplash would look against different countertop options. Once customers have a final design they like, they can share their plans by email, text, or AirDrop. The app aims to bridge the gap between imagination and reality, reducing the uncertainty often associated with home improvement projects.

"This is a transformational moment for kitchen design. Our customers can now visualize their dream kitchen in their own space, and that's incredibly exciting," said Seemantini Godbole, Lowe's executive vice president and chief digital and information officer, in a Lowe's press release.[66] "Lowe's Style Studio immerses our customers in a cutting-edge design experience enabled by spatial computing that will make home improvement easier than ever."

Sports retail giant DECATHLON also utilized the Apple Vision Pro launch as a moment to showcase its innovation in immersive shopping.[67] Customers can virtually explore DECATHLON's product range, including placing 3D models of its products in their physical space. Instead of scrolling through endless product lists online, shoppers can use the headset to interact with 3D sports equipment, apparel, and accessories models. This allows consumers to get up close with products, view them from all angles, and even head inside products such as tents to get a feel for what they are all about. The app also features video, which can be viewed on large panels within the headset.

"We are thrilled to be proposing such a unique and immersive experience to our customers on the Apple Vision Pro. We're going one step further in our commitment to innovating the world of modern sport. Customers can step inside our tents or check out our new bikes in 3D from the comfort of their own home – a revolution in the shopping experience. What comes next is bound to be exceptional, as we continue to accompany people in their sporting experiences in new and exciting ways," Barbara Martin Coppola, CEO of DECATHLON, said in a news release on the DECATHLON website.[68]

J.Crew launched its Apple Vision Pro app J.Crew Virtual Closet to reimagine its shopping experience for this spatial computer.[69] The app, created in partnership with leading immersive shopping platform Obsess, lets consumers make a personalized virtual closet by mixing and matching outfits from J. Crew's collection. The headset provides realistic 3D visualizations of how the clothes will look when worn using a life-size 3D mannequin. Customers can not only examine combinations of clothing together but also use 3D models to get close to the details, such as the texture of the fabrics. The shopping experience is set against immersive environment backgrounds designed to inspire wardrobe choices based on different types of locations.

One powerful feature in the app is the inclusion of SharePlay, which lets customers chat with friends and family to get their opinions on the looks. J.Crew is also offering the ability to chat with J.Crew expert stylists through this capability which is an excellent tip of the hat to the future of shopping in headset.

"The J.Crew Virtual Closet is a first for the fashion industry – leveraging Apple's newest technology to immerse shoppers in a hyper-realistic styling experience with our brand," said Halsey Anderson, VP of marketing at J.Crew in a press release.[70] "We're thrilled to continue our partnership with Obsess to use this cutting-edge device to bring J.Crew into an exciting new era of spatial shopping and styling. We're particularly excited for our J.Crew stylists to use Apple Vision Pro to work with customers in a more dynamic way than ever before, via SharePlay in FaceTime. This incredible technology, combined with our rich brand heritage of best-in-class service, will provide endless styling capabilities."

Alo Yoga created *alo Sanctuary* for the Apple Vision Pro to offer an immersive wellness shopping experience for headset shoppers.[71] Developed in partnership with Obsess and Ave Advisory, this spatial computing shopping experience centers on immersive environments and spatial audio, creating a serene setting to shop and meditate. The app features four hyper-realistic environments, including beach, mountains, jungle, and canyons, designed to show off a collection of

Alo Yoga apparel. Customers can view apparel in 3D on a life-sized mannequin in front of them, get close to the details, and rotate the clothing to see it from all angles. Customers can participate in guided meditations and wellness workshops, all within this immersive sanctuary. The headset provides a serene setting, enhancing the overall wellness experience. This innovative approach promotes Alo Yoga's products and fosters a deeper connection with the brand, aligning with its mission of promoting mindfulness and well-being.

"This is a new, immersive way for a visionary brand like ours to share a mindful experience that transports consumers directly into our world through interaction designed for spatial computing," said Danny Harris, cofounder and co-CEO of Alo Yoga, in a press release.[72]

e.l.f. Cosmetics also took a meditative and wellness approach to its beauty app for the Apple Vision Pro, "your best e.l.f.," created in partnership with Obsess. Users are invited to experience three different immersive environments while in the headset, each reflective of an e.l.f. beauty product also for sale within the app. The environments intend to get shoppers in the mood while they explore the product catalog, including 3D e.l.f. products. The app also features self-care activities including guided meditations, stretching exercises, and other relaxing activities such as puzzles and games.

"'Your best e.l.f.' is a game-changing beauty experience that welcomes users to relax, de-stress and focus on being their best self," said Ekta Chopra, chief digital officer, e.l.f. Beauty in a press release.[73] "Partnering with Obsess to launch one of the first beauty shopping apps for Apple Vision Pro is an evolution for our brand, which has always been digitally led. We are champions for innovation and new technology platforms. The decision to launch on Apple Vision Pro is not only natural for us; it is critical to continue to meet our community – and entertain them – wherever they are."

StockX, a popular marketplace for sneakers and streetwear, joined the brands and retailers using MR to create an immersive shopping experience on the Apple Vision Pro.[74] The app, developed in-house by StockX designers and engineers, features an immersive sneaker showcase where customers can look at the details of each shoe by grabbing them from the virtual shelves in front of them and bringing them up close to where they are. In addition, the app also gives consumers the ability to interact with visual graphs and sales information and purchase shoes within the experience.

"Nothing replaces the feeling of picking a sneaker off the shelf and holding it in your hands, but this new experience comes very close," said Greg Schwartz, StockX president and chief operating officer, in a press release.[75] "Innovation is at the heart of everything we do at StockX. We were the first to introduce stock market mechanics to the resale space, and we're proud to be one of the first marketplaces to launch a spatial app for Apple Vision Pro. It's everything you know and love about StockX, but in an entirely new dimension."

Brands are already utilizing mixed reality to create immersive, interactive, personalized shopping experiences that revolutionize e-commerce. From home improvement and sports equipment to fashion and beauty, MR headsets offer a whole new set of possibilities to engage customers and enhance their shopping journeys, and this is just the beginning. As the MR headset category continues to come together, with more options for consumers and as this device grows in adoption, it will become an integral part of the retail landscape, offering even more innovative ways to connect with consumers and transform how we shop.

Looking at Retail Through AR Glasses

It is still early for AR glasses, but brands have already begun using the devices available today to show how they will change shopping. These early adopters use this as an opportunity to experiment and learn how spatial computing will change the retail experience as much as a PR opportunity to show consumers and the rest of the market that they are willing and ready to embrace innovation and change.

Lowe's has been a pioneer in integrating AR headworn wearables into retail. Utilizing NVIDIA's Omniverse platform, Lowe's is creating interactive digital twins of its stores, which can be engaged with on a Magic Leap 2 headset to give its store employees superpowers.[76] One use case is assisting store associates with store inventory. Store associates can look at in-store shelves while wearing a Magic Leap 2 and visualize how the store shelf should look to assist in stocking. This assistive experience lets associates engage with the digital twin to help them with their jobs and can also lend the associate's eyes to remote centralized store planners to provide additional guidance. Remote associates can flag changes and suggestions using an AR sticky note that the in-store employee can see and act on. Lowe's is also using NVIDIA's Omniverse and the Magic Leap 2 headset to give employees "x-ray vision." Tapping into the digital twin, store associates can look at any in-store inventory and be provided with information. This reduces the need to get on ladders to check on the store's top stocks.

"At Lowe's, we are always looking for ways to reimagine store operations and remove friction for our customers," said Seemantini Godbole, executive vice president and chief digital and information officer at Lowe's, in a blog post on NVIDIA's website.[77] "With NVIDIA Omniverse, we're pulling data together in ways that have never been possible, giving our associates superpowers."

H&M Group collaborated with Warpin Media and Magic Leap to create an innovative retail experience called Redesign Labs to give new life to secondhand garments.[78] Customers were invited to wear the Magic Leap headset and be guided through a process to give new life to clothing. Using hand gestures, customers donned the headset and then moved through menus of motifs and styles to select new designs they could see virtually applied to physical T-shirts. Once the customer was happy with the new design they could see on the shirt, they used a gesture to confirm the design, and it was then sent off to be printed on the physical apparel.

Online retailer Wayfair explored using the Magic Leap smart-glasses to let shoppers visualize furniture and decor in their homes. Wayfair Spaces is an interior design and room planning app for the Magic Leap smartglasses.[79] This app lets shoppers view curated spaces, such as kitchens and living rooms, which feature products available on Wayfair. These 3D spaces can be viewed from a bird's-eye view. When shoppers find products they think look good in their homes, they drag individual furniture items into their space. The selected items are then anchored to the desired location using Magic Leap's spatial capabilities. Anchoring adds a sense of realism and enables the shopper to walk around the true-to-life-sized products to see if they fit the space well.

"At Wayfair, we know that visual inspiration and discovery are key to creating the best possible shopping experience for home. That's why we've always taken the lead in setting industry standards in 3D modeling and visualization, and in building innovative applications that will transform the way people shop for their homes," said Steve Conine, co-chairman and cofounder of Wayfair, in a news release on the Wayfair website.[80] "Alongside Magic Leap, we're excited to be on the forefront of one of the most visionary explorations of what's possible in retail, as mixed reality and spatial computing influence the future of the customer experience."

Porsche Cars North America is utilizing the Microsoft HoloLens 2 for post-sales support. It has sent a HoloLens to nearly 200 dealerships to give its technicians superpowers. One solution, created by CraneMorley, allows technicians to get guided 3D aid using Teams on HoloLens to call an expert in another location. Technicians wearing the device can see their surroundings and the car they're working on alongside pointers, annotations, and document sharing to help resolve tricky repair problems.

"Technicians quickly figured out that this was going to help them do their jobs better and make their customers happier. And management knows that having satisfied customers means more repeat business. So, this solution is a win for everyone," said Thomas Pratt, president of CraneMorley, in a case study on the Microsoft website.[81]

In addition, HoloLens is being used to bring detailed training to technicians at the dealership rather than requiring them to travel. Technicians can view a 3D hologram of a car and go through remote training classes. They are able to see the vehicle in their space and hide and show parts as well as virtually tear down a model of a car.

"Our technicians may go to training for weeks at a time – which means we lose them from the dealership for that period, and they're away from their lives and families," says Jarrett. "Being able to do training in-house with HoloLens 2 means a better quality of life for technicians and a significant cost savings for us. When you multiply that savings across a network of almost 200 dealer partners, it's a substantial figure," said Paul Jarrett, general manager at Gaudin Porsche of Las Vegas, in the Microsoft case study.[82]

According to the case study, the use of HoloLens by Porsche technicians "has the double benefit of getting customers' cars back quickly and giving technicians the satisfaction of working for a company that cares about their skills development and professional advancement. In an industry where technicians are in scarce supply, this is an important recruiting tool."[83]

AR glasses will revolutionize the retail industry by creating immersive shopping experiences and providing valuable post-sales support. Brands such as Lowe's, H&M Group, Wayfair, and Porsche are leading the way in showing us how. As AR glasses continue to evolve and grow in adoption, applications in retail will likely expand, offering even more innovative ways to connect with consumers and improve their shopping experiences.

On the Horizon for Spatial Sales

As MR headsets gain popularity and AR smart glasses begin to emerge for consumer use, brands must stay updated on the trends to remain competitive and relevant in selling their online and in-store products.

One key trend is the emergence of AR glasses paired with multimodal AI capabilities, which enables wearers to ask about what they see in the world around them to get information. We are already starting to see this superpower brought on by AI + AR with devices such as Ray-Ban Meta smartglasses, which combine the power of Meta AI and wearable cameras to enable the assistant to see the world with the prompt, "Hey Meta, look and ..." The AI uses the camera as its eyes and processes the image it takes with its machine learning models to surface relevant information. Today, glasses can help identify objects and places, provide you with relevant information it finds online, and then whisper these details in your ear. Tomorrow, multimodal AI smartglasses may give wearers even more real-time auditory and visual information about the world. This may include making the entire world an e-commerce opportunity by looking at what you are interested in to bring up product information and using a simple gesture or voice command to purchase anything you see throughout the day. This "see it, buy it" feature will move the online shopping experience into the physical world, making it more intuitive and relevant by inspiring purchases in a context where consumers discover the products rather than only in a retail environment.

AI-enabled wearables may go beyond just providing information and access to purchase. The combination of AI and wearables could usher in personalized shoppers. These virtual assistants will use their newfound senses and vast knowledge to tailor recommendations based on customer interactions and preferences. With this technology, you may soon be able to enter a store and be guided by your shopper, who understands your taste, suggests new items, and assists you along your journey around the store. At the start, this may be an auditory experience. Eventually, AR glasses will allow us to embody our shoppers as holograms or avatars, who may be seen walking beside us as we move about the store, pointing out different products they think we might like.

Glasses will also significantly enhance the use of AR for way-finding and navigation. While possible on mobile today, the smartphone's limited field of view and handheld nature constrains the value AR-enabled navigation can offer. With AR headworn devices, navigation facilitated by AR will feel more intuitive and integrated within the environment. AR glasses could assist with in-store navigation by guiding customers to desired products while providing information and promotions. This digital lens could be viewed from a mall, store, or brand perspective with guided tours of retail spaces designed by brands. These tours could also be curated from the perspective of an influencer, celebrity, or friend. Each lens would highlight different visual and auditory information as you walked around the retail environment, making suggestions and guiding you to other areas and products in the store.

AR glasses will also continue to give sales associates and store employees superpowers. These assistive devices will enhance everyday operations, reducing errors and omissions, increasing quality, and boosting the confidence and morale of employees. This includes applications for AR smartglasses that help team members with inventory management, remote collaboration, and customer service. Today, we have seen many pilots of these solutions. Tomorrow, store employees wearing AR glasses to help them with their jobs will become commonplace.

AR glasses could also take a shopping experience from everyday to extraordinary. The gamification of the mundane is a potential outcome of consistent use of AR headworn wearables. Relying on the spatial computer's semantic spatial understanding of the world, developers could transform grocery shopping and other retail trips into a casual or competitive game that helps you get everything on your list in a way that feels as if you were at an arcade or theme park. These same devices will reimagine store merchandising, turning stores into immersive environments that immediately get shoppers into the mood to buy the latest line of products. While these devices can change physical retail locations, they also have the ability to transform any space into a retail experience, for example, making your living room a showroom or changing room to try on clothes. Headsets will take virtual try-on and virtual try-out experiences we see today on mobile to the next level. With a headset on, you can view products in your house, on yourself, and others as if they were physically there in the space with you.

As headworn wearables become the norm, websites must be optimized for these devices. This will start with spatializing 2D websites by adding 3D models and environments to further the existing e-commerce experience on MR headsets. Eventually, however, websites will need to be reimagined as we fully enter the spatial web era with AR glasses. Brands must offer shoppers with glasses new ways to engage with online retail content. Websites may act more like portals to virtual stores and branded worlds that reimagine what a physical retail experience could be without the constraints and limitations of the physical world, including an infinite space and modified physics or world filters and lenses that augment the user's perspective of the store or the world around them as they walk about and see the world through the glasses.

The growing trend of virtual goods is something that brands must pay attention to. Today, virtual goods can be purchased for avatars, whether in traditional gaming or virtual reality. Tomorrow, virtual products will decorate our homes, embellish our outfits, and complete our looks. As glasses become something we wear daily, the sale of virtual products will become an even greater opportunity. Consumers may mix virtual goods with physical products as part of their everyday lift. This may include digital-only exclusives by brands, digital twins of physical products purchased, and even virtual perks and bonuses that get unlocked when you buy the "real" thing.

As AR glasses and MR headsets grow in adoption, companies need to keep up with the times by embracing these emerging trends as part of their sales strategy. Many opportunities that may be unlocked by consistent headworn device use are already in play on mobile. By incorporating AR and MR into their approaches, companies can develop tailored, engaging, and immersive encounters that draw in and keep customers, fostering advancement and creativity in the challenging retail environment.

Sparking Spatial Strategies

Strike up strategic dialogue about AR's role in your business with these essential conversation starters:

- **In the boardroom:** How can we leverage AR technology to enhance our customers' online and physical shopping experience?
- **For your team meeting:** How will AR features integrate with existing e-commerce systems, such as product catalogs, checkout processes, and customer databases?
- **Around the water cooler:** Have you tried any shopping experiences on MR headsets? Which ones stood out to you and why?

Share this on your socials: Did you know AR is transforming shopping? Try on clothes and makeup virtually, visualize furniture in your home, and explore immersive showrooms. From reducing returns to enhancing in-store experiences, AR is revolutionizing retail! #thenextdimensionbook

CHAPTER 9

Becoming a Spatial Computing Champion

Like video did for the internet, spatial computing will rapidly advance in the coming years to a point where 3D objects and environments are as easy to create and consume as your favorite short-form social media videos are today.

— Werner Vogels, *CTO at Amazon*[1]

Chapter Cheat Sheet Powered by AI

I asked an AI to read this chapter and create a cheat sheet. If you only have five minutes to spare, here are the three must-know insights to help you level up your spatial computing knowledge.

- ◆ **Experimentation is Key:** Cultivate a culture of testing and learning, approaching AR by starting with small-scale pilot projects and continuously iterating based on feedback and results.
- ◆ **Lifelong Learning:** Stay updated with AR trends, attend conferences, and go hands-on with AR development tools and devices to understand and innovate within the evolving technology landscape.

♦ **Strategic AR Integration:** Develop a clear, measurable AR-centric strategy that is rooted in solving customer problems, aligns with business goals, empowers teams, and remains adaptable to market changes and technological advancements.

Want to talk to an AI about this book? Scan the QR code or visit ai.thenextdimension book.com in your browser to access The Next Dimension Book GPT.

Scan Me

Spatial Computing Needs You

As someone passionate and interested in using cutting-edge technologies to advance your career and business, your curiosity about AR and spatial computing led you to pick up this book and brought you to this chapter. Whether you're already implementing AR strategies or just starting to explore the possibilities of this technology, you likely understand the advantage it can offer you and your organization. This book has introduced you to concepts and examples and has left you with questions to intensify your curiosity to continue your journey. It is meant to be one more stepping stone on your path to becoming a spatial computing champion.

Embracing new technologies requires a visionary group of individuals who can spot early opportunities and leverage the transformative potential of emerging innovations. For augmented reality and spatial computing that individual is you. Your insights and commitment to emerging technology are vital in guiding your business through a nascent space that can help your organization gain a competitive advantage and be future-proof.

This final chapter outlines strategies to advance your role as an advocate. We'll discuss ways to incorporate AR into your business strategy to ensure your organization stays at the forefront of innovation. This includes setting the right goals and solving customer challenges with this technology. Together with the ideas and real-life examples in this book, you will have a solid foundation on which to implement AR plans within your organization.

Becoming a leader in spatial computing goes beyond adopting technology. It's also about nurturing a culture of innovation in your organization. Ongoing and consistent experimenting and learning will ensure that you and your organization keep pace with this fast-moving and ever-evolving technology. By embracing these principles, you'll join a community of trailblazers reshaping industry norms and setting standards for success across industry verticals.

You can be a spatial computing champion.

Embrace Experimentation Enthusiastically and Eagerly

As AR is new and constantly developing, especially its use with head-worn wearable devices, stepping into this space requires a dedication to trying new things and being comfortable with the unknown. Despite the flux, businesses that have already adopted this mindset have shown that AR can offer possibilities for improving sales, marketing, and advertising today. To do this successfully, one must fully embrace a mindset of exploration and creativity.

To keep up with the fast-paced change of this technology, it is essential to cultivate a culture of experimentation within your organization. Give your team the time and space to experiment, test ideas, and learn. Begin with internal projects and prototypes to gain experience and tap into the wider organization to help you battle-test technologies and projects and give you feedback. This process, often called "dogfooding," can help you better identify and fix issues, demonstrate confidence in technologies and initiatives, and better understand the user experience. The learnings from this step will build confidence in using AR before moving to small test groups involving your customers.

It's beneficial for organizations to incorporate beta testing into their experimentation process. Beta testing involves trials with select customers to get valuable feedback and resolve issues before launching an initiative fully to a broader audience. Seek user feedback during these testing phases, as their perspectives can offer insights into usability, functionality, and overall user experience. Involving users in the development process ensures your AR offerings are tailored to meet their needs and expectations.

Experimentation should be an ongoing part of your business rather than a one-time occurrence. It requires a mindset of learning and adaptation, where each experiment informs the next. Collect feedback, evaluate outcomes, and make modifications along the way.

Here, it is about the journey just as much as the destination. No mistakes, just learnings. This iterative loop aids in tuning your AR tactics to ensure they align with your business objectives and meet customer expectations. The knowledge you gain from these experiments will give you an edge over competitors as you improve your use of AR as a core part of your business.

Goals and especially non-goals are both vital to experimentation. Clearly define what you intend to accomplish with your AR initiatives and what AR is not intended to solve. This clarity helps concentrate your efforts and resources on the most important areas to you and your users. While goals are key to orient decisions for your AR project, it is important to remember that experiments are about learning and not about a pass or fail. Only some AR experiments will turn out as planned. It is important to take lessons from each attempt and apply them to enhance future endeavors. Embrace a mindset that views setbacks as opportunities for growth and unexpected outcomes as aha moments. Each insight brings you closer to discovering what resonates with your customers and starts to inform your AR language. This approach nurtures a culture of resilience and ongoing progress within your company and will be key to your success in getting your business into the next dimension of computing.

Promoting creativity among your team is also essential when it comes to experimentation. New technologies require new thinking, so empowering your team to think outside the box is important. Organize brainstorming sessions, workshops, and hackathons to spark ideas. Encourage your team to play with existing AR applications. Get them access to new devices and carve out time to use them regularly to understand their potential and limitations better. It is essential to use AR tools and platforms within your organization to remain at the forefront of AR innovation. With the evolving AR landscape, new technologies and platforms emerge that can enhance your capabilities and offerings. Stay abreast of the developments in the field. Be open to experimenting with fresh tools and platforms. This approach ensures that your company stays agile and adaptable, prepared to capitalize on the advancements in AR technology for business growth. By nurturing a culture of creativity and play, you can unleash the potential of AR for your business.

To become a champion in spatial computing requires a dedication to experimentation, creativity, and continual improvement. By fostering a culture that encourages innovation, values user feedback, and sees each initiative as an opportunity to learn and improve, you will unlock the full potential of AR for your business.

Commit to Lifelong Learning

Embracing a commitment to learning is key. Like all waves of computing, advancements in AR technology are ongoing, so continual education is vital to staying at the forefront. To achieve this, it is important to prioritize learning time to ensure you and your team stay updated on AR trends, tools, and best practices.

The first step is to stay informed. Subscribe to industry publications, follow creators and influencers on social media, and attend conferences, webinars, and meetups. Events, such as AWE (Augmented World Expo), and online resources, such as AR Insider and MIXED Reality News, can help you keep close to the industry's heartbeat while introducing you to leaders and pioneers like yourself who are part of the spatial computing community. Keeping up with progress in this space will enable you to take advantage of the latest features and capabilities in your next AR project. Meeting like-minded people can provide much-needed support and unlock potential partnerships. Being well informed about industry trends allows you to anticipate shifts and adjust your strategies accordingly.

For deeper dives, joining online communities and exploring forums where discussions and threads on AR, wearable devices, and spatial computing are happening can be precious. Platforms such as Reddit, Stack Overflow, and AR channels on Slack and Discord offer opportunities to ask questions, share knowledge, and listen to what is on people's minds when it comes to this technology. Engaging with these communities can provide insights not found in mainstream publications. Additionally, enrolling in AR courses and obtaining certifications is a way to stay competitive. Many universities and online platforms offer classes specifically designed for AR technology. Completing these courses can offer a learning path and a recognized certification to showcase your expertise. Websites such as Coursera, Udemy, and LinkedIn feature courses covering topics ranging from AR basics to development techniques.

However, being informed isn't just about consuming information – it also involves actively interacting with the technology. Carve out consistent time to play with AR technologies and solutions and download smartphone applications. Visit WebAR experiences. Create videos and photos with social AR effects and lenses. Invest in new hardware, such as MR headsets and AR glasses, and engage with available content to deepen your understanding, highlight opportunities and limitations, and, most importantly, put yourself in the shoes of a user. This playtime will be essential to you and your team's success.

Engaging with development tools and creator platforms is another aspect of this hands-on learning process. Tools such as Niantic's Lightship and 8th Wall platforms, Snap AR Lens Studio, and TikTok Effect House, and popular game engines such as Unity and Unreal Engine enable you to create experiences and grasp what is needed to build an AR experience. Developing AR content can also help you and your team test out new concepts and explore new user experience patterns, which can significantly influence your strategic decisions.

One way to dedicate time to development is through hackathons. Engaging in AR hackathons is a great way to collaborate and innovate with like-minded individuals and receive feedback from industry experts. Hackathons push your limits, help you acquire skills, and often introduce you to cutting-edge tools and technologies. In addition to attending hackathons produced by the community, such as MIT Reality Hacks, there are also many workshops and hands-on courses to consider, such as those hosted by XR Bootcamp and Circuit Stream. Consider sponsoring an internal hackathon within your organization to inspire your teams to experiment, learn, and gain experience with AR technologies.

Establishing a learning community within your company is also essential. Cultivate a culture of sharing knowledge and collaboration. Provide opportunities for your team members to share their insights and experiences with AR, whether through seminars, joint projects, or informal lunch-and-learn sessions. A community of learners enhances skills and fosters collective growth and innovation. Encourage your team to remain curious and explore avenues with AR.

Focusing on learning is essential to keep your organization ahead in AR technology.

Becoming a spatial computing champion requires a dedication to learning, staying updated on industry trends, actively engaging with technology, and promoting a culture of ongoing learning within your organization. By applying these tactics, you and your team can stay at the forefront of developments, utilize the advancements in AR technology, and foster innovation in your field. This comprehensive approach will ensure that you are always ready to adapt to the changing landscape of AR technology and maintain an advantage.

Crafting an AR–Centric Strategy

As AR is a transformational technology, it is essential to devise a strategy that prioritizes its integration into business operations. This entails creating a road map rooted in your customers' problems, aligned with your business goals, and at pace with the unfolding opportunities of spatial computing technologies.

When developing a strategy centered on AR, it's essential to understand your customer base. Take the time to analyze their challenges, preferences, and behavior to pinpoint where AR can genuinely make a difference. Conduct surveys and hold focus groups. Delve into existing data to uncover how AR can address customer needs or enrich their interactions. You will also want to consider your audience's demographics to meet them where they are with their AR journey and understand what devices they are using. As you have found in previous chapters, AR resonates differently for different generations, with millennials and Gen Z more apt to adopt quickly. As most AR solutions rely on a user having access to a device, your customers' access to these devices is also something you will want to consider.

Subsequently, ensure that your AR initiatives align with your business objectives. Whether you're looking to boost sales, enhance customer satisfaction, or strengthen brand engagement, ensure your AR strategy is crafted to support these goals. Establish success metrics, such as improved conversion rates, decreased returns, or heightened engagement levels, to gauge the effectiveness of your AR endeavors. Outcome-based and measurable metrics are key to showcasing how this new technology is moving the needle within your organization. Identify ways your AR solutions can contribute to your organization's key performance indicators and north star metrics. Understanding what you want to measure and why it is essential will be critical when setting up the analytics within your solutions.

A practical approach is to kick off with a pilot project as a first step. Identify an area where AR could make an impact and test it out with a smaller group of people. Keep an eye on the results, gather feedback, and use that input to improve your strategy and planning. Highlighting feedback from customers, including testimonials or survey results, alongside quantitative data that demonstrate the impact of AR within this test can help build confidence with business leaders. When presenting the results of pilots, be sure to include a video of the experience itself and encourage business leaders to try out your AR solutions by providing access or setting up meetings dedicated to demoing the technology in action. Combining quantitative and qualitative data alongside creative output can go a long way to building a business case for your organization's outstanding use of AR.

Promoting your AR capabilities is essential for boosting adoption and engagement. Emphasize the user benefits of your AR solutions in your marketing efforts. Use captivating visuals and demonstrations to exhibit how AR can improve the customer experience. Video and GIFs are a great medium to convey the experience in 3D space. Use clear and simple messaging, especially for your call to action and onboarding materials. Avoid technical jargon and err on the side of assuming your users are new to AR. Integrate your AR campaign as part of a 360-media plan. Use media, email marketing, and other channels to connect with your target audience and generate excitement around your AR projects.

Scalability needs to be an aspect of your AR plan. Once you gather insights from pilot programs and initial rollouts, create a strategy to expand the scope of your AR experiences within your organization. Identify areas where AR can provide value and devise a plan for broadening your AR endeavors. Ensure your infrastructure and resources are equipped to meet the growing demand as you expand. Gathering and examining data is crucial for grasping the effectiveness of your approach. Use tools to monitor user interactions with your content and gather insights into their behavior. Analyze this information to spot patterns, preferences, and areas that can be enhanced. Utilize these findings to tune and improve your AR interactions.

Creating AR content requires expertise, so teaming up with AR developers and designers is wise. Work with established AR agencies, creative studios, and solution providers who have a track record of success and can help bring your ideas to fruition. Look for teams with 3D design expertise and experience building AR and MR content for various platforms. When evaluating external solution providers, look not only at the quality of their work but also inquire about the impact and performance of the content against the goals it was designed for. You may also want to understand what relationships they have with the AR platforms they are creating to see whether they are part of any early access programs, which you can, in turn, benefit from. Finally, you will want to look for teams keeping themselves updated on the latest technologies in this space. A quick review of the company's blog, podcast, or social media feeds can help you evaluate work performed and their thought leadership within the industry.

In addition to tapping external sources for your initiatives, you will also want to ramp up internal teams with spatial computing skills and expertise as part of your AR business strategy. Proper training and support for your team are crucial for implementing AR in your business operations. Provide training for your staff on how to utilize AR tools and technologies. This training could encompass workshops, online courses, or hands-on sessions. Hire individuals with 3D modeling, 3D animation, and game development backgrounds to invest in building internal expertise within your organization.

Ensure your team has access to the technology and tools they need to succeed in their roles. Instill a spirit of creativity within your team. Encourage them to explore AR concepts and technologies and create an atmosphere where originality and ingenuity are encouraged. By nurturing a culture of innovation, you can keep your organization ahead in AR advancements while increasing the satisfaction and morale of your team.

It's also crucial to think about the time horizon of your AR strategy. The AR field constantly changes, with new technologies and capabilities emerging.

To succeed, it's important to stay flexible, especially with plans that are further out in the future, and adjust your approach as necessary. Keep revisiting and refining your AR strategy to meet your business objectives and customer demands. As you integrate AR more into your business, integrating AR with your existing systems is another critical factor. Ensure that your AR solutions seamlessly blend with your IT setup, including your website, mobile applications, and back-end systems. This seamless integration will facilitate data flow and deliver a consistent user experience across all channels.

Go Forth and Be Spatial

To become a spatial computing expert, you need a blend of experimentation, continuous learning, and strategic planning. By promoting innovation, staying updated on the trends, and creating an AR–focused strategy, you can fully utilize AR for your business. While the journey may be challenging, the benefits – improved customer experiences, higher engagement, and a competitive edge – are worth it. Embrace the future of AR and guide your organization into the next dimension of computing.

To stand out as a leader in spatial computing, you must have a resilient mindset. Try AR applications, learn from successes and failures, and adjust your strategies accordingly. Stay informed about cutting-edge developments and industry trends to ensure your business stays innovative. Use this to develop an AR–focused approach that aligns with your business goals and maximizes the impact of AR across all aspects of your operations.

Becoming a champion in spatial computing requires dedication and an openness to exploring territories. Foster an environment that promotes creativity and recognizes the potential of AR.

By taking these steps, you can enhance customer interactions, create new connections, and gain a notable edge over other companies. AR's potential in the coming years is vast. Your proactive approach will establish your company as a frontrunner in this evolving sector.

Embrace the experience, explore the opportunities, and lead your business into the spatial computing era.

Sparking Spatial Strategies

Strike up strategic dialogue about AR's role in your business with these essential conversation starters:

- **In the boardroom:** How can we ensure that our investment in AR technology positions us ahead of the competition in the coming years?
- **For your team meeting:** What small-scale AR pilot projects should we consider when integrating AR into our processes?
- **Around the water cooler:** Have you seen any excellent AR applications lately that could inspire our next project?

Share this on your socials: Unlock AR's potential by embracing a culture of experimentation and creativity. Use small-scale pilot projects to test and learn, fostering continuous adaptation. Encourage team brainstorming and workshops to drive innovative AR solutions that align with business goals. #thenextdimensionbook

Endnotes

Chapter 1

1. Vinge, Vernor. *Rainbows End* (USA: Tor Books, 2006), page 37.
2. Wurmser, Yoram. (June 12, 2023). Time Spent with Connected Devices 2023. https://www.emarketer.com/content/connected-device-time-spent-2023.
3. Wikipedia. (June 13, 2024). Graphical User Interface. https://en.wikipedia.org/wiki/Graphical_user_interface.
4. IANS. (April 30, 2023). Nearly 80% of iPhone users now own an Apple Watch: Report. https://retail.economictimes.indiatimes.com/news/consumer-durables-and-information-technology/consumer-electronics/nearly-80-of-iphone-users-now-own-an-apple-watch-report/99885867.
5. Louis, Sarah. (December 1, 2023). Roughly 60% of millennials, Gen Z would rather spend money on 'life experiences' like traveling, concerts now than save for retirement – are they making a big mistake? https://finance.yahoo.com/news/roughly-60-millennials-gen-z-110000580.html.

Chapter 2

1. Stephenson, Neal. *Snow Crash* (USA: Bantam Books, 1992), page 29.
2. Apple. (June 5, 2023). Introducing Apple Vision Pro: Apple's first spatial computer. https://www.apple.com/newsroom/2023/06/introducing-apple-vision-pro.
3. Wikipedia. (May 20, 2024). Spatial Computing. https://en.wikipedia.org/wiki/Spatial_computing.
4. Wikipedia. (May 20, 2024). Spatial Computing. https://en.wikipedia.org/wiki/Spatial_computing.
5. Wikipedia. (September 8, 2023). Tom A. Furness III. https://en.wikipedia.org/wiki/Thomas_A._Furness_III.

6. Greenwold, Simon. (June 2003). Spatial Computing. Massachusetts Institute of Technology. 1.2 Definition. https://acg.media.mit .edu/people/simong/transfers/layout.pdf.

Chapter 3

1. Cline, Ernest. *Ready Player One* (USA: Ballantine Books and Crown Publishing Group, 2011), page 27.
2. Lebow, Sara. (May 31, 2023). AR/VR user growth forecast to slow ahead of Apple's headset release. https://www.emarketer.com/ content/ar-vr-user-growth-forecast-slow-ahead-apple-headset-release.
3. McKinsey & Company. (August 17, 2022). What is the metaverse? https://www.mckinsey.com/featured-insights/mckinsey-explainers/what-is-the-metaverse.
4. Laricchia, Federica. (June 12, 2024). Smartphones – statistics & facts. https://www.statista.com/topics/840/smartphones/#topic Overview.
5. Newton, Casey. (December 14, 2017). Snap releases Lens Studio, a tool for creating your own AR effects. https://www.theverge .com/2017/12/14/16770088/snap-lens-studio-snapchat-lenses-filters-download-mac-windows.
6. Constine, Josh. (September 15, 2015). Snapchat Acquires Looksery To Power Its Animated Lenses. https://techcrunch.com/2015/09/ 15/snapchat-looksery.
7. Snap Inc. (2024). Snap Inc. https://snap.com/en-US.
8. Investor Relations. (Q1 2024). Why Snap? https://investor.snap .com/overview/default.aspx.
9. Snap AR. (September 10, 2023). Snap Augmented Reality. https://ar.snap.com.
10. Young, Sue. (September 1, 2020). Expanding the Spark AR Ecosystem. https://spark.meta.com/blog/extending-spark-ar-ecosystem.
11. Logan, Dan, Erb, Danielle, and Le, Amanda. (September 28, 2023). Meta Connect 2023 Roundup. https://spark.meta.com/ blog/meta-connect-2023-roundup.
12. Meta. (August 27, 2014). A Meta Spark Update. https://spark .meta.com/blog/meta-spark-announcement/.

13. The TikTok Team. (September 17, 2021). Thanks a billion! https://newsroom.tiktok.com/en-us/1-billion-people-on-tiktok.

14. The Effect House Team. (April 2022). Effect House Exits Beta. https://effecthouse.tiktok.com/latest/news/public-launch.

15. The Effect House Team. (April 2022). Effect House Exits Beta. https://effecthouse.tiktok.com/latest/news/public-launch.

16. 8th Wall. (2024). FAQ. https://www.8thwall.com/faq.

17. Haasch, Palmer. (June 17, 2021). Why Pixar-esque cartoon faces are taking over your social media feeds. https://autos.yahoo.com/why-pixar-esque-cartoon-faces-174947302.html.

18. AR Insider. (April 11, 2024). Will Mobile AR Revenue Reach $21 Billion by 2028? https://arinsider.co/2024/04/11/will-mobile-ar-revenue-reach-21-billion-by-2028.

19. AR insider. (April 11, 2024). Will Mobile AR Revenue Reach $21 Billion by 2028? https://arinsider.co/2024/04/11/will-mobile-ar-revenue-reach-21-billion-by-2028.

20. Alsop, Thomas. (May 19, 2024). Mobile AR active users worldwide 2023, by platform. https://www.statista.com/statistics/1221439/mobile-augmented-reality-active-users-by-platform.

21. Thrive Analytics. (June 7, 2022). New Study Reveals 23 Percent of U.S. Adults Have Tried Virtual Reality. https://www.prweb.com/releases/new-study-reveals-23-percent-of-u-s-adults-have-tried-virtual-reality-801410195.html.

22. The Harris Poll. (January 25, 2022). Americans are Interested in AR, VR, and the Metaverse. https://theharrispoll.com/briefs/future-of-ar-vr-metaverse.

23. AddictiveTips. (September 14, 2023). 95% of Americans Eager to Embrace AR/VR Technology, Price and Health Concerns Holding Them Back: AddictiveTips Survey. https://www.accesswire.com/782968/95-of-americans-eager-to-embrace-arvr-technology-price-and-health-concerns-holding-them-back-addictivetips-survey.

Chapter 4

1. Tayeb, Zahra. (March 21, 2021). Pizza Hut is launching augmented reality pizza boxes that you can play 'Pac-Man' on. The company's CMO tells Insider why it's using the gaming icon in its 'Newstalgia' campaign. https://www.businessinsider

.com/pizza-hut-augmented-reality-boxes-play-pac-man-on-newstalgia-2021-3.

2. PwC. (2023). PwC's 2023 Emerging Technology Survey. https://www.pwc.com/us/en/tech-effect/emerging-tech/emtech-survey.html.

3. Hubspot. (2024). The Ultimate List for Marketing Statistics of 2024 - HubSpot Blog Marketing Trends Report, 2024. https://www.hubspot.com/marketing-statistics.

4. Alsop, Thomas. (May 22, 2024). Global mobile augmented reality (AR) user devices 2019-2024. https://www.statista.com/statistics/1098630/global-mobile-augmented-reality-ar-users.

5. Vacante, Valerie. (February 28, 2022). Retrospective: How LEGO Augments Our World. https://vrscout.com/news/retrospective-how-lego-augments-our-world.

6. Paur, Joey. (2009). Transformers 2 Augmented Reality Experience. https://geektyrant.com/news/2009/6/16/transformers-2-augmented-reality-experience.html.

7. TechCrunch. (August 20, 2009). DVD/Blu-ray Transformers: Revenge of the Fallen confirmed for October 20, augmented reality included. https://techcrunch.com/2009/08/20/dvdblu-ray-transformers-revenge-of-the-fallen-confirmed-for-october-20-augmented-reality-included.

8. Taylor, Petroc. (May 22, 2024). Number of smartphone mobile network subscriptions worldwide from 2016 to 2023, with forecasts from 2023 to 2028. https://www.statista.com/statistics/330695/number-of-smartphone-users-worldwide.

9. 8th Wall. (2024). Discover WebAR. https://www.8thwall.com/discover.

10. Vacante, Valerie. (February 28, 2022). Retrospective: How LEGO Augments Our World. https://vrscout.com/news/retrospective-how-lego-augments-our-world.

11. PTC. LEGO Powers up with Nexo Knight Toy Sets with Augmented Reality. https://www.ptc.com/en/case-studies/lego-augmented-reality-game-engine.

12. IDC. (March 19, 2024). IDC Forecasts Robust Growth for AR/VR Headset Shipments Fueled by the Rise of Mixed Reality. https://www.idc.com/getdoc.jsp?containerId=prUS51971224#:~:text=Virtual%20Reality%20headsets%20are%20forecast, training%2C%20design%2C%20and%20more.

13. Stastista Research Department. (September 22, 2015). Overall unit shipments of the Apple iPhone by model worldwide from 2008 to 2015. https://www.statista.com/statistics/519699/iphone-sales-by-model-worldwide.

14. Snap. (2022). It's time for an Augmentality Shift. https://forbusiness.snapchat.com/augmentalityshift-uk.

15. Snap. (2022). It's time for an Augmentality Shift. https://forbusiness.snapchat.com/augmentalityshift-uk.

16. Sutcliffe, Chris. (March 13, 2023). '94% increase in conversion rates': Snap on how ecommerce tech is boosting top brands. https://www.thedrum.com/news/2023/03/13/94-increase-conversation-rates-snap-how-ray-tracing-boosting-top-brands.

17. Snap. (2022). It's time for an Augmentality Shift. https://forbusiness.snapchat.com/augmentalityshift-uk.

18. Snap. (2022). It's time for an Augmentality Shift. https://forbusiness.snapchat.com/augmentalityshift-uk.

19. Feger, Arielle. (February 23, 2024). Guide to Gen Z: What matters to this generation and what it means for marketers. https://www.emarketer.com/insights/generation-z-facts.

20. Walk-Morris, Tatiana. (April 6, 2022). Snapchat: 62% of Gen Z want to use AR for shopping. https://www.retaildive.com/news/snapchat-92-of-gen-z-want-to-use-ar-for-shopping/621656.

21. Walk-Morris, Tatiana. (April 6, 2022). Snapchat: 62% of Gen Z want to use AR for shopping. https://www.retaildive.com/news/snapchat-92-of-gen-z-want-to-use-ar-for-shopping/621656.

22. Snapchat. (April 5, 2022). How Gen Z is Reshaping Communication and Redefining the Shopping Experience with AR. https://forbusiness.snapchat.com/blog/how-gen-z-is-reshaping-communication-and-redefining-the-shopping-experience-with-ar.

23. Laricchia, Federica. (March 22, 2024). Share of adults in the United States who owned a smartphone from 2015 to 2023, by group. https://www.statista.com/statistics/489255/percentage-of-us-smartphone-owners-by-age-group.

24. Flynn, Jack. (March 10, 2023). 18 Average Screen Time Statistics [2023]: How Much Screen Time is Too Much. https://www.zippia.com/advice/average-screen-time-statistics.

25. McKinsey & Company. (March 20, 2023). What is Gen Z? https://
www.mckinsey.com/featured-insights/mckinsey-explainers/
what-is-gen-z.

26. The Harris Poll. (January 25, 2022). American Are Interested
in AR, VR, and the Metaverse. https://theharrispoll.com/briefs/
future-of-ar-vr-metaverse.

27. TeamStage. (2024). Millennials in the Worksplace Statistics: Generational Disparities in 2024. https://teamstage.io/millennials-in-
the-workplace-statistics/#:~:text=How%20much%20of%20
the%20workforce,Xers%20in%20the%20US%20workforce.

Chapter 5

1. WPP. (September 30, 2021). WPP and Snap Inc. launch Augmented Reality partnership. https://forbusiness.snapchat.com/
augmentalityshift-uk/09/wpp-and-snap-inc-launch-augmented-
reality-partnership.

2. 8th Wall. (2024). Netflix | Cursed | Discover Your Power. https://
www.8thwall.com/powster/cursed-discover-your-power-demo.

3. Ankers-Range, Adele. (July 17, 2020). Netflix's Cursed: Virtual
Experience Launches Alongside Premiere. https://www.ign.com/
articles/netflix-cursed-virtual-experience-launch-premiere.

4. Baar, Aaron. (February 22, 2024). Warner Bros. teams with Snapchat for AR 'Dune: Part Two' campaign. https://finance.yahoo
.com/news/warner-bros-teams-snapchat-ar-094413023.html.

5. Spangler, Todd. (June 30, 2023). 'Barbie' Hits Snapchat: App
Launches Official AR Filter That Lets You Virtually Dress Up in
Outfits Inspired by the Movie. https://variety.com/2023/digital/
news/barbie-snapchat-filter-ar-lens-outfits-1235658170.

6. AR.Rocks Editor. (October 29, 2020). Michelob ULTRA Pure
Gold Transports Consumers to Yosemite with WeAR Portal
Experience. https://www.ar.rocks/posts/michelob-ultra-pure-
gold-transports-consumers-to-yosemite-with-webar-portal-
experience.

7. 8th Wall. (2024). Cadbury Easter Hunt. https://www.8thwall.com/
zebrar/cadbury.

8. Zebrar. (2024). Cadbury. https://www.zebrar.com/work/cadbury.

9. Vox News. (February 19, 2021). "Vagalumes", do Bradesco, se torna maior ação de realidade aumentada do mundo. https://voxnews.com.br/vagalumes-do-bradesco-se-torna-maior-acao-de-realidade-aumentada-do-mundo.

10. LLBonline.com. (October 12, 2019). Fireflies Light Up the New Year in Touching Film from Bradesco Bank. https://lbbonline.com/news/fireflies-light-up-the-new-year-in-touching-film-from-bradesco-bank.

11. 8th Wall. (2024). Bradesco Realidade Aumentada - Em 2021, volte a brilhar. https://www.8thwall.com/buudigital/bradesco-thevoice.

12. Buu Digital Group. (2021). Bradesco Realidade Aumentada. https://buudigital.com.br/bradesco-realidade-aumentada.

13. 8th Wall. (2024). Bradesco Realidade Aumentada - Em 2021, volte a brilhar. https://www.8thwall.com/buudigital/bradesco-thevoice.

14. Warner Bros. Discovery Media Release. (July 25, 2022). HBO Max Begins Global Rollout of Augmented Reality App 'House of the Dragon: DracARys'. https://press.wbd.com/us/media-release/hbo-0/house-dragon/hbo-max-begins-global-rollout-augmented-reality-app-house-dragon-dracarys.

15. HBO. (2024). What is House of Dragon: DracARys? https://www.hbo.com/house-of-the-dragon/dracarys-app-awards.

16. HBO. (2024). What is House of Dragon: DracARys? https://www.hbo.com/house-of-the-dragon/dracarys-app-awards.

17. "HBO 'House Of The Dragon: DracARys' | The Mill | Experience." Millchannel. January 23, 2023. Video, 0:01:55, https://www.youtube.com/watch?v=czWXXayBVpk.

18. BusinessWire. (March 31, 2021). Frederick Wildman & Sons Launches Augmented Reality Experience for Italian Fine Wines Brands. https://www.businesswire.com/news/home/20210331005145/en/Frederick-Wildman-Sons-Launches-Augmented-Reality-Experience-for-Italian-Fine-Wines-Brands.

19. BusinessWire. (March 31, 2021). Frederick Wildman & Sons Launches Augmented Reality Experience for Italian Fine Wines Brands. https://www.businesswire.com/news/home/20210331005145/en/Frederick-Wildman-Sons-Launches-Augmented-Reality-Experience-for-Italian-Fine-Wines-Brands.

20. FWA. (April 3, 2020). Nike: Move to Zero. https://thefwa.com/ cases/nike-move-to-zero.

21. Vatsel, Mark. (January 13, 2020). Nike: Move to Zero. https://www .unit9.com/project/nike-move-zero.

22. 8th Wall. (April 20, 2020). Nike transforms shoe boxes into interactive WebAR stories. https://www.8thwall.com/blog/post/ 62785760889/nike-creates-move-to-zero-ar-activated-shoe-boxes.

23. Wine Industry Advisor. (October 31, 2023). Rock Paper Reality Partners with Chronic Cellars to Bring First-of-Its-Kind Personalized AR Sommelier to Life. https://wineindustryadvisor.com/2023/10/31/ rock-paper-reality-partners-with-chronic-cellars.

24. Rock Paper Reality. (2023). Our Work – Chronic Cellars. https:// rockpaperreality.com/our-work/chronic-cellars.

25. Stone, Zara. (December 12, 2017). 19 Crimes Wine is an Example of Adult Targeted Augmented Reality. https://www.forbes.com/ sites/zarastone/2017/12/12/19-crimes-wine-is-an-amazing-example-of-adult-targeted-augmented-reality.

26. PTC. Case Study: 19 Crimes Augmented Reality to Differentiate Their Brand Through Innovation. https://www.ptc.com/en/case-studies/augmented-reality-19-crimes-wine.

27. Kaplan, Andrew. (August 1, 2019). How AR is Reinventing Drinks Marketing. https://daily.sevenfifty.com/how-ar-is-reinventing-drinks-marketing.

28. Wine Industry Advisor. (November 23, 2020). Snoop Dogg Goes Beyond the Bottle in New Augmented Reality Experience for 19 Crimes' Snoop Cali Red. https://wineindustryadvisor.com/ 2020/11/23/snoop-dogg-goe-augmented-reality.

29. Print Design Academy. (May 2, 2023). Immersive Packaging with AR Labels: 19 Crimes Wine + Snoop Dogg. https://www .printdesignacademy.com/blog/19-crimes-snoop-dogg-AR-labels.

30. Buckinham, Kristjan. (September 21, 2022). Watch Snoop Dogg in AR on this Sparkling Wine Label. https://screenrant.com/snoop-dogg-19-crimes-ar-sparkling-wine-label.

31. Tactic. Snoop "Cali" Wine – Web AR Experience. https://tactic .studio/snoop-cali-wines-ar.

32. 8th Wall. (March 25, 2021). Pizza Hut turns special edition pizza boxes into an augmented reality arcade. https://www.8thwall .com/blog/post/43876996201/pizza-hut-turns-special-edition-pizza-boxes-into-an-augmented-reality-arcade.

33. Pizza Hut Blog. (March 15, 2021). Pizza Hut serves up 'Newstalgia' with campaign celebrating all that fans know and love about the pizza restaurant. https://blog.pizzahut.com/pizza-hut-serves-up-newstalgia-with-campaign-celebrating-all-that-fans-know-and-love-about-the-pizza-restaurant/.

34. Hein, Kenneth. (February 17, 2022). Coke innovation platform takes flight with Ava Max & space-inspired Coca-Cola Starlight. https://www.thedrum.com/news/2022/02/17/coke-innovation-platform-takes-flight-with-ava-max-space-inspired-coca-cola.

35. 8th Wall. (April 19, 2022). Coca-Cola launches an out-of-this-world WebAR concert for the release of Coca-Cola Starlight with Ava Max. https://www.8thwall.com/blog/post/71344177808/coca-cola-launches-an-out-of-this-world-webar-concert-for-the-release-of-coca-cola-starlight-with-ava-max.

36. The Coca-Cola Company. (February 18, 2022). A Coca-Cola That's Out of This World. https://www.coca-colacompany.com/media-center/a-coca-cola-thats-out-of-this-world.

37. Jardine, Alexandra. (July 28, 2020). Rapper Tinie is debuting his new single at "The World's Smallest Gig"—on top of a Whopper. https://adage.com/creativity/work/burger-king-uk-tinie-performs-whopper/2270561.

38. 8th Wall. Burger King and Tinie Tempah host tiniest AR concer to engage Whopper Lovers. https://www.8thwall.com/customer-work/bully-whoppa-on-a-whopper.

39. Vacante, Valerie. (February 28, 2022). Retrospective: How LEGO Augments Our World. https://vrscout.com/news/retrospective-how-lego-augments-our-world.

40. Adele Feletto Publicity. (January 16, 2023). Minecraft Quest launches in Big W, via Merchantwise. https://mumbrella.com.au/minecraft-quest-launches-in-big-w-via-merchantwise-771255.

41. 8th Wall. (2024). Real World Minecraft adventure provides an immersive in-store experience for Big W customers. https://www.8thwall.com/blog/post/102376578692/real-world-minecraft-adventure-provides-an-immersive-in-store-experience-for-big-w-customers.

42. 8th Wall. (2024). Minecraft Scavenger Hunt Retail Activation. https://www.8thwall.com/intergalactic/mc-scavenger.

43. Adobo Magazine. (September 22, 2020). Campaign Spotlight: McDonald's Sweden replaces all balloons with AR balloons in effort to reduce single-use plastics and waste. https://www.adobomagazine.com/campaign-spotlight/campaign-spotlight-mcdonalds-sweden-replaces-all-balloons-with-ar-balloons-in-effort-to-reduce-single-use-plastics-and-waste.

44. Adobo Magazine. (September 22, 2020). Campaign Spotlight: McDonald's Sweden replaces all balloons with AR balloons in effort to reduce single-use plastics and waste. https://www.adobomagazine.com/campaign-spotlight/campaign-spotlight-mcdonalds-sweden-replaces-all-balloons-with-ar-balloons-in-effort-to-reduce-single-use-plastics-and-waste.

Chapter 6

1. Kelion, Leo. (October 11, 2017). Apple's Tim Cook prefers augmented reality to VR. https://www.bbc.com/news/technology-41590323.

2. Meta. (March 25, 2014). Facebook to Acquire Oculus. https://about.fb.com/news/2014/03/facebook-to-acquire-oculus.

3. Mehta, Ivan. (February 2, 2023). Samsung, Google and Qualcomm are making a mixed-reality platform. https://techcrunch.com/2023/02/02/samsung-google-and-qualcomm-are-making-a-mixed-reality-platform.

4. Meta Quest Blog. (April 22, 2024). A New Era for Mixed Reality. https://www.meta.com/blog/quest/meta-horizon-os-open-hardware-ecosystem-asus-republic-gamers-lenovo-xbox.

5. IDC Media Center. (March 19, 2024). IDC Forecasts Robust Growth for AR/VR Headset Shipments Fueled by the Rise of Mixed Reality. https://www.idc.com/getdoc.jsp?containerId=prUS51971224.

6. IDC Media Center. (March 19, 2024). IDC Forecasts Robust Growth for AR/VR Headset Shipments Fueled by the Rise of Mixed Reality. https://www.idc.com/getdoc.jsp?containerId=prUS51971224.

7. Alsop, Thomas. (April 16, 2024). Apple Vision Pro Shipment Forecast Worldwide from 2024 to 2028. https://www.statista.com/statistics/1398458/apple-vision-pro-shipments.

8. Uceda, Jorge. (June 6, 2024). 68% of businesses ready to bet big on the Apple Vision Pro. https://www.sortlist.com/datahub/reports/apple-vision-pro-for-marketing.

9. Uceda, Jorge. (June 6, 2024). 68% of businesses ready to bet big on the Apple Vision Pro. https://www.sortlist.com/datahub/reports/apple-vision-pro-for-marketing.

10. Uceda, Jorge. (June 6, 2024). 68% of businesses ready to bet big on the Apple Vision Pro. https://www.sortlist.com/datahub/reports/apple-vision-pro-for-marketing.

11. Arbanas, Jana and Auxier, Brooke. (July 7, 2023). While we wait for the metaverse to materialize, young people are already there. https://www2.deloitte.com/us/en/insights/industry/technology/gen-z-and-millennials-are-metaverse-early-adopters.html.

12. Esposito, Filipe. (April 9, 2024). Survey shows that teenagers are using more VR devices in the US. https://9to5mac.com/2024/04/09/survey-teenagers-using-more-vr-devices.

13. Arbanas, Jana and Auxier, Brooke. (July 7, 2023). While we wait for the metaverse to materialize, young people are already there. https://www2.deloitte.com/us/en/insights/industry/technology/gen-z-and-millennials-are-metaverse-early-adopters.html.

14. Arbanas, Jana and Auxier, Brooke. (July 7, 2023). While we wait for the metaverse to materialize, young people are already there. https://www2.deloitte.com/us/en/insights/industry/technology/gen-z-and-millennials-are-metaverse-early-adopters.html.

15. Arbanas, Jana and Auxier, Brooke. (July 7, 2023). While we wait for the metaverse to materialize, young people are already there. https://www2.deloitte.com/us/en/insights/industry/technology/gen-z-and-millennials-are-metaverse-early-adopters.html.

16. Bosworth, Andrew. (December 18, 2023). Living in the Future. https://about.fb.com/news/2023/12/metas-2023-progress-in-ai-and-mixed-reality.

17. Apple Newsroom. (February 1, 2024). Apple announces more than 600 new apps built for Apple Vision Pro. https://www.apple.com/newsroom/2024/02/apple-announces-more-than-600-new-apps-built-for-apple-vision-pro.

18. Deyo, Jessica. (January 30, 2024). Snickers brings AR Super Bowl experience to forthcoming Apple Vision Pro. https://www.marketingdive.com/news/snickers-apple-vision-pro-ar-super-bowl/705800.

19. Blippar. (February 7, 2024). Blippar and Snickers Bring AR Super Bowl Experience to the Apple Vision Pro. https://www .blippar.com/blog/2024/02/07/blippar-and-snickers-bring-ar-super-bowl-experience-to-forthcoming-apple-vision-pro.

20. Link, Kevin. (April 9, 2024). Kung Fu Panda: School of Chi for Apple Vision Pro helps you find inner peace with Po. https:// mixed-news.com/en/kung-fu-panda-school-of-chi-for-apple-vision-pro-released/#google_vignette.

21. IMDB. Kung Fu Panda. https://www.imdb.com/title/tt0441773.

22. PR Newswire. (March 4, 2024). DIAGEO announces its first experience with the Apple Vision Pro to bring tequila culture to fans around the world. https://www.prnewswire.com/ news-releases/diageo-announces-its-first-experience-with-apple-vision-pro-to-bring-tequila-culture-to-fans-around-the-world-302077722.html.

23. PR Newswire. (March 4, 2024). DIAGEO announces its first experience with the Apple Vision Pro to bring tequila culture to fans around the world. https://www.prnewswire.com/ news-releases/diageo-announces-its-first-experience-with-apple-vision-pro-to-bring-tequila-culture-to-fans-around-the-world-302077722.html.

24. Aten, Jason. (April 25, 2024). Gucci Made an App for Apple Vision Pro, and It's the Best I've Seen Yet. https://www.inc .com/jason-aten/gucci-made-an-app-for-apple-vision-pro-its-best-ive-seen-yet.html.

25. Barilaro, Micael. (March 17, 2024). Indulge your senses, ignite your imagination, and be inspired. https://www.linkedin.com/ pulse/indulge-your-senses-ignite-imagination-inspired-micael-barilaro-c9hxf.

26. Quantum Universe. (2023). DaVinci Motel in MIXED REALITY. https://quantumuniverse.co/en/mr-experience/davinci-motel-in-mixed-reality.

Chapter 7

1. IAB. (February 8, 2024). IAB and MRC Release Augmented Reality Measurement Guidelines For Public Comment. https:// www.iab.com/news/iab-and-mrc-release-augmented-reality-measurement-guidelines-for-public-comment.

2. 8th Wall. WebAR Delivers Real Value. https://www.8thwall.com/webar.
3. Nadia. (April 25, 2024). How Many Ads Do We See A Day? https://siteefy.com/how-many-ads-do-we-see-a-day.
4. Anish. (December 26, 2008). MINI's ad with Augmented Reality (AR) hits stands! https://mydigitalwhiteboard.wordpress.com/2008/12/26/minis-ad-with-augmented-deality-ar-hits-stands.
5. 8th Wall. WebAR Delivers Real Value. https://www.8thwall.com/webar.
6. Niantic. (June 19, 2023). Niantic Launches In-Game Rewarded AR Ad Format at Cannes Lions International Festival. https://nianticlabs.com/news/niantic-rewarded-ar-ads?hl=en.
7. Statista Market Insights. (April 2024). AR Advertising – United States. https://www.statista.com/outlook/amo/ar-vr/ar-advertising/united-states.
8. Statista Market Insights. (April 2024). AR Advertising – Worldwide. https://www.statista.com/outlook/amo/ar-vr/ar-advertising/worldwide.
9. Statista Market Insights. (April 2024). AR Advertising – Worldwide. https://www.statista.com/outlook/amo/ar-vr/ar-advertising/worldwide.
10. Baar, Aaron. (January 11, 2024). Global mobile ad spend to reach $402B in 2024 fueled by social, creators. https://www.marketingdive.com/news/global-mobile-ad-spend-402-billion-creator-social-media-report/704347.
11. Visible with help from Stacker. (April 23, 2024). Americans are more connected than ever. https://www.visible.com/blog/visible-101/americans-are-more-connected-than-ever.
12. Snapchat. Gucci Engages Snapchatters and Drives Sales with Virtual Shoe Try-on. https://forbusiness.snapchat.com/inspiration/gucci-ar-tryon.
13. Niantic. (September 23, 2023). LUNCHABLES® Teams Up with Niantic to Launch the First-Ever Rewarded AR Ads Campaign. https://nianticlabs.com/news/lunchables?hl=en.
14. Vibrant Media. (March 9, 2017). 67% of Agencies Want to See More VR and AR in Ad Campaigns. https://www.vibrantmedia.com/2017/03/10/more-vr-ar-ad-campaigns.

15. Snap and IPSOS. (September 2022). It's Time for an Augmented Reality Shift. https://forbusiness.snapchat.com/augmentalityshift-us.

16. Snap and IPSOS. (September 2022). It's Time for an Augmented Reality Shift. https://forbusiness.snapchat.com/augmentalityshift-us.

17. Walk-Morris, Tatiana. (April 6, 2022). Snapchat: 92% of Gen Z want to use AR for shopping. https://www.retaildive.com/news/snapchat-92-of-gen-z-want-to-use-ar-for-shopping/621656.

18. Accenture. (September 22, 2020). Immersive Technology to Reimagine Online Shopping Experience and Increase Consumer Purchasing Confidence, According to new Accenture Interactive Report. https://newsroom.accenture.com/news/2020/immersive-technology-to-reimagine-online-shopping-experience-and-increase-consumer-purchasing-confidence-according-to-new-accenture-interactive-report.

19. PRNewswire. (June 10, 2021). Augmented Reality Advertising Research Shows Consumers Want To See More AR Ads. https://www.prweb.com/releases/augmented-reality-advertising-research-shows-consumers-want-to-see-more-ar-ads-898723360.html.

20. PRNewswire. (June 10, 2021). Augmented Reality Advertising Research Shows Consumers Want To See More AR Ads. https://www.prweb.com/releases/augmented-reality-advertising-research-shows-consumers-want-to-see-more-ar-ads-898723360.html.

21. Teads. (June 18, 2018). Teads Launches inRead AR. https://www.teads.com/teads-launches-inread-ar.

22. PYMNTS. (April 25, 2024). Snap Reports Augmented Reality Drives User Engagement, Brand Advertising. https://www.pymnts.com/earnings/2024/snap-reports-augmented-reality-drives-user-engagement-brand-advertising.

23. PYMNTS. (April 25, 2024). Snap Reports Augmented Reality Drives User Engagement, Brand Advertising. https://www.pymnts.com/earnings/2024/snap-reports-augmented-reality-drives-user-engagement-brand-advertising.

24. PYMNTS. (April 25, 2024). Snap Reports Augmented Reality Drives User Engagement, Brand Advertising. https://www.pymnts.com/earnings/2024/snap-reports-augmented-reality-drives-user-engagement-brand-advertising.

25. Snapchat. Christian Dior Couture Drives Sales Using Sneakers Virtual Try-on. https://forbusiness.snapchat.com/inspiration/diorsneakers.

26. Snapchat. Christian Dior Couture Drives Sales Using Sneakers Virtual Try-on. https://forbusiness.snapchat.com/inspiration/diorsneakers.
27. Snapchat. Christian Dior Couture Drives Sales Using Sneakers Virtual Try-on. https://forbusiness.snapchat.com/inspiration/diorsneakers.
28. Snapchat. Volkswagen Renews its Partnership with Snapchat and Boosts its Image with Augmented Reality. https://forbusiness.snapchat.com/inspiration/volkswagen-id3-success-story.
29. Snapchat. Volkswagen Renews its Partnership with Snapchat and Boosts its Image with Augmented Reality. https://forbusiness.snapchat.com/inspiration/volkswagen-id3-success-story.
30. Snapchat. Volkswagen Renews its Partnership with Snapchat and Boosts its Image with Augmented Reality. https://forbusiness.snapchat.com/inspiration/volkswagen-id3-success-story.
31. Snapchat. Volkswagen Renews its Partnership with Snapchat and Boosts its Image with Augmented Reality. https://forbusiness.snapchat.com/inspiration/volkswagen-id3-success-story.
32. Snapchat. Total Success for McDonald's with Total Takeover on Snapchat. https://forbusiness.snapchat.com/inspiration/mcdonalds-total-takeover.
33. Snapchat. Total Success for McDonald's with Total Takeover on Snapchat. https://forbusiness.snapchat.com/inspiration/mcdonalds-total-takeover.
34. TikTok. Branded Effects Updates, a New Effect Creator Marketplace, and More. https://effecthouse.tiktok.com/latest/news/creatormarketplace.
35. TikTok. (March 27, 2023). Unleashing creative possibilities for brands with Effect House Branded Effects. https://newsroom.tiktok.com/en-us/unleashing-creative-possibilities-for-brands-with-effect-house-branded-effects.
36. TikTok. Effect House Exits Beta! https://effecthouse.tiktok.com/effect-platform/latest/news/public-launch.
37. TikTok. Success Stories: M.A.C. https://www.tiktok.com/business/en-GB/inspiration/mac-uk-branded-effect?.
38. TikTok. Success Stories: M.A.C. https://www.tiktok.com/business/en-GB/inspiration/mac-uk-branded-effect?.
39. TikTok. Success Stories: M.A.C. https://www.tiktok.com/business/en-GB/inspiration/mac-uk-branded-effect?.

40. TikTok. Success Stories: M.A.C. https://www.tiktok.com/business/en-GB/inspiration/mac-uk-branded-effect?.

41. TikTok. Success Stories: Samsung Galaxy Watch6. https://www.tiktok.com/business/en/inspiration/samsung-galaxy-watch6.

42. TikTok. Success Stories: Samsung Galaxy Watch6. https://www.tiktok.com/business/en/inspiration/samsung-galaxy-watch6.

43. TikTok. Success Stories: Samsung Galaxy Watch6. https://www.tiktok.com/business/en/inspiration/samsung-galaxy-watch6.

44. TikTok. Pepsico Pakistan. https://www.tiktok.com/business/en-US/inspiration/pepsico-pakistan.

45. TikTok. Pepsico Pakistan. https://www.tiktok.com/business/en-US/inspiration/pepsico-pakistan.

46. TikTok. Pepsico Pakistan. https://www.tiktok.com/business/en-US/inspiration/pepsico-pakistan.

47. TikTok. Pepsico Pakistan. https://www.tiktok.com/business/en-US/inspiration/pepsico-pakistan.

48. Perez, Sarah. (May 4, 2023). Meta pitches augmented reality to advertisers with new AR Reels Ads and Facebook Stories. https://techcrunch.com/2023/05/04/meta-pitches-augmented-reality-to-advertisers-with-new-ar-reels-ads-and-facebook-stories.

49. Facebook. Case study: Coors Light. https://www.facebook.com/business/success/3-coors-light.

50. Facebook. Case study: Coors Light. https://www.facebook.com/business/success/3-coors-light.

51. Facebook. Case study: The Walt Disney Company France. https://www.facebook.com/business/success/2-the-walt-disney-company-france.

52. Facebook. Case study: INFINITI Canada. https://www.facebook.com/business/success/infiniti-canada.

53. Facebook. Case study: INFINITI Canada. https://www.facebook.com/business/success/infiniti-canada.

54. Facebook. Case study: INFINITI Canada. https://www.facebook.com/business/success/infiniti-canada.

55. Facebook. Case study: Focus Features. https://www.facebook.com/business/success/focus-features.

56. Facebook. Case study: Focus Features. https://www.facebook.com/business/success/focus-features.

57. Facebook. Case study: Focus Features. https://www.facebook.com/business/success/focus-features.

58. Niantic. (June 19, 2023). Niantic Launches In-Game Rewarded AR Ad Format at Cannes Lions International Festival. https:// nianticlabs.com/news/niantic-rewarded-ar-ads?hl=en.

59. Deyo, Jessica. (June 22, 2023). Circle K pilots new Rewarded AR ads in Pokémon GO. https://www.marketingdive.com/news/ circle-k-pilots-niantic-rewarded-ar-ads-pokemon-go/653548.

60. Niantic. (June 19, 2023). Niantic Launches In-Game Rewarded AR Ad Format at Cannes Lions International Festival. https:// nianticlabs.com/news/niantic-rewarded-ar-ads?hl=en.

61. Niantic. (June 19, 2023). Niantic Launches In-Game Rewarded AR Ad Format at Cannes Lions International Festival. https:// nianticlabs.com/news/niantic-rewarded-ar-ads?hl=en.

62. Shaul, Brandy. (September 29, 2023). Lunchables Uses Rewarded AR Ads to Reach Pokémon GO Players. https://www.adweek .com/brand-marketing/lunchables-rewarded-ar-ads-pokemon-go.

63. Niantic. (September 29, 2023). LUNCAHBLES Teams Up with Niantic to Launch the First-Ever Rewarded AR Ads Campaign. https://nianticlabs.com/news/lunchables?hl=en.

64. Niantic. (September 29, 2023). LUNCAHBLES Teams Up with Niantic to Launch the First-Ever Rewarded AR Ads Campaign. https://nianticlabs.com/news/lunchables?hl=en.

65. Aryel. (March 21, 2023). Aryel & Teads: A Powerhouse Partnership for Brining 3D/AR in Advertising. https://aryel.io/blog/ aryel-teads-a-partnership-to-bring-3d-ar-in-advertising.

66. Shaul, Brandy. (November 17, 2023). These AR Ads Helped Marcolin Promote Eyewear Through a Try-On Feature. https://www .adweek.com/brand-marketing/these-ar-ads-helped-marcolin-promote-eyewear-through-a-try-on-feature.

67. Teads. (November 19, 2023). Case Study: Teads & Intarget's Augmented Reality (AR) Campaign Elevates Marcolin's Guess Brand in Five Countries. https://www.teads.com/case-study-teads-marcolin-guess-augmentedreality-ar.

68. Teads. (November 19, 2023). Case Study: Teads & Intarget's Augmented Reality (AR) Campaign Elevates Marcolin's Guess Brand in Five Countries. https://www.teads.com/case-study-teads-marcolin-guess-augmentedreality-ar.

69. Teads. (November 19, 2023). Case Study: Teads & Intarget's Augmented Reality (AR) Campaign Elevates Marcolin's Guess Brand in Five Countries. https://www.teads.com/case-study-teads-marcolin-guess-augmentedreality-ar.

70. Teads. (June 28, 2023). Coty & Teads Deliver Festive Success Through Augmented Reality for Lacoste. https://www.teads .com/lacoste-augmented-reality-christmas-campaign.

71. Teads. (June 28, 2023). Coty & Teads Deliver Festive Success Through Augmented Reality for Lacoste. https://www.teads .com/lacoste-augmented-reality-christmas-campaign.

72. Baar, Aaron. (April 10, 2024). How Christian Dior made virtual try-ons a luxury experience. https://www.marketingdive.com/ news/christian-dior-luxury-virtual-try-on-teads-marketing-results/711597.

73. Baar, Aaron. (April 10, 2024). How Christian Dior made virtual try-ons a luxury experience. https://www.marketingdive.com/ news/christian-dior-luxury-virtual-try-on-teads-marketing-results/711597.

74. XR Today. (December 23, 2021). Emodo Builds Broadway Ad with New AR Studio. https://www.xrtoday.com/augmented-reality/ emodo-builds-broadway-ad-with-new-ar-studio.

75. Emodo. (December 15, 2021). Ericsson Emodo Launches First 5G-Powered Augmented Reality Ads For Mobile Advertising. https://www.emodoinc.com/news-posts/ericsson-emodo-launches-first-5g-powered-augmented-reality-ads-for-mobile-advertising.

76. Emodo. (December 15, 2021). Ericsson Emodo Launches First 5G-Powered Augmented Reality Ads For Mobile Advertising. https://www.emodoinc.com/news-posts/ericsson-emodo-launches-first-5g-powered-augmented-reality-ads-for-mobile-advertising.

77. XR Today. (December 23, 2021). Emodo Builds Broadway Ad with New AR Studio. https://www.xrtoday.com/augmented-reality/ emodo-builds-broadway-ad-with-new-ar-studio.

78. Williams, Robert. (March 21, 2019). Burger King sets rivals' ads aflame with AR app. https://www.marketingdive.com/news/ burger-king-sets-rivals-ads-aflame-with-ar-app/551020.

79. LLBonline. (December 7, 2021). Singer Anne-Marie Launches Global and Barclaycard's Summer Gig Series with AR Campaign. https://lbbonline.com/news/singer-anne-marie-launches-global-and-barclaycards-summer-gig-series-with-ar-campaign.

80. Visualise. Capital WebAR Experience with Anne-Marie. https:// visualise.com/case-study/capital-webar-experience-with-anne-marie.

81. Visualise. Capital WebAR Experience with Anne-Marie. https://visualise.com/case-study/capital-webar-experience-with-anne-marie.

82. AR. Rocks Editor. (July 31, 2020). Aircards Create WebAR Retail Experience With ABInBev And BonV!V Spiked Seltzer. https://www.ar.rocks/posts/aircards-webar-retail-experience-abinbev-bonv-v-spiked-seltzer.

83. 8th Wall. Bon V!V creates immersive OOH AR experience for its Spiked Seltzer. https://www.8thwall.com/customer-work/bon-viv-spiked-seltzer.

84. AEG. (February 6, 2023). LA Kings Legend Dustin Brown Lifts Stanley Cup on Sprawling 3D Billboard in Downtown Los Angeles. https://www.aegworldwide.com/press-center/press-releases/la-kings-legend-dustin-brown-lifts-stanley-cup-sprawling-3d-billboard.

85. 8th Wall. (February 23, 2023). The LA Kings Honor Dustin Brown with an Immersive WebAR Experience. https://www.8thwall.com/blog/post/103874459177/the-la-kings-honor-dustin-brown-with-an-immersive-ar-experience.

86. AEG. (February 6, 2023). LA Kings Legend Dustin Brown Lifts Stanley Cup on Sprawling 3D Billboard in Downtown Los Angeles. https://www.aegworldwide.com/press-center/press-releases/la-kings-legend-dustin-brown-lifts-stanley-cup-sprawling-3d-billboard.

87. PRWeb. (January 14, 2021). Porsche Promote All-Electric Taycan Using Web-based Augmented Reality Print Advertising With Blue Logic and Aircards. https://www.prweb.com/releases/porsche-promote-all-electric-taycan-using-web-based-augmented-reality-print-advertising-with-blue-logic-and-aircards-852649612.html.

88. 8th Wall. (December 19, 2019). It's a very merry WebAR holiday: activations from Baileys, Purolator and Leo AR. https://www.8thwall.com/blog/post/41177027222/its-a-very-merry-webar-holiday-activations-from-baileys-purolator-and-leo-ar.

89. 8th Wall. (August 8, 2022). Warner Bros Pictures brings the DC League of Super-Pets characters to life through Amazon boxes. https://www.8thwall.com/blog/post/81430093593/warner-bros-pictures-brings-the-dc-league-of-super-pets-characters-to-life-through-amazon-boxes.

90. Zou, Michel. (April 23, 2024). IAB/MRC Includes Niantic's Rewarded AR Ads in AR Measurement Guidelines. https://nianticlabs.com/news/aradstandards?hl=en.

91. Zou,Michel.(April23,2024).IAB/MRCIncludesNiantic'sRewarded AR Ads in AR Measurement Guidelines. https://nianticlabs.com/news/aradstandards?hl=en.

92. Zou, Michel. (April 23, 2024). IAB/MRC Includes Niantic's Rewarded AR Ads in AR Measurement Guidelines. https://nianticlabs.com/news/aradstandards?hl=en.

93. IAB. (April 23, 2024). IAB/MRC Augmented Reality Measurement Guidelines. https://www.iab.com/guidelines/iab-mrc-augmented-reality-measurement-guidelines.

94. IAB & MRC. Augmented Reality (AR) Advertising Measurement Guidelines 1.0. https://mediaratingcouncil.org/sites/default/files/Standards/IAB-MRC-Augmented-Reality-AR-Measurment-Guidelines-April-2024.pdf.

95. Roblox. Documentation: Immersive Ads. https://create.roblox.com/docs/production/monetization/immersive-ads.

96. Keiichi Matsuda. Hyper-Reality. http://hyper-reality.co.

97. Keiichi Matsuda. Hyper-Reality. http://hyper-reality.co.

Chapter 8

1. Cook, Allan V., Ohri, Lokesh, Kusumoto, Reynolds, Chuck Reynolds, and Schwertzel, Eric. (January 10, 2020). Augmented shopping: The quiet revolution. https://www2.deloitte.com/us/en/insights/topics/emerging-technologies/augmented-shopping-3d-technology-retail.html .

2. OpenPR. (June 24, 2024). Augmented Reality Software and Services Market Set to Surge: $333.06 Billion Growth Forecast by 2033. https://www.openpr.com/news/3550807/augmented-reality-software-and-services-market-set-to-surge.

3. Aiello, Cara, Bai, Jiamei, Schmidt, Jennifer and Vilchynskyi, Yuril. (June 12, 2022). Probing reality and myth in the metaverse. https://www.mckinsey.com/industries/retail/our-insights/probing-reality-and-myth-in-the-metaverse.

4. Sabanoglu, Tugba. (December 19, 2023). Forecast share of consumers who will have used AR when buying products online worldwide by 2025, by country. https://www.statista.com/statistics/1270070/ar-use-forecast-in-buying-online.

5. Reydar. Augmented Reality Retail: Stats, Benefits and Examples. https://www.reydar.com/augmented-reality-retail-stats-benefits-examples/#:~:text=Research%20highlights%20that%2061%25%20 of,channels%20and%20insights%20to%20exploit. .

6. Walk-Morris, Tatiana. (April 6, 2022). Snapchat: 92% of Gen Z Want To Use AR for Shopping. https://www.retaildive.com/news/ snapchat-92-of-gen-z-want-to-use-ar-for-shopping/621656/ #:~:text=Ninety%2Dtwo%20percent%20of%20Gen,using%20 AR%2C%20per%20the%20report.

7. Walk-Morris, Tatiana. (April 6, 2022). Snapchat: 92% of Gen Z Want To Use AR for Shopping. https://www.retaildive.com/news/ snapchat-92-of-gen-z-want-to-use-ar-for-shopping/621656/ #:~:text=Ninety%2Dtwo%20percent%20of%20Gen,using%20 AR%2C%20per%20the%20report.

8. Walk-Morris, Tatiana. (April 6, 2022). Snapchat: 92% of Gen Z Want To Use AR for Shopping. https://www.retaildive.com/news/ snapchat-92-of-gen-z-want-to-use-ar-for-shopping/621656/ #:~:text=Ninety%2Dtwo%20percent%20of%20Gen,using%20 AR%2C%20per%20the%20report.

9. Popov, Kosta. (August 17, 2023). How AR Technologies Can Help Retailers Enhance Customer Experience and Increase Sales. https://www.supplychainbrain.com/blogs/1-think-tank/ post/37894-how-ar-technologies-can-help-retailers-enhance-customer-experience-and-increase-sales.

10. Muzzi, Charlotte. (January 24, 2024). The Thrilling Evolution: 3D Ecommerce and a New Era of Retail. https://www.shopify.com/ blog/3d-ecommerce.

11. Dopson, Elise. (2024). Ecommerce Returns: Expert Guide to Best Practices (2024). https://www.shopify.com/enterprise/blog/ ecommerce-returns.

12. PYMNTS. (February 12, 2024). L'Oréal Sees 150% Increase in Virtual Try-Ons as Consumers Seek AR Immersion. https://www .pymnts.com/news/retail/2024/loreal-sees-150percent-increase-in-virtual-try-ons-as-consumers-seek-ar-immersion.

13. PYMNTS. (February 12, 2024). L'Oréal Sees 150% Increase in Virtual Try-Ons as Consumers Seek AR Immersion. https://www .pymnts.com/news/retail/2024/loreal-sees-150percent-increase-in-virtual-try-ons-as-consumers-seek-ar-immersion.

14. PYMNTS. (February 12, 2024). L'Oréal Sees 150% Increase in Virtual Try-Ons as Consumers Seek AR Immersion. https://www.pymnts.com/news/retail/2024/loreal-sees-150percent-increase-in-virtual-try-ons-as-consumers-seek-ar-immersion.

15. PYMNTS. (February 12, 2024). L'Oréal Sees 150% Increase in Virtual Try-Ons as Consumers Seek AR Immersion. https://www.pymnts.com/news/retail/2024/loreal-sees-150percent-increase-in-virtual-try-ons-as-consumers-seek-ar-immersion.

16. Marin-Lopez, Xanayra. (October 12, 2023). Walmart app to bring virtual makeup try-on to customers. https://www.retaildive.com/news/walmart-virtual-makeup-try-on-perfect-corp/696521.

17. Business Wire. (October 11, 2023). Perfect Corp. and Walmart to Offer Innovative AR-Powered Makeup Virtual Try-On Experience to Customers. https://finance.yahoo.com/news/perfect-corp-walmart-offer-innovative-104500557.html.

18. Business Wire. (October 11, 2023). Perfect Corp. and Walmart to Offer Innovative AR-Powered Makeup Virtual Try-On Experience to Customers. https://finance.yahoo.com/news/perfect-corp-walmart-offer-innovative-104500557.html.

19. Neirynck, Kristof. Avon Sees 320% Boost in Conversion, 33% Increase in Average Order Value Using Perfect Corp. Virtual Try-On. https://www.perfectcorp.com/business/successstory/Avon-Sees-Boost-in-Conversion-Perfect-Corp-Virtual-Try-On.

20. Neirynck, Kristof. Avon Sees 320% Boost in Conversion, 33% Increase in Average Order Value Using Perfect Corp. Virtual Try-On. https://www.perfectcorp.com/business/successstory/Avon-Sees-Boost-in-Conversion-Perfect-Corp-Virtual-Try-On.

21. Williams, Robert. (June 28, 2019). Gucci adds AR sneaker try-ons to its mobile app. https://www.marketingdive.com/news/gucci-adds-ar-sneaker-try-ons-to-its-mobile-app/557838.

22. Wanna. Wanna x Gucci. https://wanna.fashion/gucci.

23. Wanna. Wanna x Gucci. https://wanna.fashion/gucci.

24. Chakravarty, Sayan. (August 25, 2020). Gucci's smartphone app now lets you try on its watches virtually using augmented reality. https://luxurylaunches.com/fashion/guccis-smartphone-app-now-lets-you-try-on-its-watches-virtually-using-augmented-reality.php.

25. 8th Wall. Try on wireless audio products from the comfort of your home with JLab's virtual fitting room. https://www.8thwall

.com/blog/post/43145903960/try-on-wireless-audio-products-from-the-comfort-of-your-home-with-jlabs-virtual-fitting-room.

26. JLab Audio. https://www.bestbuy.com/site/brands/jlab-audio/pcmcat1532008148252.c?id=pcmcat1532008148252.

27. Gartenberg, Chaim. (February 4, 2019). Warby Parker's new app combines AR and face mapping so you can try on virtual glasses. https://www.theverge.com/2019/2/4/18205654/warby-parker-ar-iphone-face-id-mapping-glasses-try-on-app.

28. McKeel, Brock. (June 23, 2022). New Features Put AR Shopping Experiences Right in Customers' Pockets – At Home and In Stores. https://corporate.walmart.com/news/2022/06/23/new-features-put-ar-shopping-experiences-right-in-customers-pockets-at-home-and-in-stores.

29. Takahashi, Dean. (July 1, 2024). Walmart shows off its progress with augmented reality showrooms. https://venturebeat.com/ai/walmart-shows-off-its-progress-with-augmented-reality-showrooms.

30. Berthiaume, Dan. (September 14, 2023). Amazon enhances online shopping experience with AI, AR. https://chainstoreage.com/amazon-enhances-online-shopping-experience-ai-ar.

31. AMZ Prep. (February 28, 2024). Enhance Amazon Sales with Captivating 3D Visuals: Revealing the Advantages. https://amzprep.com/3d-content-amazon.

32. AMZ Prep. (February 28, 2024). Enhance Amazon Sales with Captivating 3D Visuals: Revealing the Advantages. https://amzprep.com/3d-content-amazon.

33. Connolly, Brian. (May 5, 2024). Amazon AR (Augmented Reality): How to Add 3D Content to Your Amazon FBA Listings. https://www.junglescout.com/resources/articles/amazon-ar.

34. Auganix. (August 18, 2020). Saatchi Art launches 'View in a Room' Augmented Reality feature powered by 8th Wall's WebAR platform. https://www.auganix.org/saatchi-art-launches-view-in-a-room-augmented-reality-feature-powered-by-8th-walls-webar-platform.

35. 8th Wall. WebAR Case Study: Saatchi Art lets customers view over 1 million works of art in their home using WebAR. https://www.8thwall.com/customer-work/saatchi-art-integrates-largest-deployment-of-webar-ecommerce.

36. IKEA newsroom. (September 12, 2017). IKEA Place app launched to help people virtually place furniture at home. https://www .ikea.com/global/en/newsroom/innovation/ikea-launches-ikea-place-a-new-app-that-allows-people-to-virtually-place-furniture-in-their-home-170912.

37. Dent, Steve. (June 22, 2022). IKEA's latest AR app can erase your furniture to showcase its own. https://www.engadget .com/ikea-ar-app-lets-you-preview-its-furniture-in-your-own-house-130004284.html?src=rss.

38. Cripps, Coral. (May 19, 2023). Crocs launches interactive AR game experience with Minecraft. https://www.prweek.com/article/ 1823541/crocs-launches-interactive-ar-game-experience-minecraft.

39. 8th Wall. Minecraft x Crocs x Gravity Road | Choose Your Mode AR Games. https://www.8thwall.com/powster/choose-your-mode.

40. Waldman, Sophie. (July 18, 2022). RTFKT x Nike AR Hoodie Set to Launch This Week. https://hypebeast.com/2022/7/rtfkt-x-nike-ar-hoodie-set-to-launch-this-week.

41. OpenSea. RTFKT X NIKE AR HOODIE FORGED. https://opensea .io/collection/rtfkt-nike-ar-hoodie.

42. Hahn, Jennifer. (March 19, 2021). Gucci releases first virtual sneaker that can only be worn in digital environments. https:// www.dezeen.com/2021/03/19/virtual-25-gucci-wanna-digital-sneaker.

43. Servantes, Ian. (March 17, 2021). Gucci knows NFTs are hot, starts selling virtual sneakers. https://www.inverse.com/input/style/ gucci-virtual-sneakers-nft-wanna-fashion-augmented-reality.

44. Hirschmiller, Stepanie. (July 19, 2022). Digital Fashion Brand DRESSX Joins Balenciaga, Prada, and Friends at Meta's Avatar Store. https://www.forbes.com/sites/stephaniehirschmiller/2022/ 07/19/digital-fashion-brand-dressx-launches-on-metas-avatar-store.

45. Hirschmiller, Stephanie. (December 1, 2023). What DRESSX's New Desktop Camera Means For Brands & Video Conferencing. https:// www.forbes.com/sites/stephaniehirschmiller/2023/12/01/ what-dressxs-new-desktop-camera-means-for-zoom-google-meet-teams.

46. DREESSX. https://pro.dressx.com.

47. Farra, Emily. (September 16, 2020). This Is the First Augmented Reality Experiment of Spring 2021. https://www.vogue.com/article/khaite-spring-2021-augmented-reality-experience.

48. 8th Wall. WebAR Case Study: KHAITE saw a 4x increase in shoe sales with its SS21 WebAR-enabled lookbook. https://www.8thwall.com/customer-work/khaite.

49. Yotka, Steff. (March 9, 2021). Simone Rocha x H&M Launches an Augmented Reality Pop-Up Book With Painter Faye Wei Wei. https://www.vogue.com/article/simone-rocha-hm-faye-wei-wei-augmented-reality-pop-up-book.

50. 8th Wall. H&M: AR pop-up book. https://www.8thwall.com/unit9/h-m-3069.

51. 8th Wall. (June 23, 2021). C&A brings it's Autumn/Winter Collection '21 to life through augmented reality magazine. https://www.8thwall.com/blog/post/49357505108/winter-collection-21-to-life-through-augmented-reality-magazine.

52. 8th Wall. (June 23, 2021). C&A brings it's Autumn/Winter Collection '21 to life through augmented reality magazine. https://www.8thwall.com/blog/post/49357505108/winter-collection-21-to-life-through-augmented-reality-magazine.

53. 8th Wall. Bloomingdale's celebrates 150th anniversary with AR enabled catalog. https://www.8thwall.com/blog/post/88912934021/bloomingdales-celebrates-150th-anniversary-with-ar-enabled-catalog.

54. 8th Wall. Bloomingdale's celebrates 150th anniversary with AR enabled catalog. https://www.8thwall.com/blog/post/88912934021/bloomingdales-celebrates-150th-anniversary-with-ar-enabled-catalog.

55. Auganix. (April 14, 2021). BMW launches its 'Virtual Viewer' web browser-based Augmented Reality experience powered by 8th Wall. https://www.auganix.org/bmw-launches-its-virtual-viewer-web-browser-based-augmented-reality-experience-powered-by-8th-wall.

56. Auganix. (April 14, 2021). BMW launches its 'Virtual Viewer' web browser-based Augmented Reality experience powered by 8th Wall. https://www.auganix.org/bmw-launches-its-virtual-viewer-web-browser-based-augmented-reality-experience-powered-by-8th-wall.

57. Auganix. (April 14, 2021). BMW launches its 'Virtual Viewer' web browser-based Augmented Reality experience powered by 8th Wall. https://www.auganix.org/bmw-launches-its-virtual-viewer-web-browser-based-augmented-reality-experience-powered-by-8th-wall.

58. Yahoo Finance. (March 22, 2024). ARway.ai Announces Major 300,000 SQ FT or 30,000 M. Retail Store Pilot of its AR Navigation Platform. https://finance.yahoo.com/news/arway-ai-announces-major-300-113000457.html.

59. Berthiaume, Dan. (May 22, 2024). CSA Q&A: Macy's enables virtual AR try-on at in-store Disney shop. https://chainstoreage.com/csa-qa-macys-enables-virtual-ar-try-store-disney-shop.

60. Milnes, Hilary. (May 5, 2023). Coach's AR try-on window will stop shoppers in the street. https://www.voguebusiness.com/technology/coachs-ar-try-on-window-will-stop-shoppers-in-the-street.

61. LinkedIn. Zero10. "Did you know that AR fashion market is predicted to grow to $26B by 2028? We believe in this prediction, and here's why". https://www.linkedin.com/posts/zero10ar_did-you-know-that-ar-fashion-market-is-activity-71036628 51793297411-E4yG.

62. 8th Wall. Selfridges AW22 In-Store AR. https://www.8thwall.com/rosedigital/selfridges-ar.

63. XR Today. (August 31, 2023). How Google and Adobe are Bringing AR Experiences to Retail. https://www.xrtoday.com/augmented-reality/how-google-and-adobe-are-bringing-ar-experiences-to-retail.

64. Dream Syndicate. Nike "Play New" In-Store WebAR. https://dreamsyndicate.com/nike-play-new.

65. Lowe's. (February 1, 2024). Lowe's Unveils Lowe's Style Studio for Apple Vision Pro. https://corporate.lowes.com/newsroom/press-releases/lowes-unveils-lowes-style-studio-apple-vision-pro-02-01-24.

66. Lowe's. (February 1, 2024). Lowe's Unveils Lowe's Style Studio for Apple Vision Pro. https://corporate.lowes.com/newsroom/press-releases/lowes-unveils-lowes-style-studio-apple-vision-pro-02-01-24.

67. DECATHLON. (February 2024). DECATHLON unveils a cutting-edge immersive experience on Apple Vision Pro. https://www

.decathlon-united.media/pressfiles/decathlon-apple-visio-pro-immersive-experience.

68. DECATHLON. (February 2024). DECATHLON unveils a cutting-edge immersive experience on Apple Vision Pro. https://www.decathlon-united.media/pressfiles/decathlon-apple-visio-pro-immersive-experience.

69. Berthiaume, Dan. (February 2, 2024). J.Crew expands metaverse effort with Apple Vision Pro styling app. https://chainstoreage.com/jcrew-expands-metaverse-effort-apple-vision-pro-styling-app.

70. PRWeb. (February 2, 2024). J.Crew Brings Virtual Closet Experience to Apple Vision Pro in Partnership with Obsess. https://www.prweb.com/releases/jcrew-brings-virtual-closet-experience-to-apple-vision-pro-in-partnership-with-obsess-302051423.html.

71. Marin-Lopez, Xanayra. (February 7, 2024). Alo Yoga debuts immersive shopping app for Apple Vision Pro. https://www.retaildive.com/news/alo-yoga-app-apple-vision-pro/706646.

72. PRWeb. (February 2, 2024). Alo Yoga Launches "alo Sanctuary," One of the First Wellness Shopping Experiences for Apple Vision Pro, Developed in Partnership with Obsess and Ave Advisory. https://www.prweb.com/releases/alo-yoga-launches-alo-sanctuary-one-of-the-first-wellness-shopping-experiences-for-apple-vision-pro-developed-in-partnership-with-obsess-and-ave-advisory-302051446.html.

73. PRWeb. (February 2, 2024). e.l.f. Cosmetics Launches its First Beauty Shopping Experience for Apple Vision Pro: a Multi-Sensory, Immersive visionOS App, Developed by Obsess. https://www.businesswire.com/news/home/20240202593487/en.

74. Walk-Morris, Tatiana. (March 6, 2024). StockX releases immersive shopping experience for Apple Vision Pro. https://www.retaildive.com/news/stockx-releases-immersive-shopping-experience-for-apple-vision-pro/709291.

75. StockX. (March 4, 2024). StockX Among the First to Launch Immersive Shopping Experience for Apple Vision Pro. https://stockx.com/about/stockx-among-the-first-to-launch-immersive-shopping-experience-for-apple-vision-pro.

76. Edwards, Cliff. (September 20, 2022). Reinventing Retail: Lowe's Teams With NVIDIA and Magic Leap to Create Interactive Store Digital Twins. https://blogs.nvidia.com/blog/lowes-retail-digital-twins-omniverse.

77. Edwards, Cliff. (September 20, 2022). Reinventing Retail: Lowe's Teams With NVIDIA and Magic Leap to Create Interactive Store Digital Twins. https://blogs.nvidia.com/blog/lowes-retail-digital-twins-omniverse.

78. Warpin Reality. Augmented Reality Cases: Redesign Lab by H&M Group. https://warpinreality.com/cases/redesign-lab.

79. Wayfair. (October 10, 2018). Introducing Wayfair Spaces, the First-Ever Interior Design and Room Planning App on Magic Leap One. https://investor.wayfair.com/news/news-details/2018/Introducing-Wayfair-Spaces-the-First-Ever-Interior-Design-and-Room-Planning-App-on-Magic-Leap-One/default.aspx.

80. Wayfair. (October 10, 2018). Introducing Wayfair Spaces, the First-Ever Interior Design and Room Planning App on Magic Leap One. https://investor.wayfair.com/news/news-details/2018/Introducing-Wayfair-Spaces-the-First-Ever-Interior-Design-and-Room-Planning-App-on-Magic-Leap-One/default.aspx.

81. Microsoft. (April 13, 2023). Porsche Cars North America delivers world-class service with Microsoft mixed reality and HoloLens 2. https://ms-f1-sites-02-we.azurewebsites.net/en-sg/story/1523387086361264063-porsche-cars-north-america-automotive-dynamics-365-guides-dynamics-365-remote-assist-hololens.

82. Microsoft. (April 13, 2023). Porsche Cars North America delivers world-class service with Microsoft mixed reality and HoloLens 2. https://ms-f1-sites-02-we.azurewebsites.net/en-sg/story/1523387086361264063-porsche-cars-north-america-automotive-dynamics-365-guides-dynamics-365-remote-assist-hololens.

83. Microsoft. (April 13, 2023). Porsche Cars North America delivers world-class service with Microsoft mixed reality and HoloLens 2. https://ms-f1-sites-02-we.azurewebsites.net/en-sg/story/1523387086361264063-porsche-cars-north-america-automotive-dynamics-365-guides-dynamics-365-remote-assist-hololens.

Chapter 9

1. Buck, Heidi. (February 9, 2023). Exploring the Spatial Computing Spectrum: From 3D to Simulation. https://aws.amazon.com/blogs/spatial/exploring-the-spatial-computing-spectrum-from-3d-to-simulation.

Acknowledgments

I want to express my heartfelt gratitude to everyone who supported me in creating this book. To my family, John Emrich, Nancy Emrich, Belinda-Shade Moore, Amanda Brennan, and Bob Brennan, thank you for being my biggest cheerleaders during the writing process.

Special thanks to Amy LaMeyer, Dana Murphy-Chutorian, Erik Murphy-Chutorian, Maryam Sabour, Alexander Hague, Vicki Fountain, Julie Den Tandt, Sheri Stroh, Seray Zurnacioglu, Sean Mayers, Rana June, Rehana Logel, Cara Hack, Paula Kwan, and Amanda Cosco. Your constant check-ins, willingness to let me bounce ideas off you, and invaluable feedback over texts and calls have been immensely helpful – a huge high five to Lakshmi Lakshmanan for inspiring me to create a GPT to let readers talk to an AI about this book.

A huge thank you to my editor, Kelly Talbot, for your insightful feedback. To the entire Wiley team, including Christina Rudloff and Purvi Patel, thank you for your unwavering support and belief that this book needs to exist in the world. Lily Snyder, thank you for providing an early set of eyes on the material. To the team at EyeJack, thank you for creating a powerful WebAR experience powered by 8th Wall that lets this book walk the walk.

Finally, thank you to my incredible husband, Jonathan Carver Moore, for your infinite patience, endless love, and boundless support. Your understanding and encouragement throughout this book-writing process have been my greatest strength. Thank you for believing in me and for always being my rock. I couldn't have done this without you.

About the Author

Tom Emrich is a recognized pioneer in AR, virtual reality (VR), and wearable technology. With over 15 years of experience in the space, Tom has been at the forefront of spatial computing and has a track record of providing strategic direction for powerhouse brands and organizations using emerging technology.

As a product leader, Tom has inspired teams, shaped solutions, and created developer ecosystems for some of the most influential AR/MR platforms, including those from Niantic and Meta. As VP of Product at 8th Wall, the WebAR platform now part of Niantic, Tom was instrumental in enabling agencies and brands with tools to create browser-based AR content for business growth. Some of the brands that launched WebAR campaigns powered by 8th Wall include Nike, Porsche, Sony Pictures, Burger King, General Mills, Heineken, McDonald's, Red Bull, and COACH. At Meta, Tom is a product lead for the Horizon OS development platform, empowering developers with the tools they need to succeed across the developer journey in creating mixed reality content for headsets such as the Meta Quest.

Tom has been critical in building the AR/VR/wearables community. In 2013, Tom founded We Are Wearables, which he grew to become the largest wearable tech community before it was acquired. He also co-produced AWE, the world's #1 spatial computing event series, for nearly six years, expanding and growing this community globally.

An investor with a sharp eye for the future of spatial computing, Tom was a founding partner of Super Ventures, a VC fund for early-stage AR investments. He continues to invest in this space as an angel investor.

Tom's thought leadership is widely recognized in the media and industry events. His insights have been featured in *CNN, BBC, Forbes, Adweek, and The New York Times,* and he has been a sought-after speaker at TEDx, CES, SXSW, Festival de Cannes, and Elevate. His background as a freelance journalist and recurring wearable tech expert on Canada's largest TV morning show underscores his ability to communicate complex technological concepts in an accessible and engaging manner to a broad audience. Now a "Top Voice" on LinkedIn, Tom has written about wearable technology for over a decade.

Tom's unparalleled experience and innovative mindset make him a leading authority in AR and VR. His book, *The Next Dimension*, offers invaluable insights into leveraging these technologies for business growth, making it a must-read for business leads looking to stay ahead of the curve.

Follow Tom on LinkedIn at http://www.linkedin.com/in/thomase mrich.

Index

213